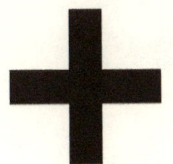

First established in 2004, the DATA browser book series explores new thinking and practice at the intersection of contemporary art, digital culture and politics. The series takes theory or criticism not as a fixed set of tools or practices, but rather as an evolving chain of ideas that recognize the conditions of their own making. The term "browser" is useful here in pointing to the framing device through which data is delivered over information networks and processed by algorithms. Whereas a conventional understanding of browsing suggests surface readings and cursory engagement with the material, the series celebrates the potential of browsing for dynamic rearrangement and interpretation of existing material into new configurations that are open to reinvention.

Series editors:

Geoff Cox
Joasia Krysa

Volumes in the series:

DB 01 ECONOMISING CULTURE
DB 02 ENGINEERING CULTURE
DB 03 CURATING IMMATERIALITY
DB 04 CREATING INSECURITY
DB 05 DISRUPTING BUSINESS
DB 06 EXECUTING PRACTICES

www.data-browser.net

This volume produced by Critical Software Thing with support from Participatory IT Research Centre, Aarhus University & Exhibition Research Lab, Liverpool John Moores University

DATA browser 06
EXECUTING PRACTICES

Geoff Cox
Olle Essvik
Jennifer Gabrys
Francisco Gallardo
David Gauthier
Linda Hilfling Ritasdatter
Brian House
Yuk Hui
Marie Louise Juul Søndergaard
Peggy Pierrot
Andy Prior
Helen Pritchard
Roel Roscam Abbing
Audrey Samson
Kasper Hedegård Schiølin
Susan Schuppli
Femke Snelting
Eric Snodgrass
Winnie Soon
Magdalena Tyżlik-Carver

DATA browser 06
EXECUTING PRACTICES

Edited by Helen Pritchard,
Eric Snodgrass and Magda
Tyżlik-Carver

Published by
Open Humanities Press 2018
Copyright © 2018 the authors

This is an open access book,
licensed under the Creative
Commons Attribution By Attribution
Share Alike License. Under this
license, authors allow anyone to
download, reuse, reprint, modify,
distribute, and/or copy their work
so long as the authors and source
are cited and resulting derivative
works are licensed under the same
or similar license. No permission
is required from the authors or the
publisher. Statutory fair use and
other rights are in no way affected
by the above. Read more about
the license at creativecommons.org/
licenses/by-sa/4.0/

Freely available at
data-browser.net/db06.html

ISBN (print): 978-1-78542-056-6
ISBN (PDF): 978-1-78542-057-3
ISBN (ePUB): 978-1-78542-058-0

DATA browser series template
designed by Stuart Bertolotti-Bailey.

Book layout and typesetting by
Mark Simmonds & Esther Yarnold

The cover image is derived from
Multi by David Reinfurt, a software
app that updates the idea of the
multiple from industrial production
to the dynamics of the information
age. Each cover presents an iteration
of a possible 1,728 arrangements,
each a face built from minimal
typographic furniture, and from
the same source code.
www.o-r-g.com/apps/multi

Contents

7 **Acknowledgements**

9 **Executing Practices**

25 **Preface: The Time of Execution**
Yuk Hui

35 **Modifying the Universal**
Roel Roscam Abbing, Peggy Pierrot, Femke Snelting

55 **RuntimeException() — Critique of Software Violence**
Geoff Cox

69 **On Commands and Executions: Tyrants, Spectres and Vagabonds**
David Gauthier

85 **Deadly Algorithms: Can Legal Codes Hold Software Accountable for Code That Kills?**
Susan Schuppli

99 **Executing Micro-temporality**
Winnie Soon

115 **The Spinning Wheel of Life**
Winnie Soon

117 **Synchronising Uncertainty: Google's Spanner and Cartographic Time**
Brian House

127 **Loading... 800% Slower**
David Gauthier

137 **BUGS IN THE WAR ROOM — Economies and/of Execution**
Linda Hilfling Rittasdatter

159 **Erasure**
Audrey Samson

171	**Posthuman Curating and Its Biopolitical Executions. The Case of Curating Content** Magdalena Tyżlik-Carver
191	**Ghost Factory — Posthuman Executions** Magdalena Tyżlik-Carver & Andy Prior
197	**Bataille's Bicycle: Execution and/as Eroticism** Marie Louise Juul Søndergaard & Kasper Hedegård Schiølin
218	**The Chance Execution** Olle Essvik
237	**What Is Executing Here?** Eric Snodgrass
261	**Critter Compiler** Helen Pritchard
279	**Shrimping Under Working Conditions** Francisco Gallardo & Audrey Samson
295	**Afterword: Reverse Executions in the Internet of Things** Jennifer Gabrys
303	**Biographies**
309	**Index of all elements leading to the end of the world (in this book)** Linda Hilfling Ritasdatter

Acknowledgements

This book is a result of collective energy that brought together a group of artists, researchers and practitioners. Their different practices and approaches to the question of execution sparked a desire to carry out a project where thinking about software is entangled with various practices of computationally-informed executions. We want to acknowledge all the group members and workshop participants: Anuradha Venugopal Reddy, Audrey Samson, Brian House, David Gauthier, Eric Snodgrass, Fran Gallardo, Geraldine Juárez, Helen Pritchard, Lea Muldtofte, Linda Hilfling Ritasdatter, Magdalena Tyżlik-Carver, Marie Louise Juul Søndergaard, Michelle Westerlaken, Molly Schwartz, Olle Essvik, Thomas Bjørnsten and Winnie Soon, and thank them for carrying out this project in its many forms and towards its execution as a published book.

Critical Software Thing emerged spontaneously after a research workshop at the School of Creative Media, City University of Hong Kong in October 2014, co-organised with *A Peer-Reviewed Journal About*, Aarhus University and transmediale. It was because of the conversations during this event that the question of execution became a prominent research focus for some of the workshop participants, leading to Critical Software Thing group activities. We want to acknowledge Kristoffer Gansing (transmediale) and Jane Prophet, who was at the time at the School of Creative Media, City University of Hong Kong, as well as Geoff Cox and Christian Ulrik Andersen (Aarhus University) as partly responsible for Critical Software Thing's beginnings.

This book would not have been possible without support and encouragement from colleagues who also acted as respondents during our meetings at Aarhus University (2015) and Malmö University (2016). We would like to thank Wendy Hui Kyong Chun, Geoff Cox, Susan Schuppli, Femke Snelting, Peggy Pierrot and Roel Roscam Abbing who delivered provocative keynote talks at the two events, and who, together with Christian Ulrik Andersen, Søren Pold, Cornelia Sollfrank, Susan Kozel, Bo Reimer, Maria Hellström Reimer and Nikita Mazurov, responded to early versions of the contributions to this collection. We want to thank them all for their constructive criticism and inspiring conversations. For documentation from both events, see: http://softwarestudies.projects.cavi.au.dk/

index.php/*.exe_(ver0.1) & http://softwarestudies.projects.cavi.au.dk/index.php/*.exe_(ver0.2).

We are very grateful to Jennifer Gabrys and Yuk Hui who wrote on the subject of execution in response to the articles in the book, and offered their texts to open and close the collection. Their original approaches to the subject of the publication have expanded and enriched perspectives offered here.

We are grateful to many organisations and institutions who offered their generous support and hosted our activities, including Digital Aesthetics Research Center (DARC), Aarhus Institute for Advanced Studies (AIAS), Medea and the School of Arts and Communication (K3) at Malmö University, the Making Sense of Data research project, Graduate School, Arts, Aarhus University, The Contemporary Condi-tion research project, The Centre for Advanced Visualization and Interaction (CAVI), Centre for Participatory Information Technology (all at Aarhus University), Carlsberg Foundation in Denmark and transmediale.

We want to thank all collaborators and co-writers. It has been a very ambitious plan to have this book ready after just over a year since the first meeting of the group in Aarhus. We want to thank all who contributed to achieving this. In particular, huge thanks go to Esther Yarnold, for her generous work on the book, dedicating hours of computer time to produce the final copy for print. Many thanks also to Stuart Bertolotti-Bailey for the book design. Many other individuals helped at various stages of producing the book: Ben Carver, Winnie Soon and Joasia Krysa read the extracts and gave feedback. A very special thank you to Geoff Cox, one of the series editors of the Data Browser series, for encouraging us to take up the project and his brilliant support in finalising the book for publication.

Executing Practices

Helen Pritchard, Eric Snodgrass, Magdalena
Tyżlik-Carver

Towards the end of a keynote address on "Theory and Practice" presented in 1989 at the 11th World Computer Congress, the well-known computer scientist and mathematician Donald Knuth suggests a challenge to his audience.
> *Make a thorough analysis of everything your computer does during one second of computation. The computer will execute several hundred thousand instructions during that second; I'd like you to study them all.*
> (Knuth [1989] 1991, 12–13)

There is an expectation that comes from a technical understanding of execution that it is a straightforward running of a task. For instance, in computing, execution is often associated specifically with the fetch–decode–execute instruction cycle, during which a computer's central processing unit (CPU) retrieves instructions from its memory, determines what actions the instructions dictate and proceeds to carry out those actions. But of course the instruction cycle does not encompass execution's impact and embeddedness in the world, and it is this that contributors to this book elaborate and expand upon critically. As Knuth notes, "[e]ven when the machine's instructions are known, there will be problems" (13).

Contained in every "blip" of execution is a range of technical and cultural issues to be addressed, with one operational experience of executing practices opening onto another (Fuller 2003).[1] *Executing Practices* brings attention to what Isabelle Stengers (2005) describes as the particular demands of practices that propel execution. Practices are parsed as processes by which execution stabilises and takes hold in the world (Stengers, in Gabrys 2016, 9). Rather than considering the stability of execution as the norm, which we might approach with dystopic or paranoid dread, the authors in the book engage with and make interventions on the problems of execution.

Executing Practices alerts us that access to instructions that drive execution is only one account, and even then, our understanding of execution might always remain partial and speculative. If we approach Knuth's challenge through an engagement with practices, it becomes apparent that processes of computation have particular obligations that infringe upon those who practise or are affected by it. Through geographic, temporal and material specificity the chapters attend both to the practices of execution and their differing research practices. The focus is on complexities inherent to different forms of execution, while also recognising an understanding of execution as a performance of step-by-step instructions. The outcome of this is a collection of research practices that intervene in executing processes at differing points and locations to engage with the most important aspect of Knuth's challenge—*the problems* of execution.

"Uwaga... Start!!": Experiences of Execution

The practices of the women who devised and implemented the programming for ENIAC (Electronic Numerical Integrator And Computer) in the 1940s might offer a useful orientation when addressing Knuth's challenge. If we consider one second of computing in this example it becomes clear that it is not just algorithmic calculations that have to be attended to but also women setting values, connecting switches and wiring cables and plugs between different parts of the machine (what is now referred to as "direct programming"). At a time when there was no computer language and no operating system as such, "the women had to figure out what a computer was, how to interface with it, and then break down a complicated mathematical problem into very small steps that the ENIAC could then perform" (Kathy Kleinman, in Sheppard 2013; see also Chun 2004, Hayles 2005, Balsamo 1996). The working system which supported their invention of coding, with its various hierarchies and divisions of labour, was described by Jean Jennings, one of the ENIAC operators, in the following way:

> *Betty and I were the workhorses, finishers, tying up all the loose ends. Kay was often more creative, suggesting clever ways to reduce total size of the program. Marlyn and Ruth agreed to generate a test trajectory, calculating it exactly the way the ENIAC was to do it so we could check the detailed steps once it was on the ENIAC. We spent a lot of time working on programming notation so we could keep track of the timing of program pulses and digital operations. The ENIAC was a parallel machine, so the programmer had to keep track of everything,*

whether interdependent or independent. (Jennings, in Fritz 1996, 20)

Computing here, as well as being a physical execution of calculations that require wiring by hand, is also a task of military labour which is divided according to skills that demand an intimate understanding of the machine and processes required to run it. Situating ENIAC's practices is also important. ENIAC was initially sponsored by the US military as a general-purpose electronic computer for calculating artillery-firing tables (the settings used for different weapons under varied conditions for target accuracy), and later for other tasks such as numerical weather prediction and the working out of implosion problems relating to the ongoing development of the hydrogen bomb. In this account of computational practices, the problems of execution are historically situated and entangled with the contingent forces of machines, bodies, institutions, military labour practices and geopolitics, rather than simply a set of instructions that are outside of life.

Another example that highlights differing experiences of execution is the idiosyncratic coding practice of Radiokomputer that developed in Poland in the late 1980s. Radiokomputer illustrates the distributed relations to be taken into account when thinking about execution and how execution might be experienced. Radiokomputer[2] was a radio programme broadcast on Polish National Radio between 1986 and the early 1990s, transmitting via shortwave frequencies computer programs and games for early home computers such as Atari, ZX-Spectrum and Commodore 64. A similar distribution of music via radio was commonly practiced for most of the 1980s, when radio presenters would broadcast boths sides of vinyl LPs delivered or smuggled to Poland from West Europe. Political restrictions on culture and commerce at the time influenced and generated particular ways of sharing foreign pop culture. It is not surprising that this model was also used for distributing computer programs, which were radiocast for the listeners to record onto a cassette tape. At 4pm on Fridays after a brief introduction, the radio presenter would announce the transmission with a warning to listeners: "Uwaga... Start!!" which would mark a moment to press the record button on a tape recorder, after which a nationwide broadcast of noise would follow. As one of the programme listeners recalls, Spectrum sounds would differ from Atari, and Commodore would also sound recognisably different.[3] Unfortunately, this cacophony of sounds would not always deliver, as any interference in radio waves could corrupt the program. According to computer users at the time, there was an estimated 70% success rate for this form of program recording, with Atari being the most amenable to this method and Spectrum being least open to it. To aid the process, the radio presenter wrote an article advising the best recording practice, which was then published in *Bajtek*, a monthly journal dedicated to computers and related technologies (for more details, see Jordan 1986). The articles included step-by-step instructions, with information about what hardware to use (Polish cassettes produced by Stilon were not recommended because of the low level of iron necessary for better quality of recording) and how to set up for best results (including the advice to turn off all unnecessary electrical devices in the house, such as washing machines, hoovers, etc.).

Practices such as these highlight what are perhaps less familiar experiences of computing. In Radiokomputer, the socio-political situation and lack of copyright laws regarding software in Poland at the time generated a practice of national broadcast radio for free transmission of code. On Friday afternoons, as long as the radio was tuned to the right station, it was possible to listen to code and hear its crackling noises while attempting to record it so that it could be executed again as a game. This example is another instance of an executing practice which, together with the example of ENIAC, points to localised and physical experiences of code. A multiplicity of relations are highlighted in such executions, which, as well as including hardware and software, are also dependent on laws, cables, the electromagnetic spectrum, minerals, histories, gender relations, economies and so on. Issues of maintenance and instantaneous debugging are at the very centre of this form of code writing, inscribing computational ecologies as unexpected systems that are as temporary as they are concrete in the moment of their execution. And so investigations of execution pay attention to which stories of execution we choose to tell and which are forgotten in the history of software.

Where should we conclude this readily sprawling task of practicing and working through execution as inquiry? This is a key question, and as contributions to this volume suggest, whilst accounts might reveal the terminal character of computation, there is no end to such investigations. For instance, Knuth's challenge could be considered to be a practical study in which one remains within the physical confines of the machine itself: a world of circuitry-registers, operational codes, scan codes, glyph selections, screen renderings, non-keyboard inputs and the like. In addition, this "your computer" is itself connected to the distributed services of the Internet, subject to and executing within "local" and "global" experiences of packet switching, resolutions of internet protocols, scripts, multiple caches and loads, and so on. And what then of the busy electrons and swerving atoms charging the "bare metal" and flowing onwards within greater infrastructures of electricity, optical fibre, manufacturing and so on? And what of the different collective entities and bodies that necessarily act as transducers for such energies? Knuth's problem opens further still and in come the uninvited guests of perspectivalism, political economy and the general meshed nature of the world. In the meantime, the complexity and amount of actions performed by a typical computer have increased exponentially. As one commenter on a *Hacker News* thread replied to the question of what happens when you type Google.com into your browser and press enter? "Somebody also needs to talk about what's happening in the CPUs, with 3 billion or so instruc-tions per CPU core every second, all devoted to looking up a cat video for you. When you play a cat video, more computation occurs than was done in the history of the world prior to 1940" (Animats 2015).

Beyond standard attempts aimed at unpacking discrete instances of execution—typically carried out with the intention of optimising the executing processes involved—the notion of tracking execution and its many shifting parts over a particular instance of time has produced a variety of responses on the part of practitioners and artists. In *Diff in June* (2013), artist Martin Howse uses a small bit of custom script to track whenever a bit of data is changed between one day and the next within the file system of an IBM x60 machine. Running the script results in a 1,673 page transcript that creates a narrative of "a day in the life of a personal computer written by itself in its own language, as a sort of private log or intimate diary focused on every single change to the data on its hard disk" (Howse 2013). In this book, David Gauthier's contribution *Loading... 800% Slower* enacts a method of détournement that willfully slows down the bitrate of an internet connection, making audible the many "timely designed assaults" of the invisible scripts involved in composing a particular web page. Magdalena Tyżlik-Carver and Andrew Prior assemble code, interface, texts and sound in a *Ghost Factory* experiment that makes recursivity available to participating bodies, whether human or not. Elsewhere, the excessive character of execution as a form of eroticism is hacked by *Marcelle*, a pair of white cotton briefs equipped with vibrators that respond to surrounding WiFi networks. An intervention by Marie Louise Søndergaard which, as further discussed in her joint article with Kasper Hedegård Schiølin, functions as a conceptual tool that posits eroticism as "an inherent aspect of computational culture and history". Meanwhile, Olle Essvik investigates execution as a practice of bookbinding that incorporates book-end papers bought at an auction in Sweden. In the process he explores random noise generation and "chance executions" by referencing situated material histories whose traces are found on the purchased papers and then performed in the making of the book. Such methods and their often performative modes of "parasitic rendering" (Gauthier) bring to the fore inflecting and productive relations of even the most minor executing procedures.

The contributors to this collection account for both the practical specificities of computing and a range of matters both very close to and also, seemingly, very far from the machine itself. In particular, the book presents why, and in which ways thinking through a notion of execution can be useful. Each piece in the book provides its own response. Some work towards defining a particular mode or process of execution, and others use execution as a concept through which to study a variety of issues and their relations to one another. As writers such as Karen Barad (2007) make clear, the path towards answering a question such as Knuth's will say much about the ontologies, epistemologies and various ensembles of objects and entities brought together in answering it. It is because of this complex character of computation that questions such as Knuth's are commonly brought up during job interviews in computing and related fields. Ask a Java programmer what they understand execution to mean and you will likely get a rather different answer to that of someone involved with physical computing or a researcher working within the fields of queer theory or software studies. Such accounts of execution point to complex relations that are highlighted in practices, opening up an understanding of execution to its different experiences.

While each contribution in the book covers differing experiences of execution, we will highlight a few tentative themes shared by many of the chapters. The intention is not to categorise the contributions or map out a definitive set of themes, but rather to give a sense of some of the directions which working through a notion of execution takes us.

Executing Temporalities

Today it is no longer a couple of hundred thousand instructions executing per second (as Knuth suggests in 1989), but rather an accelerating number of potential instructions at any one time. One practical way in which to deal with Knuth's suggestion on the typically much faster machines of the present would be to cut a single second into a more manageable unit of time: perhaps a nanosecond (one billionth of one second), the time it typically takes to execute one machine cycle on a 1 GHz microprocessor. If we take computational time to be linear — in the way that Knuth's challenge might suggest — the focus is on that moment in read-write culture where the computer program "does what it says". Execution is often considered as a culminating step in writing a program, yet at the same time it is but a split moment in computer time: a second that is instantaneous with another second, and another so on.

As Winnie Soon's and Brian House's essays in this book both argue, computation depends upon increasingly brief and strictly maintained micro-temporalities, in which the maintaining of a consistency in signal processing is essential for the establishing of clock cycles, both in local and more global instances of computation. Thus, as House's essay explains, Google Spanner's "TrueTime" Application Programming Interface (API) is a practical method for synchronising the executing uncertainties of individual computer time in relation to the various needs of Google's globally networked systems. Nevertheless, like the many timekeeping strategies before it, in the process of doing so, Google Spanner inevitably has a direct role in establishing various forms of "micro-experiences" for the many users that come within its sweep (House). Soon traces this microtemporality of computers and the network back from the planetary scale to the rather more mundane instance of a "throbber", those pulsating images of spinning wheels that for Internet users signify a time of waiting for a stream of information to resolve itself. As Soon explains: "a throbber icon acts as an interface between computational processes and visual communication", thus echoing Wendy Chun's well-known statement that software creates an invisible system of visibility by obfuscating certain structures while revealing others (2004, 27). In this sense, the throbber can be understood as an obfuscation of the necessarily discontinuous executing processes of discrete computing, replacing the asynchronous and uncertain clockworks of these tasks with an intentionally smoothed-out visual presentation of the network. Thus a throbber, like Google Spanner's TrueTime, is itself yet another cultural and computational practice that plays a role in "constantly rendering the pervasive and networked conditions of the *now*" (Soon).

In his preface to this book, Yuk Hui notes that "[e]xecution is always teleological because to execute means to carry out something which is already anticipated before the action". Any particular *telos* can be reached according to different methods, each with their own temporalities and often isometric worldviews. Hui traces the way in which a largely linear temporality with predefined sequential procedures and relative logical certainty—such as one finds in eighteenth and nineteenth century forms of mechanisation—represents both an intuitive and simple method of application in executing procedures. At the same time, such perspectives can be seen to readily coevolve with the material and economic conditions of the time in question. The eventual arrival of general-purpose electronic computing machines in the twentieth century sees an explosion of linearity into non-linear recursive cycles of execution. In the process, this introduces different potential rhythms of mechanisation and related paradigms for understanding the world; with the implications of automation and the steady rise of platform capitalism posing particularly urgent questions for enquiry.

In his separate article contribution, Gauthier interrogates misplaced notions of executions as apodictic commands to be followed. In opposition to this sense of command as control, he highlights practices of debugging as illustrative of the continual and unpredictable itineration of signs and signals working themselves through the architectures of any given machine at a given time. The term execution and the way in which it emphasises a sense of a decisive moment can risk a similar emphasis on foreclosure. In contrast, the equally common terminology of running a program has the effect of shifting the focus to a sense of the durational aspects of live execution (runtime) and the ongoing, necessary processes of maintenance involved in executing systems—a topic which Linda Hilfling Ritasdatter's article explores. Her ethnographic investigation in Chennai, South India into the Y2K problem at the turn of the millennium gives a poignant example that links maintenance to a number of problems, including those of computation and its economic conditioning as well as particular colonial and other historical trajectories.

Executing Ecologies

As contributions to this book show, execution is not simply a clean delivery of a task. Command and control is never absolute. This is not to say that a program does not do what it says. Rather, the authors focus on what execution is, how it operates and what might be obscured in the process. The history of computing is one in which computation, in its actual execution and spreading into domains of all kinds, inevitably grows *wild*. As media theorist Friedrich Kittler aptly states,

> *David Hilbert's dreamlike program to clear out the opacity of everyday language once and for all through formalization is undone not only at the clear, axiomatic level of Gödel or Turing, but already by the empiricism of engineers. Codes with compatibility problems begin to grow wild and to adopt the same opacity of everyday languages that have made people their subjects for thousands of years.* (Kittler 1997, 167)

Knuth himself, in an aside during the same keynote, hints at this unruly expansiveness of computing in the world. He refers to a recent experiment carried out by researchers looking to identify and count each tree in a tropical forest. By Knuth's reckoning, the process of counting 250,000 trees in the arboreal survey was roughly equivalent to the number of instructions in a second of computing at the time (Knuth 1991, 13). What, one may ask, is the point of this seemingly off-handed comparison, in which Knuth sees fit to even include detailed photocopied samples from the article on the tree survey in his slides for the keynote presentation? A response suggested by this book would be that enumeration, as a theory and practice lying at the core of computing, puts into motion further modes of counting and calculative execution. Francisco Gallardo and Audrey Samson give the example of Charles Darwin's work on evolutionary deviation from the norm, highlighting how, with the gradual maturation of statistics, theory becomes fully provable as a "thing that holds" (Alain Desrosière, cited in Gallardo and Samson); in other words, as a theory that becomes a fully executable practice. To parcel out the mathematical or the technical from the many other relations that Gallardo and Samson point to, is to miss one of the key qualities and emphases of execution as the direct experimentation with various materially directed affordances and relationalities. This becomes that, and along the way, becomes something entirely else, with each execution posing further correlations, problems and interpretations to be addressed (Snodgrass).

As Jennifer Gabrys notes in the collection's afterword, execution "is a process and condition that might unfurl through code, but also overspills the edges of code". Such intensifications of computation into the lived, everyday experience and its situated applications introduce ecologies that bring other figures of execution that operate outside of a relatively stabilised domain of computation. Contributions in this book include sound, image, user practices, popular culture and shrimping alongside computation. In these instances, execution is often treated as a bio-geo-political process that engages complex terrains. The skins of mammals become sites for pincer-like executions by tick or computer (Snodgrass). Transgenic fish and microbes become organisms where execution is increasingly instantiated (in both a metaphysical and computational sense) by the extension of computation into biotic subjects (Pritchard). Brown shrimp (*Crangon crangon*), fishing trawlers and mechanised modes of automation exist within critical territories of extinction (Gallardo and Samson). In other articulations of natureculture, content curating functions through practices of linking, liking, reposting, RSS feeds or even contouring, while making users' bodies operational for the purposes of big data (Tyżlik-Carver). Hard-coded forms of self-representations such as one finds in the example of emoji character sets are governed by Unicode protocols and the dominant corporate interests of the present (Pierrot, Roscam

Abbing and Snelting). Bodies of many kinds become malleable materials that introduce both flexibility, resistance and often unruly factors of contingency into execution.

Executing Politics

Computing, as an endeavour which emerges out of concerted efforts at command and control, has demonstrated a propensity for furthering the range of executable tasks towards which it can be applied. We find ourselves in an era of an Internet of Things in which computation insinuates itself into objects such as fridges (Gabrys), deadly executions by remotely controlled and autonomous drones (Schuppli) and executions that take place in toxic and polluted landscapes (Pritchard). This increasingly wide range of executing things and practices has the effect of entering into and rerouting a wide range of endeavours. If Marx's dictum that "the hand-mill gives you society with the feudal lord; the steam-mill, society with the industrial capitalist" (Marx, cited by Hui), what is it that a distributed army of Internet-connected web cameras rerouted to carry out a denial of service (DDoS) attack against websites and web hosts (Gabrys) can be said to represent? As Gabrys's afterword on these new methods of making things operational puts it: "Within the Internet of Things, what programs are to be run? Who decides which programs are to be prioritised? And how are the conditions of the executable shifting to give rise to new problems of execution?" At a time when the iconic spectacle of execution by guillotine has been replaced with that of execution by an opaque and rapid agglomeration of black-boxed algorithms fed into remote drone operations, the task becomes that of developing "a politics appropriate to these radical modes of calculation" (Schuppli).

The term execution is often associated with death and the taking of life. Its histories include *l'exécuteur du testament*, from twelfth-century France, designating the executor of the will.[4] In such a manifestation, a specific practice of execution is already embedded in regulatory forms of bureaucracy. As Susan Schuppli highlights in her contribution on "Deadly Algorithms", the etymological and genealogical roots of the term can take on further meanings in the contemporary context of drone warfare, in which "it is only by executive decision that the US President can execute the kill order, which in turn executes a coding script that operates the remote-controlled drone, that is itself engaged in acts of summary execution". Similarly, Geoff Cox, explains how, as with the act of entering into language, there is a similar, perhaps even more overt and inherent violence to the imposition of entering into an interaction with software, particularly for the way in which "[w]ith program code, it not only symbolises but enacts violence on the thing during runtime: it quite literally executes it" (Cox). This kind of "softwar" (Angela Mitropoulos, cited in Cox) of aggression is exerted not only in overt practices of violence but also in everyday interactions with software.

It is not only that contemporary modes of execution can be seen to enact particularly strong impositions within the domains in which they operate, but also that, in many cases, these impositions come with their own forms of exception. Is it unreasonable to take an algorithm to court? What is the responsibility of an individual (human or nonhuman) in a complex computational configuration? Accountability, whether individual or collective, is buried in a mesh of technical, legal and administrative complexity. Peggy Pierrot, Roel Roscam Abbing and Femke Snelting give an example of such complexities in their chapter on the Unicode Consortium's implementation of a skin tone modifier mechanism for emoji. Their chapter highlights how the various technology corporations involved in the Unicode Consortium (such as Apple, Google and Microsoft) claim reputational victories for themselves in relation to a particular implementation, while never considering the colonial assumptions inherent within systems of encoding. As the authors highlight, in such a strategy of exception and deferral,[5] "the companies hide behind the limitations of the standard if necessary, and break out of its confines when desirable" (Pierrot, Roscam Abbing, Snelting). And if drone strikes during Obama's presidency are one instance of executing practices, Donald Trump's election in late 2016 signals emerging ways in which politics is executed on a global scale. As (at the time of writing) Trump is ushered into office on a cresting wave of Twitter updates, election hacking controversies, algorithmically supported fake news items (so-called post-truth politics), the mainstreaming of a slew of long brewing far-right movements is taking hold in violent ways. This situation asks one to, once again, "radically rethink what it means to say 'everyone'", particularly when the de facto standpoint of the majority of the dominant corporations involved in providing the infrastructures and platforms of online expression is one of employing an "a-politicised and egalitarian discourse of diversity" (Pierrot, Roscam Abbing and Snelting).

In response to practices where various states of exception are executed, one oppositional strategy can be to uncover and create various forms of oversight and forms of accountability. Tyżlik-Carver's chapter highlights the continuous editing by many users of the Wikipedia entry on "curator", from its first registered entry at 23:19 on 6 December 2003, delivered by the IP address 131.211.225.204, to an entry in Summer 2016 that includes a fork in the main definition and describes "technology curators" as those "able to disentangle the science and logic of a particular technology and apply it to real world situations and society, whether for social change or commercial advantage". In these works we see what Tyżlik-Carver describes as the way in which executing practices of different kinds are "distributed across and performed by agents of different orders". Samson's additional contribution to the book highlights several different forms of "erasures" and the ways in which they can be seen to "execute knowledge production". Samson gives a range of examples, such as the case of University of California Davis's hiring of reputation management firms to delete an incriminating photo of a pepper spray incident on their campus, so as to avoid negative coverage of the event. Meanwhile, Hilfing Ritasdatter's essay gives a report of acts of black-boxing that sometimes unwittingly become apparent in moments of actual or potential breakdown. The anxieties and worries concerning a breakdown of global systems, caused by the Y2K bug, opens up a moment in which the many complex internal technical, economic and geopolitical relations come into focus. Hilfing Ritasdatter shows how these relations uphold the networked global economy and point towards "the neo-colonial divides" that are maintained and supported by such "anxious" executing flows.

These processes work their way across the spectrum of the political and beyond. We live and die with/in their executions. As Schuppli points out, their significance is manifest and everywhere to be seen and experienced:

> *Algorithms have long-adjudicated over vital processes that help to ensure our wellbeing and survival, from pacemakers that maintain the natural rhythms of the*

> *heart, genetic algorithms that optimise emergency response times by cross-referencing ambulance locations with demographic data, to early warning systems that track approaching storms, detect seismic activity, and even prevent genocide by monitoring ethnic conflict with orbiting satellites.* (Schuppli)

Such executing devices are charged by existing modes of politics, just as they might enable or be reoriented to execute other potential politics. Together with them, various forms of life might be inscribed, curated, supported, destroyed or left to wither away. In Helen Pritchard's chapter on "Critter Chips", we see how organisms are held in semi-living yet enduring states by computational practices, and in Gallardo and Samson's contribution we see this in their example of how populations of brown shrimp are manipulated in ways that mutate the notion of extinction itself, highlighting neoliberalism's dependably thorough ability to financialise all aspects of life and death. Specifically, their example of shrimping involves the bringing together of the fields of computation, statistics, economics and boat design to generate a category of "commercial extinction". This is a slowly fluctuating mode of deadening as a possible mode of life—what Gallardo and Samson describe as "a comfortable form of catastrophe". This almost undead, inexhaustible drive of executable code in its ideal form is readily put into practice by neoliberal, neo-colonial and/or necropolitical (Mbembe 2003) forces in modes of operation that often veer towards exhaustion. As further evidenced in the examples of the forkbomb (Cox) and the example of the Mirai botnet DDoS attack (Gabrys), one can in these instances witness the full undead force and "ability of processes of execution to destroy the very infrastructure of the executable" (Gabrys).

In the face of any such apparent "destiny of execution" (Hilfling Ritasdatter), the direction of many of the contributions here is to suggest a politics of critique as invention, reverse engineering, intervention, repair, resistance and configuration. As the wide variety of topics and examples covered in this book acknowledge, there is an inherent excess and immanence to execution. Automation continually opens onto contingencies, breakdowns and unexpected new terrains of the executable. Similarly, execution has the quality of being both a thought experiment at the same time that it is a matter of *practising* this experiment in the world. The apt inscription and salute of executability—"Hello, world!"—captures this sense of both a putting into practice of a particular instantiation amongst many others as well as a following of its encounters and iterations in the world. In this mesh of executing practices, the potential for configuration continues to make itself available, whether at the level of mass intervention or in the tweaking of a single line or second of code.

Notes

1. See also Fuller's brief discussion of Knuth's challenge in this same book (Fuller 2003, 17).

2. For more details, see http://atariki.krap.pl/index.php/Radiokomputer (in Polish).

3. See http://suchar.net/forum/viewtopic.php?t=15335&sid=0f308438cf03ed15f3eb13d8b6d073b7 (in Polish).

4. For a further exposition on execution, see the entry on "Execution", jointly written by several contributors to this collection, in Braidotti and Hlavajova's forthcoming Posthuman Glossary collection).

5. At the first Execution symposium (2015) held in Aarhus, Denmark, it was pointed out that such protological commands and manoeuvres on the part of contemporary modes of power can be seen to be summed up in the exultant refrain of a song from a comic opera of Gilbert & Sullivan's: "Defer, Defer, to the Lord High Executioner!" ([1885] 1992). For documentation and coverage from each of the two Execution events, see the following links: http://softwarestudies.projects.cavi.au.dk/index.php/*.exe_(ver0.1) & http://softwarestudies.projects.cavi.au.dk/index.php/*.exe_(ver0.2).

References

Animats. 2015. "What happens when you type Google.com into your browser and press enter?" *Hacker News*, January 17. https://news.ycombinator.com/item?id=8902105.

Balsamo, Anne Marie. 1996. *Technologies of the Gendered Body: Reading Cyborg Women.* Durham, North Carolina: Duke University Press

Barad, Karen. 2007. *Meeting the Universe Halfway: Quantum Physics and the Entanglement of Matter and Meaning.* London: Duke University Press.

Critical Software Thing. Forthcoming. "Execution." In *Posthuman Glossary*, edited by Rosi Braidotti and Maria Hlavajova. London: Bloomsbury Press.

Chun, Wendy Hui Kyong. 2004. "On Software, or the Persistence of Visual Knowledge." *Grey Room* 18 (Winter): 26–51.

Fritz, W. Barkley. 1996. "The Women of ENIAC." *IEEE Annals of the History of Computing* 18 (3): 13–28.

Fuller, Matthew. 2003. *Behind the Blip: Essays on the Culture of Software.* Brooklyn, New York: Autonomedia.

Gabrys, Jennifer. 2016. *Program Earth: Environmental Sensing Technology and the Making of a Computational Planet.* Minneapolis, University of Minnesota Press.

Hayles, N. Katherine. 2005. *My Mother was a Computer. Digital Subjects and Literary Texts.* Chicago:

Chicago University Press.
Howse, Martin. 2013. *Diff in June*. Brescia: Link Editions. http://linkeditions.tumblr.com/howse.
Jordan, Tomasz. 1986. "Uwaga... Start!!! Radiokomputer." *Bajtek* 11 (Listopad): 28.
Kittler, Friedrich. 1997. *Literature, Media, Information Systems*, edited by John Johnston. Amsterdam: Overseas Publishers Association.
Knuth, Donald. (1989) 1991. "Theory and Practice." *Theoretical Computer Science* 90 (1): 1–15.
Mbembe, Achille. 2003. "Necropolitics." *Public Culture* 15 (1): 11–40.
Ede, Lisa and Andrea A. Lunsford. 2001. "Collaboration and Concepts of Authorship." *PMLA* 116 (March): 354–69.
Sheppard, Alyson. 2013. "Meet the 'Refrigerator Ladies' Who Programmed the ENIAC." *Mental Floss* UK, October 13. http://mentalfloss.com/article/53160/meet-refrigerator-ladies-who-programmed-eniac.
Stengers, Isabelle. 2005. "Introductory notes on an ecology of practices." *Cultural Studies Review* 11 (1): 183.
Sullivan, Arthur, and W. S. Gilbert. (1885) 1992. *The Mikado*. New York: Dover Publications.

Preface: The Time of Execution

Yuk Hui

Since the late twentieth century, one can clearly observe how the word "execution" has expanded its meaning from its main use in administrative, bureaucratic and juridical milieu since the fourteenth century into the operations of machines and weapons. What exactly the watershed moment was remains a historical question to be debated. However, its signification today has become an urgent social and political question. It marks a paradigm shift from human management to machine management of almost everything: drone killings, DDoS attacks, deep packet inspection, etc. We may want to ask: what does this change of semantics mean? And how is one to understand "execution" in the age of machine automation?

Paradoxically, words such as "machine" and "automation" have become more and more abstract, while both hardware and software have become increasingly concrete. The process of concretisation (Simondon 2012, 21–26)[1] is reflected in the constant amelioration of different layers (e.g. from the microphysical layer to that of the high level application layer) and the transductive operations between and beyond them. It is necessary to investigate the concretisation of technical and digital objects in order to understand such a shift. At the same time, it is important to avoid romanticising a human machine complex as "machine assemblages". I see this volume and the invaluable effort of the authors to be motivated by an urgency to seriously inquire into practices and their relation to the question of execution.

* * *

Execution is always teleological because to *execute* means to carry *out* something which is already anticipated before the action: execution of laws, execution of a plan, execution of a criminal. The *telos* can be reached in variable paths with different temporalities. The intuitive and simplest form of execution is linear, driven by pre-defined procedures. For example, we can see this in recipes: the subject follows step by step instructions until the goal is reached. In the relation between one step and the next step, there is a normalised necessity that assures the orientation.

This linearity is present in the mechanisation of the world that we still read today in the work of René Descartes amongst others, characterised by the geometrical clarity and logical certainty exhibited in the axiomatic. We may want to consider the making of automata as the realisation of this linearity. There, movement is generated by a set of sequential actions executed by elements installed inside the automaton. For example, springs turn gears which then drive another component initiating the automaton's movement. Indeed, Descartes's fascination with automata is well known. They are regularly referred to in the "Second Meditation" of his *Meditation on First Philosophy*, in which the philosopher looks out of the window and asks if the people passing by are not automata wearing coats and hats and powered by springs (Vizier 1996).

The Defecating Duck (1738) by the Frenchman Jacques Vaucanson and Mechanical Turk (1769) by the Hungarian engineer Wolfgang von Kempelen are examples of applying Cartesian thinking to automation at the time. They are also examples of confining technological thinking, and to a large extent philosophical thinking, to a linear and rational mode of thinking. Such an attitude partly comes out of material and energy constraints, that is to say, these conditions limit the types of discursive relations[2] to be realised as physical contacts. Even though Descartes distinguishes man from automata for the reason that the former has soul while the latter doesn't, we must also notice that the linearity of operation is applicable to both of Descartes's dual substances, *res cogitans* and *res extensa*. As Gilbert Simondon pointed out, "the 'long chains of reasons' carry out a 'transport of evidence' from the premises to the conclusion, just like a chain carries out a transfer of forces from the anchoring point to the last link" (Simondon [1961] 2009, 17). This does not mean at all that non-linear thinking didn't yet exist, but rather that linearity as *cognitive schema* of machines was dominant because of its compatibility with classical physics supported by the limited material resources and conditions available at the time. Marx's famous critique of Proudhon's *The Poverties of Philosophy*, where he says "the handmill gives you society with the feudal lord; the steam-mill, society with the industrial capitalist" (Marx 1971, 109; Mackenzie 1984, 473), carries the same sense: the compatibility between material condition and techno-scientific development produces a specific economical structure. This critique can be extended and today it can also include the current computational and networked infrastructures which give us society with platform capitalists.

Indeed, we must acknowledge that there is a temporal gap between philosophical and scientific thinking and technical realisation. This gap constantly creates antagonism and melancholia, which to some extent is inherited in what we call *critique* today. Indeed, non-linear thinking present since the eighteenth century could be seen as a reaction against the animal-machine and man-machine metaphors set up respectively by Descartes and Julien Offray de La Mettrie. It was demonstrated by new discoveries in the natural sciences that gave rise to a new discipline which was later named as biology in 1802 by the German naturalist Gottfried Reinhold Treviranus (1776–1837). During the same time period another German biologist Johann Friedrich Blumenbach (1753-1840) had a great influence on Kant's *Critique of Judgement*. He provided Kant with the scientific resources to inquire into the concept of beauty as "purposiveness without purpose" (*Zweckmäßigkeit ohne Zweck*) in the first part of the critique and the relation between biology and teleology in the second part.[3] The Post-Kantian philosophies such as romanticism and idealism embraced the notion of the *organic form* (notably in the work of Schelling, Hegel and the Schlegels) as the foundation of philosophical systems and mobilised it as a fierce critique against the mechanistic model of Descartes.

Nevertheless, the linear time of execution foregrounds a non-linear historical temporality and functions as a decisive factor of a future to come. The cognitive schema of linear operation provided a temporally stable foundation for social and economic analysis during the modern period, as evident in the work of Adam Smith, Charles Babbage and later Karl Marx. A sufficient example of this can be witnessed in the memorable and well known passage in Adam Smith's *An Inquiry into the Nature and Causes of the Wealth of Nations*, in which a boy transforms the linear execution of his labour into a mechanical execution:

> *In the first fire-engines, a boy was constantly employed to open and shut alternately the communication between the boiler and the cylinder, according as the piston either ascended or descended. One of those*

> *boys, who loved to play with his companions, observed that by tying a string from the handle of the valve which opened this communication to another part of the machine, the valve would open and shut without his assistance, and leave him at liberty to divert himself with his playfellows. One of the greatest improvements that has been made upon this machine, since it was first invented, was in this manner the discovery of a boy who wanted to save his own labour.* (Smith [1776] 2005, 13)

This is paragraph eight of the first chapter "On the Division of Labour", where the concept of automation is introduced. Thanks to this anonymous boy who stretched the ideas of the inventors of the fire-engines to a new terrain, work took another rhythm and the factory another form of organisation. If the temporality of the "machine assemblage" of the boy and the fire-engine consists of a homogenous linear system now, it is because of the desire of the boy to *have time* to play with his companions. Such a temporal structure is bifurcated in the way that the time of the boy and the time of the machine are separated because the mechanical energy of the fire-engine is recycled and thus replaces the labour-energy of the boy. Yet, what is interesting in this passage is the relation between automation and freedom, which remains a very actual question for us today concerning the arrival of full-automation, as some ideologists have claimed (Mason 2015).

The question of automation bifurcated into two opposing thoughts that can be found later in the work of Karl Marx. On the one hand, there is a possibility of the liberation of workers from labours as well as professions, so that they can become free. This joyful picture of the "free man" is described by Marx and Engels in the *German Ideology*, where they say that communism "makes it possible for me to do one thing today and another tomorrow, to hunt in the morning, fish in the afternoon, rear cattle in the evening, criticise after dinner, just as I have a mind, without ever becoming hunter, fisherman, herdsman or critic" (Marx and Engels [1846] 2005, 53). There is a similarity between the desire to hunt, fish and rear cattle, and the boy's desire to play with his companions. Yet, as Marx argued in the "Fragment on machines", there is a great danger embedded in this mode of production, as "not-yet-full-automation" reduces workers to merely "conscious linkages" (*bewußte Glieder*) (Marx [1857] 1973, 620). On the one hand, alienation of workers and Marxist humanism find their common root in the automation of technology. And on the other, the same technology generates sentiments that lead to condemnation and sabotage of machines as a reactionist politics.

* * *

It is evident today that non-linear thinking has pervaded into different domains such as physics, chemistry, economy, etc. and consequently has become a paradigm. It becomes more important to look into the specificity of non-linear thinkings and their compatibilities with each other across different domains. The French philosopher Gilbert Simondon, in an essay entitled "Technical Mentality" (believed to have been written in the early 1960s), suggests cybernetics to be a second cognitive schema in addition to the Cartesian one. The concept of feedback in cybernetics introduced a new temporal structure, one that was no longer based on a linear form but rather was more like that of a spiral. In this schema, the path towards the telos is no longer linear but rather one of a constant *self-regulatory process*, which Simondon himself described as "an active adaptation to a spontaneous finality" (2009, 18). Simondon was fascinated by the concept of feedback, translating it differently on various occasions as "internal resonance", "contra-reaction", "recurrence of causality" and "circular causality".[4] These distinct explanations of feedback are important to his theory of individuation and individualisation. However, as a result of these different translations, it is sometimes confusing that these notions are separate from those of cybernetics and as such should be considered as alternatives to the cybernetic notion of "feedback".

It is from this second cognitive schema described by Simondon that another concept of execution is proposed, one that is very different from the automation described by Smith and Marx. The question that I would like to raise concerning Simondon's classification, and I have tried to respond to it in my own work (Hui 2015a, 2016b), is to move from feedback to recursion. One reason for this is because I see recursive functions as concrete and formal expressions of the concept of feedback[5] which is realised in *every* computational device today.

Indeed, it always appears to me rather surprising that Simondon didn't engage with the concept of recursion. This could be due to the fact that Simondon paid more attention in his research on individuation to quantum physics, biology and psychology than to logic and mathematics (though Simondon also recognised that cybernetics has its foundation in mathematics) (Simondon 2009, 18). In effect, what can be noticed is that in his work, Simondon prioritises transduction over inference in classical logical thinking (2009, 18). And this might also be an explanation for why Simondon had never (at least not in his posthumous publications) elaborated on the concept of "algorithm".

Let us firstly establish the rapports between execution and algorithm. Instead of following the conventional interpretation of Wienerian cybernetics, it is important to re-read Kurt Gödel when addressing our question concerning execution and algorithm. The mathematical development on the question of recursion and its realisation in the universal Turing Machine during the 1930s corresponds to the emergence of what I call "algorithmic thinking" (Hui 2015b). Many people, including computer scientists and social scientists, when explaining what an algorithm is, often compare it to recipes. This is not completely wrong, since an algorithm does specify certain procedures and rules that it has to follow; but it is also absolutely incorrect, since a recipe cannot explain at all what an algorithm of our time is. Algorithm belongs only to the first cognitive schema that we have discussed above.

I would like to put forward that algorithmic thinking should be understood from the concept of recursion. A recursive function simply means a function that calls itself until a halting state is reached. Douglas Hofstadter, in his *Gödel, Escher, Bach: An Eternal Golden Braid*, explains with a joke that, if we were to imagine a German professor giving a lecture in one long sentence with a lot of *Nebensätze*, in the end he would only have to pronounce verbs in order to complete each interaction (Hofstadter 1999, 131). To explain further, let us consider a simple example of computing the Fibonacci number (1, 1, 2, 3, 5, 8, 13, 21...): in the recursive step, the function calls itself, and enters a "spiral" operation until it arrives at its halting status, e.g. when the value of the variable number becomes 0.

```
long fibonacci(long number) {
if ((number == 0) || (number == 1))
return number;
else // recursion step
```

>   return fibonacci(number - 1) + fibonacci(number - 2);
> }

In the non-recursive way, the function will have to create a repetitive loop repeating *n* times (*n* being equal to the value of the input variable, e.g. a long number). From mere repetition to recursion there is a significant change in the cognitive schema. By referring back to Kurt Gödel's work on recursive functions, we may be able to simplify here. His consists of two important steps. Firstly, he developed what is now known as Gödel numbering to arithmetize the quantifiers and operators of the logical propositions in the *Principia Mathematica* of Bertrand Russell and Alfred North Whitehead. This decisive move to numeration turns all symbolic operations into numerical operations and here we observe that it is no longer the physical contacts between different physical parts concretising the discursive relations, as in the example of automata, but rather *data*. Secondly, Gödel developed what he calls general recursivity, which considers logical proofs as arithmetic calculations, or more precisely, as a set of number theoretic functions whose values can be recursively derived. Gödel's development of the recursive function can originally be found in his 1931 paper titled "On Formally Undecidable Propositions of *Principia Mathematica* and Related Systems", and later the general recursive function that he pronounced in Princeton in 1934 can be seen to anticipate the papers from Alan Turing and Alonzo Church (also invoked in this collection by David Gauthier).[6] It is in the question of recursivity that we encounter the notion of computability, since if a natural number is not computable it means that it cannot be recursively deduced from an algorithm, and hence runs into infinite looping, which finally leads to the exhaustion of resources such as memory.

We may want to say: to execute is to compute. This dictum is almost self-evident in many domains of our everyday life: financial markets, social networks, online marketing, etc. What lies in recursivity is another temporal complex which I call *computational hermeneutics* (Hui 2016a, 238–244). It differs from the machine-boy assemblage and from the linear automation implemented by the boy. Computa-tional hermeneutics has its own dynamics resembling a self-regulating, self-learning process (in this sense, we clearly see that all machine learning algorithms are recursive). The paths towards the *telos* are not predefined, rather they are heuristics which are more or less like trial and error, like reason coming back to itself in order to know itself.

In various recursive functions, there is often an opacity into which the human capacity of calculation cannot penetrate. It produces a cognitive opacity which is known under the notorious name of "black box". It is an illusion to ask for more advancement of technology and finer division of labour while longing for the transparency of a society whose existence is no longer sure. Something other than the opposition between transparency and opacity has to be sought. Let us raise the question in another way in light of the shift in the cognitive schemas: which role do human beings occupy in executions characterised by recursivity, especially recursivity of machines? Users is the intuitive answer that we may want to give. We are all users.

Intuitively we may notice that users are part of an algorithm. Not only is the temporality of each user recorded as part of a database, but the existence of the user constitutes partly the executability. In addition, the users are also responsible for dealing with any catastrophic consequences due to errors and contingencies. For example, in the "flash crash" of a financial market, it is not the algorithms but the users (though probably in the end it is the non-users) who are responsible for the aftermaths. Instead of an illusory intimacy, the relation between human and machine has to be accessed from a higher cognitive level and a generalised "algorithmic thinking". It is on this question of execution and algorithm that we find Gilles Deleuze's 1990 essay "Postscript on the Societies of Control" relevant. Deleuze might not have thought about algorithms as we do today, but his philosophical intuition allowed him to see a new form of organisation based on a "modulation" that was taking place and that had to be distinguished from the governmentality that Foucault had analysed.[7] Modulation is distinguished from the rule imposition paradigm characteristic to the disciplinary society, because it operates not on constraints but on "freedom", or more precisely, "free space".[8] In other words, modulation relies on an operation consisting of different heuristics that orients itself towards a certain goal without strictly predefined rules. We may want to point out here that it is executability (we can also consider it as "recursivity") rather than "data empiricism" that constitutes the foundation of an "algorithmic governmentality", as the Belgian researchers Antoinette Rouvroy and Thomas Berns (2013) have convincingly argued.

* * *

To conclude let us go back to the classical opposition between "free man" and "conscious linkages" (or slaves) — two different consequences of the application of automation that we have seen in the first part of this essay. A question that is worth asking is whether this opposition continues in the automation-execution paradigms that we witness today, which are largely different to those observed by Marx in the nineteenth century? Or, does the shift of the cognitive schemas (from linearity to recursivity) in the last centuries displace or transform these oppositions (freedom/slave, opacity/transparency) and the binary choices available to us? For the latter, perhaps we will need a Nietzschean transvaluation [*Umwertung*] of these values in order to proceed further without prisoning ourselves in the choices already given in the last centuries due to the limited understandings of automation and the limitations of automation itself. This transvaluation will also be the beginning of a re-appropriation of automation in order to invent new choices (Stiegler 2016).

Notes

1. I take the concept of concretisation from Gilbert Simondon, in *Du mode d'existence des objets techniques* [On the Mode of Existence of Technical Objects]. He developed this concept to understand the evolution of technical objects and their relations to norms and schemes, in hope of re-integrating technology into culture (Simondon 2012, 15). To Simondon the relation between technology and culture was completely broken in the 18th century and consequently gave rise to an antagonism originated from ignorance and misunderstanding.

2. I develop the concept of discursive relations and existential relations in *On the Existence of Digital Objects*. The former refers to relations that can be said, while the latter refers to temporal relations which escape formalisation; they are the reformulation of the notion of *relationes secundum dici* (relations according to speech) and *relationes secundum esse* (relations according to being) in medieval philosophy.

3. Kant wrote to Blumenbach in a letter dated august 1790, "Your works have taught me a great many things; indeed your recent unification of the two principles, namely the physico-mechanical and the teleological — which everyone had otherwise thought to be incompatible — has a very close relation to the ideas that currently occupy me but which require just the sort of factual confirmation that you provide" (Lenoir 1980, 78).

4. For Simondon's relation to cybernetics, see Yuk Hui, "Qu'est ce que la marge d'indétermination" (2016b), and also Yuk Hui, "Simondon et la question de l'information" (2015a).

5. The role of recursivity (as concrete expression of "feedback") is even more obvious when we consider the recursivity in the second order cybernetics, for example system theory and autopoiesis.

6. For a more detailed analysis of this history, see Hui, *On the Existence of Digital Objects*, Chapter 6.

7. For a detailed explanation on the concept of modulation and its relation to Deleuze's philosophy in general and to the societies of control in specific, please refer to Yuk Hui, "Modulation after control" (2015c).

8. Retrospectively, if we want to understand that modulation is a concept taken from Simondon, then the analysis of the societies of control according to modulation still has to be supplemented by another dimension, since modulation is only one of the two parts of what Simondon calls allagmatic, which is a theory on the dynamics between operation and structure.

References

Deleuze, Gilles. 1992. "Postscript on the Societies of Control." *October* 59: 3–7.

Hofstadter, Douglas. 1999. *Gödel, Escher, Bach. Anniversary Edition: An Eternal Golden Braid*. New York: Basic Books.

Hui, Yuk. 2015a. "Simondon et la question de l'information." *Cahiers Simondon* 6: 29–47.

———. 2015b. "Algorithmic Catastrophe—the Revenge of Contingency." *Parrhesia—a Journal of Critical Philosophy*, 23: 122–143.

———. 2015c. "Modulation after control." New Formations 84/85: 74–91.

———. 2016a. *On the Existence of Digital Objects*. Minneapolis: University of Minnesota Press.

———. 2016b. "Qu'est ce que la marge d'indétermination." *Implications Philosophiques*, http://www.implications-philosophiques.org/actualite/une/quest-ce-que-la-marge-dindetermination/.

La Mettrie, Julien Offray de. 1960 *L'Homme Machine,* 1748.

Lenoir, Timothy. 1980. "Kant, Blumenbach, and Vital Materialism in German Biology." *Isis* 71 (1): 77–108.

Mackenzie, Donald. 1984. "Marx and the Machine." *Technology and Culture* 5 (3): 473–502.

Mason, Paul. 2015. *PostCapitalism: A Guide to Our Future*. London: Penguin.

Marx, Karl. 1971. *The Poverty of Philosophy*. New York: International Publishers.

———. 1973. *Outlines of the Critique of Political Economy*. Trans. Martin Nicolaus, London: Penguin.

Marx, Karl, and Friedrich Engels. 2004. *The German Ideology Part One*. New York: International Publishers.

Rouvroy, Antoinette and Thomas Berns. 2013. "Gouvernementalité algorithmique et perspectives d'émancipation : le disparate comme condition d'individuation par la relation? Politique des algorithmes. Les métriques du web." *RESEAUX* 31 (177): 163–196.

Smith, Adam. 2005. *Wealth of Nations*. Raleigh: Hayes Barton Press.

Simondon, Gilbert. 2009. "Technical mentality." *Parrhesia* 7: 17–27.

———. [1958, 1989] 2012. *Du mode d'existence des objets techniques*. Paris: Aubier.

Stiegler, Bernard. 2016. *The Automatic Society. Volume 1: The Future of Work*. London: Polity.

Vizier, Alain. 1996. "Descartes et les automates." *MLN* 111 (4): 688–708.

Modifying the Universal

Roel Roscam Abbing, Peggy Pierrot, Femke Snelting

In 2015, The Unicode Consortium decided to add five "skin tone modifiers" to the Unicode 9.0 core specifications, a standard that encodes more than a thousand emoji characters. This event triggered a series of reflections and collective actions through which we tried to address how specific entanglements of technology, representation and normativity (re)appear.

While you could consider emoji a pop curiosity — a light-hearted way to inject some humour, emotions or flirtation into otherwise dry text messages — their popularity has coincided with a rising awareness of issues associated with identity politics, resulting in, for example, the implementation of custom gender options in Facebook.[1] With the surge of instant messaging on both mobile and desktop-based applications, the significance of emoji have moved far beyond smiley faces or emoticons typed in e-mails by combining semicolons and brackets. This text documents a period of collective inquiry into the various mechanisms involved in establishing emoji standards. It follows the discussions and conversations that emerged between us while we were trying to intervene into the process via the official channels for public feedback provided by the Unicode Consortium. The text reflects upon how various concerns developed as we tried to decode what was happening before our eyes.

Emoji are one of many examples where technological systems intensely interact with diverse physical bodies. In this allegedly "post racial" and "post gender" era, we witness a racist and sexist backlash, in terms of the intensified discrimination of minorities and women on one side, and the development of affirmation strategies on the other side. In times of Black Life Matters and with Gamergate still raging, the emoji case shows how we might need to radically rethink what it means to say "everyone". It is no surprise though that the very companies that provide the infrastructures for on-line expression (Facebook, Twitter, Google, etc.) avoid engaging in the issue by employing an a-politicised and egalitarian discourse of diversity, and this with increasing ease and success.

The process of implementing emoji modifiers stages race, gender and technologies in a way that seems exemplary of how identity politics is being transformed from a cultural issue into a technical challenge and eventually into a commercial asset. It shows how "identity washing" operates not only in city marketing or official international politics, but also at the level of inter-personal electronic communication. Throughout this process, the politics of anti-racism and anti-sexism are being emptied out of their sense and meaning for the sake of a commodified version of equality.

The two subsequent changes to the emoji standard that we report on in this text are an example of how identity politics have been appropriated by global capitalism, and are being used to supplement and strengthen commercial strategies. Our collective inquiry was also an opportunity to test the (im)possibility for intervening into the formation of technologised representation.

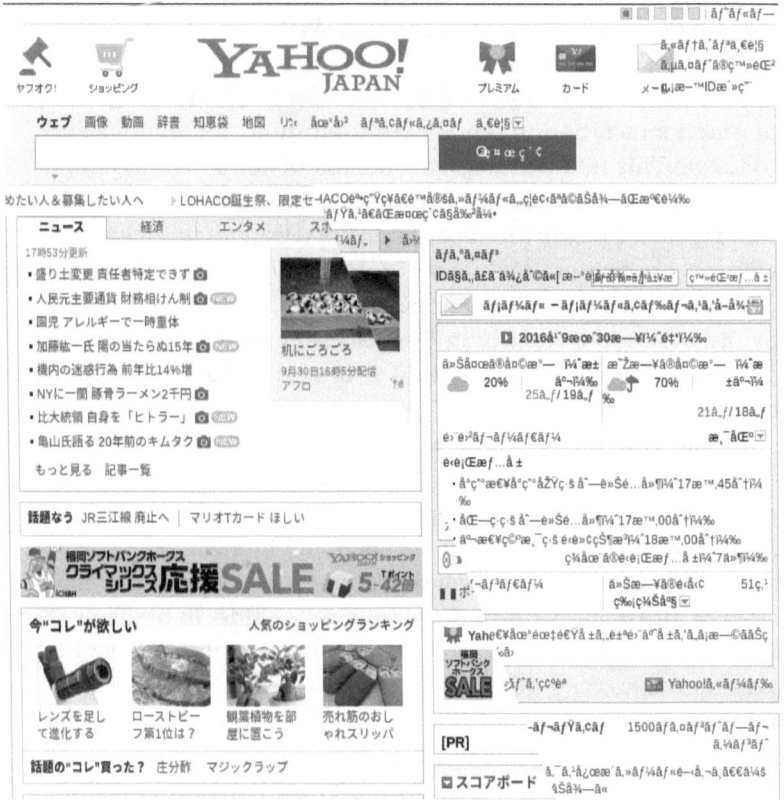

Figure 1. Left: Japanese website written and displayed in a Japanese language encoding. Right: the same website displayed with the American ASCII encoding applied.

The Unicode Standard

Unicode is a non-profit organisation concerned with universal character encoding standards and responsible for a key infrastructure that impacts all use of text on computers, mobile devices and the web. The Unicode standards are designed to normalise the encoding of characters, to efficiently manage the way they are stored, referred to and displayed in order to facilitate cross-platform, multilingual and international text exchange. The Unicode Standard is mammoth in size and covers well over 110,000 characters, of which only around 1,000 are technically considered emoji. Despite their relative marginal presence in the set, emoji currently generate most of the public attention for the Unicode standard and the activities of the Consortium.[2]

The process of standardisation within Unicode is presented as open to discussion. The procedure for adding new characters, for example, relies on a public reviewing of issues and feedback, and the Consortium welcomes proposals for new additions. However, voting members that have the power to decide if a proposal is accepted or rejected each pay $18,000 per year.[3] Most of the current individual members work for one of the nine organisations that hold full membership in the Consortium, and seven of these are US-based technology companies: Adobe, Apple, Google, IBM, Microsoft, Oracle and Yahoo. The Consortium primarily communicates in English, which is the language spoken at most companies involved in Unicode.[4] An obvious bias in this so-called universal project can be found at the heart of the standard itself. With English as an exception, many writing systems use special combinations of letters and accents. Only with some effort can they fit into a single character based paradigm that the Consortium decided to be the basic organisational grid of the Unicode standard. As a result, most languages other than English struggle with the standard to some degree (Jacquerye 2015, 261–268).

More generally, the problem of universality begins with the assumption that anything can and should be encoded in symbolic logic (Blas and Cárdenas 2013). The idea of universality underlies all things software and computer related, such as programming languages and internationalisation processes. This latent universality permeates all layers of communication technology and is strongly normative (MacKenzie 2008, 156).

The universal ambition of Unicode itself can be traced back to its inception in the late eighties. As electronic text was increasingly being exchanged online and between language areas, issues emerged when text encoded in one language was shared and read on systems assuming an encoding in another language. Unicode was a response to the incompatible text encoding standards that were proliferating. When different encodings assign the same binary numbers to different characters, this results in illegible documents. The solution, partly made possible by increased computing capacity, was to strive for a single universal encoding which would encompass all writing systems in the world. This encoding can be thought of as a single gigantic table that indexes all available characters to unique binary numbers, thus circumventing the issue of different encodings with overlapping character assignments.

Maintaining this table and deciding what should be stored in it and where is still the core activity of the Unicode Consortium. It is crucial to understand that the Consortium only deals with the assignment of numbers to characters and not with the way they are rendered. In other words, what Unicode maps is the "idea" of, for example, the Latin capital "A" to a specific binary number. How that "A" itself is represented (italic, Gothic type, big, small, etc.) is the responsibility of glyph and font designers, and not the Unicode Consortium. Furthermore, the standard is non-binding and the actualisation of its universality depends on the willingness of soft- and hardware manufacturers to implement the recommendations of the Consortium.

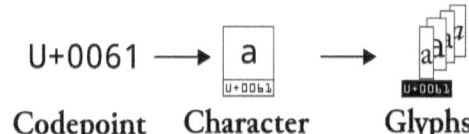

Codepoint   Character   Glyphs

Figure 2. The difference between a code point, a character and a glyph. The Unicode Consortium only concerns itself with the allocation of codepoints to characters and not with glyphs. Pierre Huyghebaert (2015).

Because one face does not fit all

The proliferation of smart-phones and fierce competition between vendors accelerates the attention given to emoji. The cute characters became a surprisingly important argument for buying a new iPhone, iPad or Android phone. In 2015, Apple launched their latest model with a completely redesigned emoji set, now proudly featuring emoji for gay and lesbian couples. The updated Apple designs were breaking with the flat, graphic rendering of emoji images and expressed volume and realism. They cemented the impression that emoji had evolved from visual aids to communicate emotion towards representations of the self. It was also painfully clear that these stand-ins for the human body looked very pale.

Once Apple had launched its high-resolution, pink-hued emoji set, discussions flared up all over the web. The supposed realism of these renderings made people feel "not represented" and subsequently users started to question the yellow base-color of emoji as well. Several petitions asking Apple to increase the diversity in its emoji set attracted thousands of signatures.[6]

The demands to technology giants to fix emoji diversity fell on fertile ground. The protest happened at a moment when US-based technology companies such as DropBox, Pinterest, Airbnb and Twitter had published statistics on the lack of women and people of colour in their workforces, thereby publicly acknowledging their issues with diversity.[7] Each of the companies had hired so-called diversity managers that were tasked with correcting these problems.

The Unicode Consortium, made up of several of these same companies, was put in charge of responding to the pressure.[8] A problem that in essence was caused by an awkward design-decision from Apple, conveniently became a problem to be solved on the abstract level of the Unicode standard. In this meta-context it was clear that the issue could only be addressed through technological means.[9]

Figure 3. Yellow base character rendered with a brown FITZPATRICK TYPE-5 modifier. Screenshot from the Unicode Technical Report 51: http://www.unicode.org/reports/tr51/.

The solution that the Unicode Consortium decided to implement was to add "skin tone modifiers", six new characters that could modify only a designated set of emoji that they considered to represent or include humans. Using essentially the same mechanism that is used to create ligatures,[10] these skin tone modifiers allow users to specify any of six different shades of brown for emoji faces. If the device of the sender or receiver has a modifiable icon set available, the emoji is rendered with that shade of brown. If not, the "default" face will be shown next to the selected colour swatch.

The Consortium based the shades on the Fitzpatrick scale, an existing standard developed for measuring the sensitivity of skin to sun exposure. From the little documentation of this surprising choice, we understand that it was believed that the Fitzpatrick scale could pass without triggering a complicated debate on the representation of ethnicity.[11] Using any scale to differentiate people according to the colour of their skin already implies a colonial gaze, since the modelling of "racial types" has been used to de-humanise whoever was not viewed as a white European. Additionally, the Consortium conflated a medical standard for the sensitivity of human skin to UV exposure with a way to represent skin colour.[12] By carelessly merging the two lightest skin tones, Type 1 and 2, into one single modifier, the Consortium underlined that light skin functions outside this colonial gaze.

The introduction of the modifiers meant that the yellow emoji began to function as a white base, with darker skin colours positioned as an add-on. After Apple had started this confusion between yellow and white, it hardly comes as a surprise that the modifiers were seen as a "blackface" move and a bastardised version of white superiority.[13]

Unlike the rigour that the Consortium usually applies to changes in the standard, the skin tone mechanism was implemented in a relatively short time. The documents available at the Consortium website avoid any reference to possible problematic consequences, and the argumentation for the mechanism comes across as hastily put together. The sub-committee involved with its implementation judged it sufficient to bring in entrepreneur Katrina Parott as an expert, in lieu of the usual dialogue with a supposed user-community. Parrott developed the successful iDiversicon project in response to the on-line protests, but can hardly be considered to single-handedly represent the complex issues of representation that were at stake.[14]

The users' demand for the diversification of emoji points to the way in which on-line representations might operate on the actual through the virtual, and opens up possibilities of representation that are not available in the physical world. But should we see the addition of modifiers as an example of such a potential? Is it a successful form of user-agency, of powerful citizen action? Does the mechanism of skin tone modifiers really bring diversity to the emoji project?

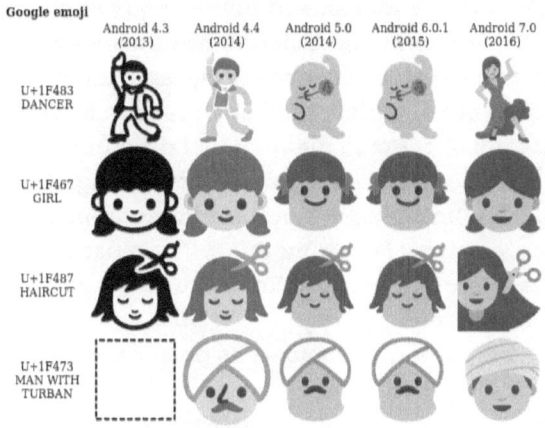

Figure 4. Google's Android has depicted the same emoji characters in different ways over the years, alternating between yellow and pink.

Cross-platform consistency

In April 2015, as soon as the updated Unicode standard was released, Apple integrated the skin tone options on their iPhones. It was celebrated as a victory that vendors were finally taking diversity into account.[15]

Interestingly, Google did not implement the modifiers on their Android platform and continued to render all humanoid emoji as Barbapapa-style blobs in unrealistic yellow. A Google spokesperson indicated that this was a deliberate choice: "[Google's] emoji faces are playful and are all about conveying the emotion you're feeling. They aren't designed to look human or reflect human characteristics".[16] The characters in Unicode that are tagged "emoji" are in fact a hybrid collection of images, each with their own visual language and culture of use. It includes icons originally designed to be displayed on Japanese broadcast screens, map symbols used in institutional communication, typographic dingbats, cute decorative elements and e-mail emoticons for inter-personal messages. At first the heightened presence of emoji on communication devices and applications gave prominence to the expression of emotions. Down the slippery slope, emoji have become a pre-coded form of identification. The skin tone modifier mechanism insists that you are what you type. You are typed.

Standardising this solution for diversity had another unexpected normative consequence. Vendors such as Google, who chose to use less humanised renderings of emoji, or Microsoft, who kept with the Unicode design specifications and rendered the characters with grey skin, came under pressure to normalise their set. A widely published research article into the cross-platform use of emoji claimed that different renderings of the characters could lead to misunderstandings (Miller et al. 2016, 9). A smiling blob + modifier did not render in the same way as a smiling face + modifier. The message you send or receive is altered by those different renderings not only in style, but also in meaning.

At this point, Google changed its position, as explained by Jeremy Burge on *Emojipedia*:

> *While cross-platform consistency was one reason for getting rid of the blob-people, another was to pave way for support of skin tone modifiers. It stands to reason that the blobs look great in yellow, but would look a bit weird if they had skin tones applied.*[17]

In essence, the implementation of skin tone modifiers forced emoji representations into another level of realism, reduced the possibility for different renderings and eventually had the effect of making all emoji look like Apple Color Emoji. In this context, the space for imagining other characters narrowed dramatically, forcing users into labelling themselves according to pre-set categories of gender and ethnicity.

As long as the emphasis is on the action or emotion expressed by the cute yellow, asexual characters, thoughts about gender, race and ability might go away. But the project to encode diverse representations into Unicode can only work if we assume that emoji are representing humans to begin with. Who or what is the template for this "universal" character? Should these complex questions be in the hands of the Unicode Consortium, specialised in finding technical solutions for implementing "all the living languages possible"?

We felt that the blobs and grey characters were at least attempts to widen the possibility for representation in digital communication. And now, even that space is gone.

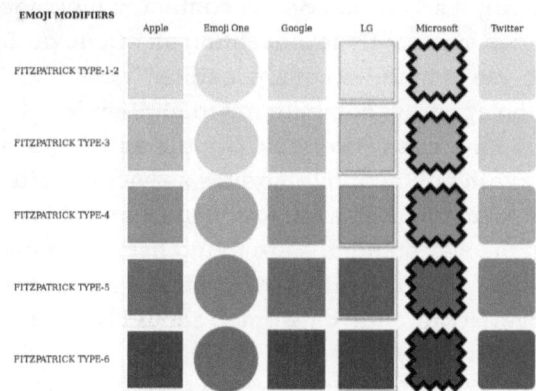

Figure 5. Different implementations of Emoji Modifiers based on the Fitzpatrick scale. The distinction between skin Type 1 and 2 has been conflated into one single "pink" modifier.

Technologies for segregation

In March 2016, Facebook proudly announced their use of ethnic affinities profiling, a thinly veiled form of racial market segregation.[18] For the promotion of the Universal motion picture *Straight Outta Compton*, two trailers were edited. One was targeting "general population (non-African American, non-Hispanic)" and another "African-American" audiences. The commercially successful campaign was the result of a close collaboration between diversity teams in both companies.[19] Despite users' refusal to provide information on their ethnic background, Facebook felt entitled to guess their "ethnic affinity" through analysis and categorisation of the data that they have access to. Segregation based on personal electronic communication had become "marketing as usual".

Emoji skin tone modifiers have of course been used to construct racist comments[20] and there is a documented case of an Instagram search that returns different results depending on emoji with the skin tone modifier applied.[21] Should a Unicode compliant search engine offer to sort results the same way? While Russia investigates if it can sue Apple for their representation of sexual diversity,[22] app stores refuse sex-positive emoji because they do not permit "sexual content".[23] Activists from Turkey were arrested because of their social network accounts, while Libya used Big Data to target its opponents (Manach and Nicoby 2015, 38, 47-48). When social networks can target ads based on the content of messages and user preferences apparently representing an ethnic profile, where will the use of modified emoji lead us?

Despite the apparent commitment to implement encryption, we have seen Facebook, Google and Apple all too easily comply with police or intelligence services to aid the global war on terror. In such a charged landscape, it is difficult to think about the way standards are being handled without a sense of paranoia, and the willingness of these companies to implement diversity through cute emoji should be met with at least some reservations.

The responsibility for instituting the potential for segregation lies not (only) with the vendor who implements such systems, but also with the one who initiates, negotiates and defines the standard. Unicode cannot neglect to consider such consequences.

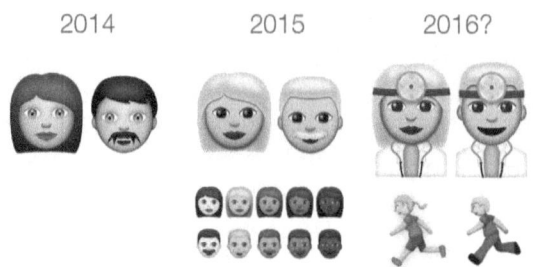

Figure 6. Sketches on emojipedia.org speculating about gender modifiers. Screenshot from http://blog.emojipedia.org/unicode-and-the-emoji-gender-gap/.

Pandora's box

In February 2016, following the perceived success of the modifier mechanism, the Unicode Consortium introduced TR#52, a proposal to allow further customisations of Unicode emoji characters.[24] If accepted, it would ensure that gender variants (such as female runners or males raising a hand), hair colour variants (a red-haired police woman) and directional variants (pointing a gun or a crocodile to the right, rather than only to the left) could be encoded.

The mechanism would use the same principle as the skin tone modifiers, allowing only certain emoji to be altered by certain modifiers. But even if one could now type a message with a female police officer or construction worker, why is there no female dancer wearing a sari, or is U+1F473, MAN WITH TURBAN the only man able to wear a turban? What about hairstyles and different traditions of gesturing, let alone representation?[25]

In their proposal, the Consortium insists on using a limited palette for haircolour because of the "cartoon style" nature of emoji and refers to the US Online Passport application form as the "standard" to follow when choosing this limited palette.[26] The way the U.S. State Department chooses to view and categorise people is a particular expression of how the border control agency sees a person. The aggressive border-profiling that targets young brown men, for example, should not have to make its way into our daily communications. Additionally, the implementation of the proposed gender variants (male, female, neutral) does not address more complex gendered formations such as transgender or transsexuality.

By further expanding the modifier mechanism, the Consortium persisted in addressing diversity through altering a so-called "neutral" base. One only has to imagine the consequences of adding "disability" as a modifier to future Unicode specifications in order to understand this tension. Disability should obviously never be conceived of as a condition of modification to a base-line standard. In practice however, it would have to be implemented exactly in this way. By continuing to naively treat these images as "just like any other character", the Unicode Consortium opened a Pandora's box of implications even wider.[27]

It was with this observation that we arrived at the *Execution* event in Malmö, a three day study session where academic researchers, practitioners and artists from around Europe gathered to question *"the cultural, material and political implications of* execution*"*.[28] We contributed with a talk and a workshop around the question of skin tone modifiers and emoji. At the workshop, participants brought their own expertise and perspectives on the emoji project within Unicode. We proposed to use the space of the workshop to write a collective response to TR52, using the channel for public feedback provided by the Unicode Consortium. After some initial reservations about the way critique would be possible or impossible within the confined space proposed by the Consortium, we began writing as a group.[29]

We agreed on arguing against implementing the proposal based on four points, leaving out a fifth comment on the commercial drive of the Unicode Consortium that we feel is actually at the root of the problem.

> *1. By positing a "normal" baseline against which difference is to be measured, the mechanism sets up problematic relations between the categories that act as modifiers and the pictographs that they modify.*
> *2. To express diversity as a "variant" is a reductive response to the complexity of identities and their representational needs.*
> *3. The Consortium should take into account how, once implemented, the modifiers will function in today's media environment. Should Unicode-compliant search engines differentiate results according to modifier categories?*
> *4. The proposed modifiers for skin tone and hair colour are both based upon questionable external standards. In the case of the Skin Tone Modifiers, the Consortium has chosen to use the Fitzpatrick scale in an attempt to find a "neutral" gauge for skin tone.*

With the comment, we attempted to argue that it does not make sense to fix these issues by finding a less controversial standard for expressing skin tone, or to solve the problem by adding yet more variables, as the mechanism of varying between binary oppositions itself is fundamentally flawed. We felt that the combination of the representational turn and market pressure produced unavoidable and unsolvable problems that the Unicode Consortium tried to respond to through the warped logic of the modifier mechanism. By holding on to the extended modifiers as if they were actually moving in the right direction, the Consortium demonstrated a lack of commitment to actual, complex needs for human communication.

We sent the comment as soon as the workshop ended, a day before the request for comments closed. To our surprise, besides a confirmation of receipt, we did not receive any response. Soon after-wards, we realised that the work on the new mechanism had been suspended:

Work on UTS 52 will be suspended for now in favour of an alternative (ZWJ) approach, focusing on female emoji, that allows for shorter development time and better fallback behavior on older systems.[30]

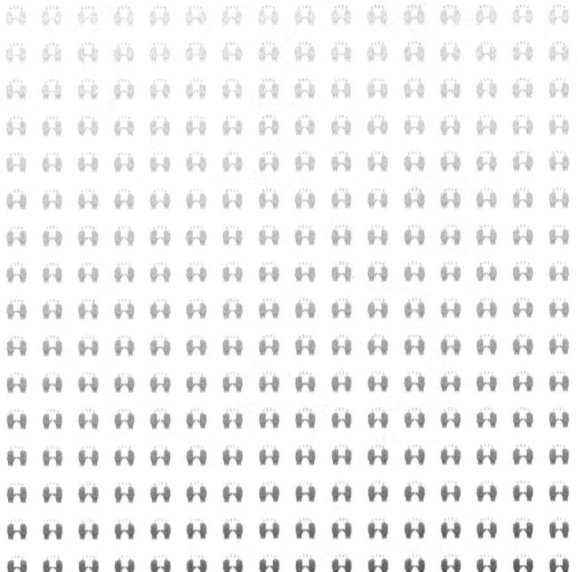

Figure 7. More resolution is no solution

It is all about implementation

But why was the work really suspended? The following is a reconstruction, based on documents available on Unicode.org:

Between the 9th and 13th of May 2016, the Unicode Technical Committee met in San Jose, California in a meeting hosted by Adobe. Among the things up for discussion was the Technical Report #52 on the Emoji Modifiers. In the weeks leading up to the meeting, the members of the Unicode Consortium had asked for and received public input for TR#52 and the proposed meetings, including our comment. On the 10th of May the Emoji Subcommittee and the voting members of the Consortium went through the agenda, reviewing the proposals and comments. This happened during the lunch-break in a so called "ad-hoc session" of which there are no minutes. During this session, Google presented a document which reads as a press release rather than a technical document. It was entitled "Expanding Emoji Professions:

Reducing Gender Inequality"[31] and was simultaneously released to the public. *The Guardian* and several other major news outlets ran a story on Google's proposal that same day.[32] After a short break, a consensus was reached to suspend any work on UTR#52 and to pursue "an alternative approach using ZWJ for representing female emoji", referring to Google's proposal.[33]

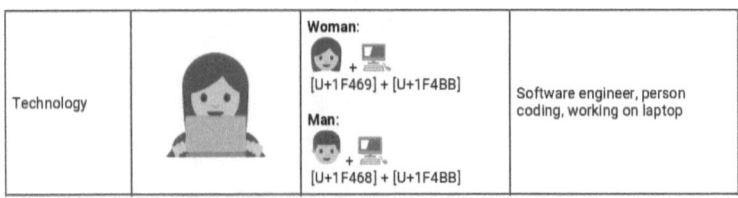

Figure 8. Detail from the Google proposal/press release demonstrating the technological fix where the ZWJ mechanism could be used to quickly create additional diversity without having to deal with the lengthy Unicode process. Screenshot from http://unicode.org/L2/L2016/16160-emoji-professions.pdf.

These events interestingly shifted the responsibility and agency for implementing diversity back to the vendors themselves and away from the Unicode Consortium. This time Google had made sure that the spotlight for making diversity happen, pointed on them, and not on Apple. The proposed change was in favour of using the ZWJ (Zero-Width-Joiner) mechanism rather than a "modifier" or modifier tag mechanism, as was originally proposed. The ZWJ is an invisible character already used in Unicode to denote the combination between two separate characters. This is being used for example in the family emoji, where the Unicode characters for man, woman and child are written in combination with ZWJ. It is then up to the vendor to implement this as a family emoji and to decide on how it shows up on a device. The important shift here is that new emoji can thus be created by making combinations of existing symbols, rather than having to propose new modifiable emoji. This means that any new emoji can be invented (and implemented) by vendors, without having to go through the Unicode Consortium. In effect this is a de-politicization of Unicode, since any move towards representing "diversity" via emoji can now happen through the vendors themselves. Google, for example, "claims" gender with their hyper-mediated introduction of gendered professions and the addition of a rainbow flag.[34]

The event also represents a typical case of do-ocracy, in which a (nominally) open and discursive process of negotiation is sidelined by presenting faits-accomplis. Do-ocracy is a mode of decision-making popular in technical circles for its speed and decisiveness. Having done the task also becomes the justification and validation for it: "Why do we actually use ZWJ emoji? because Google just did it!" Do-ocracy assumes that everyone is able to "act" with the same power and when you want to oppose a decision, you just "do" something else. Whereas Unicode nominally leaves space for individuals and small organisations to participate in the discourse and creation of standards, these individuals and small organisations can never compete with the power of Google do-ocracy. It turns the Unicode Consortium into what so many open standards bodies have become, a rubber-stamping entity to validate unilateral decision-making by large commercial players.

Solutions or diversity and potential for multiplicity

The Unicode Consortium is largely made up of technology giants like Apple and Google. It seems that the Consortium offers them an institutional front in a game of smoke and mirrors. The companies hide behind the limitations of the standard if necessary, and break out of its confines when desirable.

Our participatory observation (and practice-based research) of the decision making process at the Unicode Consortium allowed us to study the technical and social implications. On the one hand, we looked at emoji as a language and how it is perceived, and on the other hand, at the processes at work in social and economic terms. As socio-technical objects, emoji are at the heart of a biopolitical framework. They materialise in the space of communication at a moment when representational policies and politics are being reorganised according to ethnic faultlines with the help of, for example, the big-data-isation of real, marketed or perceived identities.

We observed how major economic actors in the field of communication technologies operate, adapt to external constraints or impose their choices. Technical decisions are sometimes taken without thorough reflection on their implications, whether historical or scientific, let alone on their social consequences. The proposals by the Unicode Consortium are merely techno-centric patches, engineering solutions in response to the increasing complexity of cross-device and cross-cultural computing that actually demands a rethinking of compatibility/translation in terms of difference.

Our collective enquiry was an opportunity to analyse how the Unicode Consortium slid from dealing with cross-language document exchange to a sort of creative political position, without demonstrating any self-awareness of the political nature of its actions. Yet the Unicode Consortium operates as much more than just an IT standardisation of existing languages. Through the encoding of emoji, it creates and normalises a set of representations of humanity. It projects how human bodies must be for them and for numerous other computing companies: industrious, athletic, healthy, stable and classifiable in distinct market categories. As a consequence, possible projections of the body and non-standardised languages are being reduced to stereotypes while sexual or sexually connoted deviant uses of emoji are controlled. Meanwhile, racism and ethnic profiling are not only allowed but encouraged and valued for the sake of their economic potential.

We observed how in our techno-capitalist society identity politics is recycled and reduced to the most congruous, superficial representation of a projected self for marketing purposes. We can only wonder how this will be further used in a changing political context where cultural or "ethnic" profiling of Internet users has become normal. Superficial colour-blindness abounds while a wide wave of reactionary movements—from anti-gay marriage rallies to Alt-rights, Tea Parties and National Fronts of all kind—appear with newly polished faces. Meanwhile, in reaction to radical Islamic bombings all over the world, restrictions of civil liberties are implemented through social media and communications technology. Not at any moment are the colonial assumptions underlying the system of encoding being questioned: the assumption that everything can and should be encoded into the same system.

It is urgent that we develop possibilities for multiplicity, but this means a shift of paradigm. We cannot expect to buy solutions for diversity with the next update because the one-dimensional relation between client and vendor is precisely what produces such superficial implementations in the first place. We need to collectively engage in rigorous discussions about device platforms and the consequences of standardisation processes. Unicode could provide such a platform if it took its own potential more seriously and opened up the process of technology making and standard-forming to the larger public. This is not about having a voice in which emoji should be included into the standard. It is a plea for getting involved in the way technological systems are being drawn up, and to demand more from communication standards than appeasement or soothing ways to solve difference.

When we get together to finish this text a few months later, after a few hours of browsing Unicode repositories, we find the agenda for the meeting in which our comment should have been discussed. The emoji subcommittee has dismissed it with a cryptic: *"Snelting et al: Too late for ESC*[36] *response"*.[37]

Full-color images can be found in the pdf-version available here: http://data-browser.net/db06.html

Notes

Unless otherwise noted, images composed by the authors. Image source files from Unicode.org and *Emojipedia*.

1. "When you come to Facebook to connect with the people, causes, and organizations you care about, we want you to feel comfortable being your true, authentic self." Facebook Diversity, February 2014 https://www.facebook.com/photo.php?fbid=567587973337709.

2. Interview with Mike Davis, Time Tech, March 2016 http://time.com/4244795/emoji-Consortium-mark-davis.

3. Prices are listed in USD only. http://unicode.org/Consortium/levels.html.

4. http://www.unicode.org/consortium/members.html.

5. http://www.unicode.org/reports/tr17/#CharactersVsGlyphs.

6. Two petitions ran simultaneously, http://web.archive.org/web/20140730201055/https://www.dosomething.org/petition/emojis and https://www.change.org/p/groupme-and-emoji-developers-add-more-diversity-to-the-emojis?recruiter=7740596&utm_campaign=twitter_link&utm_medium=twitter&utm_source=share_petitionb The campaign was championed by pop singer Miley Ray Cyrus on Twitter https://twitter.com/hashtag/emojiethnicityupdate.

7. Twitter: "We're committing to a more diverse Twitter" https://blog.twitter.com/2015/we-re-committing-to-a-more-diverse-twitter Apple: "Inclusion inspires innovation" https://www.apple.com/diversity Google: "A diverse mix of voices leads to better discussions, decisions, and outcomes for everyone." https://www.google.com/diversity Facebook: "We are dedicated to creating an environment where people can be their authentic selves" https://www.facebook.com/facebookdiversity/about.

8. "When we originally designed emoji, the goal was to be as neutral

as possible. The emoji charts that Unicode supports are black and white and other people will interpret them in color for realism ... we struggled with how to deal with [diversity] for a bit because what we didn't want to do is multiply the emoji tremendously." Interview with Mike Davis, Time Tech, March 2016 http://time.com/4244795/emoji-Consortium-mark-davis.

9. "Tim (Tim = Tim Cook, CEO of Apple) forwarded your email to me. We agree with you. Our emoji characters are based on the Unicode standard, which is necessary for them to be displayed properly across many platforms. There needs to be more diversity in the emoji character set, and we have been working closely with the Unicode Consortium in an effort to update the standard." Katie Cotton, vice president of worldwide corporate communications for Apple, March 2014 https://www.yahoo.com/news/the-emoji-diversity-lobby-emoji-design-kevin-119455434306.html

10. A ligature occurs when two or more letters are joined into a single glyph, for example the character æ in English, combining the letters a and e.

11. "The Fitzpatrick scale was developed for use in dermatology, it is also used in cosmetology and fashion design (and) it has the advantage of being recognized as an external standard without negative associations" http://www.unicode.org/L2/L2014/14213-skin-tone-mod.pdf

12. http://www.beauty-review.nl/wp-content/uploads/2014/04/The-validity-and-practicality-of-sun-reactive-skin-types-I-through-VI.pdf

13. "These new figures aren't emoji of color; they're just white emoji wearing masks" https://www.washingtonpost.com/posteverything/wp/2015/04/10/how-apples-new-multicultural-emojis-are-more-racist-than-before

14. Parrott recently added a section "people with disabilities" to her commercially available emoji set. "Because One Face Does Not Fit All" http://www.idiversicons.com

15. "UPDATE: WE WON! You signed the petition. Now Apple is diversifying its Emojis!" http://web.archive.org/web/20140730201055/https://www.dosomething.org/petition/emojis

16. "Android 6.0.1 Emoji Changelog", *Emojipedia,* December 2015 http://blog.emojipedia.org/android-6-0-1-emoji-changelog

17. "Android N Drops Gender-Neutral Emojis", emojipedia, April 2016, http://blog.emojipedia.org/android-n-drops-gender-neutral-emojis

18. "Facebook's ad platform now guesses at your race based on your behavior", *Ars Technica*, March 2016 http://arstechnica.com/information-technology/2016/03/facebooks-ad-platform-now-guesses-at-your-race-based-on-your-behavior

19. "(Doug) Neil (Universal's EVP of digital marketing) credited part of this (project) to a specialized Facebook marketing effort led by Universal's "multicultural team" in conjunction with its Facebook team. They created tailored trailers for different segments of the population." http://www.businessinsider.com/why-straight-outta-compton-had-different-trailers-for-people-of-different-races?r=US&IR=T&IR=T

20. "Apple's ethnic emojis are being used to make racist comments on social media. They were intended to promote harmony, but have achieved the opposite" *The Independent*, April 2016 http://www.independent.co.uk/life-style/gadgets-and-tech/features/apples-ethnic-emojis-are-being-used-to-make-racist-comments-on-

social-media-10182993.html

21. http://rhizome.org/editorial/2015/dec/08/uif618-your-ascii-goodbye

22. "Russia could be investigating Apple over 'gay propaganda' because of emoji" *Silicon Republic*, September 2015 https://www.siliconrepublic.com/companies/apple-under-investigation-in-russia-for-same-sex-emoji-reports

23. 'We'd love to build an app with all the Flirtmoji, but the Google Play Store and Apple App Store don't allow (see: censor) all sexually explicit content.' https://www.flirtmoji.co/pages/faq

24. "Proposed Draft Unicode® Technical Standard #52" http://www.unicode.org/reports/tr52/tr52-3.html

25. "In addition to gender bias, the clothing emoji are biased towards western and Japanese culture, so clothing items from other cultures might also need to be considered for inclusion. I think this is only the beginning of a discussion to make clothing items more gender & culturally inclusive, or to decide to what extent that is a goal." www.unicode.org/review/pri321/.

26. http://www.unicode.org/reports/tr52/tr52-1.html#Introduction.

27. When discussing the issue with Hin-Tak Lueng, developer of a font-validator aiming for full Unicode coverage, responded: "It was like they scratched an itch and then their whole skin fell off" Hin-Tak Leung at Libre Graphics Meeting London, April 2016.

28. Executions: conversations on code, politics & practice, Malmö University, Malmö, Sweden, April 2016 http://softwarestudies.projects.cavi.au.dk/index.php/*.exe_(ver0.2).

29. The comment was collaboratively written by Geoff Cox (Associate Professor, Aarhus University, Denmark), Linda Hilfling Ritasdatter (PhD candidate, Malmö University), David Gauthier (PhD candidate, University of Amsterdam), Geraldine Juárez (MFA candidate, Valand Academy, University of Gothenburg, Sweden), Marie Louise Juul Søndergaard (PhD candidate, Aarhus University, Denmark), Helen Pritchard (Research Fellow, Goldsmiths, University of London), Susan Schuppli (Senior Lecturer, Goldsmiths University of London), Molly Schwartz (PhD candidate, Malmö University), Eric Snodgrass (PhD candidate, Malmö University), Winnie Soon (PhD candidate, Aarhus University Denmark), Magdalena Tyzlik-Carver (Research Fellow, University of Sussex, Brighton, UK). Available here: http://possiblebodies.constantvzw.org/.

30. http://www.unicode.org/review/pri321/.

31. http://www.unicode.org/L2/L2016/16160-emoji-professions.pdf.

32. "Google proposes new set of female emojis to promote equality", *The Guardian*, 11 May 2016 https://www.theguardian.com/technology/2016/may/10/female-emojis-google-equality.

33. http://www.unicode.org/reports/tr52/.

34. http://blog.emojipedia.org/gendered-emojis-coming-in-2016/ and http://blog.emojipedia.org/rainbow-flag-emoji-details-published/.

35. "Instagram blocks 'offensive' eggplant emoji hashtag", *CNN*, April 2015 http://money.cnn.com/2015/04/29/technology/eggplant-instagram-offensive/index.html.

36. ESC = Emoji SubCommittee.

37. http://www.unicode.org/L2/L2016/16130-emoji-subcom.pdf.

References

Blas, Zach, and Micha Cárdenas. 2013. "Imaginary computational systems: queer technologies and transreal aesthetics." *AI &*

Society 28, no. 4: 559–566.

Jacquerye, Denis. 2015. "Unicodes." In *I think that conversations are the best, biggest thing that Free Software has to offer its user*, edited by Femke Snelting and Christoph Haag. Brussels: Constant.

MacKenzie, Adrian. 2008. "Internationalization." In *Software Studies: A Lexicon*, edited by Matthew Fuller. The MIT Press.

Manach, Jean-Marc, and Nicoby. 2015. *Grandes oreilles et bras cassés*. Futuropolis.

Miller, Hannah, Jacob Thebault-Spieker, Shuo Chang, Isaac Johnson, Loren Terveen, and Brent Hecht. 2016 "'Blissfully happy' or 'ready to fight': Varying Interpretations of Emoji." *ICWSM'16*. Menlo Park, CA: AAAI Press.

RuntimeException()
—Critique of Software Violence

Geoff Cox

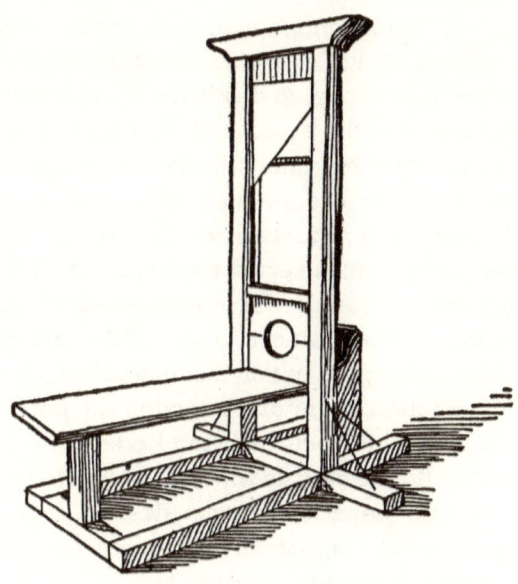

There is an inherent violence of software.[1] Our network operations are dominated by violent acts against us in the form of viruses, spam, phishing and botnets, and more to point, violence is encoded in software itself. As with language, we enter informational infrastructures antagonistically — echoing Judith Butler's observation that we come into language antagonistically from our beginnings (Butler 1997, 1; Cox & McLean 2013).[2] Butler's point is that violence is embodied in language, not simply in the way it might be used to incite a violent action or in the ways that language reflects social domination more generally — such that it can be injurious, as in the case of hate speech (against refugees, for instance). But, as Slavoj Žižek has also pointed out (after Hegel), language also is violent in the way that it produces meaning. There is something inherently violent in the capacity of language to represent a thing, what he calls "its essencing ability" (Žižek 2008, 52), equivalent to its symbolic death. As it stands in for something, "it dismembers the thing, destroying its organic unity", and forces the thing into a field of meaning that is outside of itself (58). This also happens at the level of software, and perhaps in a more overt manner, as programming languages extend natural languages through their protocological address to humans and machines. With program code, it not only symbolises but enacts violence on the thing during *runtime*: it quite literally *executes* it.

The term execution combines parallel understandings of violent, computational and legal acts, including, for instance: putting a condemned person to death; the act of performing something successfully; the process of carrying out an instruction by a computer during the runtime phase; the completion of a legal instrument such as a contract so that it becomes legally binding and enforceable; a routine court order that attempts to enforce a legal judgment; the act of accomplishing some aim or executing some order, unlawful premeditated killing of a human being by a human being, and so on.[3] Beyond symbolic violence and the deadly assault on meaning, it indicates how the completion of an action, order or instruction can produce violent consequences with real effects on living bodies. This is perhaps what artist Martin Howse signals with his work *pain registers* (2011), in which a pin penetrates human flesh as a consequence of instructions from the computer's processor when performing the simple operations of web browsing.[4]

In this essay I want to draw out some of these tensions between execution and decision-making at an operational level—where cultural and computational logics collide— or, in other words, my aim is to examine the intersection of sovereign code and law, and moreover, how contemporary forms of sovereignty execute commands or indeed refuse to execute them. The example from Mladen Dolar's book *A Voice and Nothing More* comes to mind, in which a group of soldiers repeatedly fail to execute the order of their general to attack their enemy and instead contemplate the beauty of his voice (2006, 3).

In terms of further reference points, and at the time of writing, it is also hard not to be distracted by recent terrorist events that make parallels between execution at the level of a successful completion of a task and its deadly consequences. When does the logic of one form of execution serve the other? Incidents in Paris and Brussels and the empathetic hysteria that ensued come to mind (#prayforparis/brussels),[5] as does the French-speaking context more generally invoking the republican use of the guillotine to execute the ruling elite as well as anti-fascist and anti-imperialist revolutions in North Africa. One of the famous scenes from the film *The Battle of Algiers* makes the inherent duplicity of the moral order apparent: a reporter asks the captured terrorist leader Ben M'hidi: "Isn't it cowardly to use your women's baskets to carry bombs, which have taken so many innocent lives?"; he responds, "Isn't it even more cowardly to attack defenseless villages with napalm bombs that kill many thousands of times more? Obviously, planes would make things easier for us. Give us your bombers, sir, and you can have our baskets" (1966). The assumption in this essay is that software offers the potential to be a parallel response.[6]

* * *

But before discussing these issues with respect to software, I will firstly introduce the subject of violence in more detail. As is probably clear at this point, the subtitle of this essay refers explicitly to Walter Benjamin's 1921 essay "Critique of Violence" (1996).[7] For Benjamin, at issue is not whether violence is a means to a just or unjust end, but whether violence can be a moral means in itself. As he puts it, "a more exact criterion is needed, which would discriminate within the sphere of means themselves, without regard for the ends they serve" (1996, 236). So rather than simply reconciling just ends by a justification of the means, or vice versa, the required focus becomes "the question of the justification of certain means that constitute violence" (237).

As far as the state is concerned, violence exercised by individuals, or its legal subjects, is a threat to the legal system that uses violence for legal ends that the law itself legitimates (such as police or military violence). This indicates the law's "monopoly on violence" as Benjamin puts it, in not simply preserving legal ends but more importantly in preserving the institution of the law itself. It also affirms the threat of actions that are outside of the law, and how even oppositional kinds of action or protests are tolerated because they affirm the power of the law to guarantee certain freedoms. The right to free speech is an example of this technique of power for example and I will return to this later in the essay.

Another important exception has been the right of workers to strike, conceded by the state in recognition of the inevitability of antagonism in the workplace. Whether overtly violent or not, the motivation to strike is to address the violence already imposed on the worker by the employer. In this way, and as Leon Trotsky pointed out in his essay "Terrorism" (1911), arguments against the use of violence are inherently hypocritical: "And the only question remaining is whether the bourgeois politicians have the right to pour out their floods of moral indignation about proletarian terrorism when their entire state apparatus with its laws, police, and army is nothing but an apparatus for capitalist terror!"

On the one hand terrorist violence is seen to be inadmissible by the moral order, and yet on the other, in *exceptional* circumstances it is seen to be necessary according to the self-interest of the state apparatus.

Much the same duplicity applies in contemporary discussions, wherein the "state of exception" becomes the justification for the erosion of human rights and freedoms in the paranoid context of securitisation.[8] The duplicity is evident in the way those deemed a danger to national security can be taken into custody and detained without trial or other sovereign states can be invaded in contravention with international law. The examples are well known by now. This paradoxical condition has been discussed in depth in Giorgio Agamben's *State of Exception* (2005), extending Carl Schmitt's *Politische Theologie* of 1922 that established the contiguity between sovereignty and the state of exception ("the sovereign is he who decides on the exception"). Agamben argues that the state of exception, although first described as a provisional measure in exceptional circumstances, has become the working paradigm of modern government (2001).[9] Under this logic, state power uses violence against an identifiable enemy—often preemptively—so that its use of power appears necessary and legitimate despite the active contradiction with its own legal and natural laws. When the required ends cannot be guaranteed by the legal system alone, the repressive state apparatus further exercises violence in the name of counter-terrorism or interests of national security.

If the parallel development of security and liberalism has already been well established (by Foucault), the issue of security today seems almost reducible to the challenge of managing the inherent vulnerability of networked relations. Software running over networks is increasingly regarded as a threat to security in this way and profitable commercial industries support this strategy of governance. In *The Exploit*, Alexander Galloway and Eugene Thacker identify how networks and sovereignty are indeed not incompatible but exceptional — together related as "sovereignty-in-networks" (2007). Correspondingly, the recommendation to those developing oppositional tactics is to take advantage of the vulnerabilities in networks by exploiting power differentials that are inherent to the networked system (Deleuze 1992). This is precisely how software developers and malware (malicious software) developers operate, as they exploit vulnerable operating systems, internet service and security software.

Software violence and counter-violence is propagated through such means to exploit known and potential vulnerabilities. Malware is usually installed via worms, trojan horses or backdoors under a common command and control infrastructure. For instance, a program installed by a botnet can violate a system's hard disc and monitor user's keystrokes to gather private data (such as sensitive financial information, including credit card numbers and passwords for bank or Paypal accounts) and then distribute the retrieved data over the internet back to the computer running the malware (a so-called zombie computer). In the example below, the function names and keywords below are taken from a popular bot with packet sniffing capabilities to capture online credentials and other information (Ianelli & Hackworth 2005).

> *bool IsSuspiciousVULN(const char *szBuf) – looks for keywords that indicate vulnerable server versions. Examples include:*
> • *"OpenSSL/0.9.6"*
> • *"Serv-U FTP Server"*
> • *"OpenSSH_2"*
> *bool IsSuspiciousHTTP(const char *szBuf) – may attempt to gather HTTP based authentication credentials and other valuable data. In this sample bot, the keywords appear to target paypal cookies.*
> • *"paypal"*
> • *"PAYPAL"*
> • *"PAYPAL.COM"*
> • *"paypal.com"*
> • *"Set-Cookie:"*

There are countless other examples that illustrate how vulnerabilities can be exploited and how botnets can cause severe disruption to targeted sites. A botnet can control a set of "hijacked" systems to target systems (e.g. a commercial or government website) with information requests in a distributed denial of service (DDoS) attack.[10] The hacktivist tactics of Lizard Squad, Anonymous, or of LulzSec, the splinter group of Anonymous who have been "Laughing at your security since 2011!" exemplify such an approach (Coleman 2014). These loosely associated networks of activists and hactivists have coordinated various DDoS attacks using forums and social media websites, where instructions were disseminated on how to download attack software to bombard websites with data to try to throw them offline. "Operation Payback" is one such example from 2010, targeting sites that had cut ties with WikiLeaks (such as MasterCard, Visa and PayPal).[11] More currently, Anonymous considers itself to be "at war" with the Islamic State following the recent terrorist attacks in Europe as a continuation of its "#OpISIS" campaign.[12]

These computational lines of attack, whether overtly violent or not, address the violence already imposed on the user if we follow the logic of the argument thus far. In what Angela Mitropoulos has referred to as "softwar" (2007), violence is exerted on software users in everyday circumstances, not least forcing them to pay and upgrade regularly when there are viable free alternatives as in the case of proprietary forms, and thus demanding a response. Mitropoulos refers to the issue of intellectual property and related conflicts over sharing digital content, such as those over P2P file sharing. Double standards are expressed when the user agrees to the terms of service that disallow certain actions that are inherent to the technology. Furthermore, the moral ambiguities of software licenses and duplicities of the law are plain to see, and at the heart of all terms of service agreements and copyright regimes. To break a contract thereby is to activate the threat of violence enforced by the law, whereas — as I am arguing — the greater violence has already been committed and gone unpunished in the first place. Whistleblowing is another good example of this faulty logic, or the Wikleaks project more broadly that stresses the ethical position of many who choose to break the law for the greater good. When no other choice is possible, software insurgency might be a justifiable response, founded on some of the ethical standards that the hacker movement has strived to promote:

> *Access to computers—and anything that might teach you something about the way the world really works—should be unlimited and total. Always yield to the Hands-On Imperative!
> *All information should be free.
> *Mistrust authority—promote decentralization.
> *Hackers should be judged by their acting, not bogus criteria such as degrees, age, race, or position.
> *You can create art and beauty on a computer.
> *Computers can change your life for the better.
> *Don't litter other people's data.
> *Make public data available, protect private data..[13]

In following these principles, it should be stressed that the majority of hackers condemn malign attacks. The use of *non-violent* direct action and tactical media is more commonplace, such as the FloodNet DDoS software developed in 1998 by the Electronic Disturbance Theater, and used by the Zapatistas against Mexican and American governments websites.[14] Although for many hackers the ethical practices of free software represent a move away from the use of overt violence, the paradoxes of power simply cannot be avoided as *violence is inherent to software*. Perhaps more contemporary examples of online violence serve to emphasise how software itself contains active contradictions that oscillate between truth and falsity (like Boolean logic), between violence and non-violence, and yet where both states are necessary for logical relations in networked sovereignties.

Lizard Squad's DDoS attack on the free software Tor browsing network in January 2015 makes another good example.[15] The attack aimed to highlight vulnerabilities with respect to Tor's ability to enable anonymity on the Internet and thereby to remain outside the reach of government monitoring agencies like the NSA. By attacking nodes used to relay information between peers, and setting up new relays called "LizardNSA", Lizard Squad could begin to piece together communications that were transmitted under the belief that the information was anonymous. The action enraged other hacker groups such as Anonymous who released the following Twitter message: "Hey @LizardMafia don't f--k with the Tor network. People need that service because of corrupt governments. Stand the f—k down" (Plummer 2015).

Responding to debates about Internet freedom in such a way operates in parallel to the paradoxes of free software and free speech as if they were not already problematic concepts.[16] The ethics of free software emerged out of the hacker communities yet the ambiguities of free speech as the central analogy have not been critically developed inasmuch as it is enshrined in the liberal tradition that recognises that suppressing freedom of speech is a crude tactic of governance. Instead the state, for the most part, opens up the widest possible domains for the expression of opinions that become constituent of its own exercise of power protected under international law. The Universal Declaration of Human Rights states that: "Everyone has the right to freedom of opinion and expression; this right includes freedom to hold opinions without interference and to seek, receive and impart information and ideas through any media and regardless of frontiers."[17] Article 10 of the European Convention on Human Rights similarly provides the right to freedom of expression, but like Article 19 is also subject to certain restrictions that are deemed "necessary in a democratic society".[18] Certain restrictions are implemented when deemed necessary in the interests of national security, or public order, or protection of public health and morals, and so on.

This leaves freedom on the Internet, as with life in general, subject to both state and (free) market regulation, further compromised by the pervasive use of filtering software and dataveillance practices. Antoinette's Rouvroy's notion of "algorithmic governmentality" resonates with these practices and our (in)ability to intervene in processes of government (2013). Subjectivities are produced in relation to what algorithms understand about our intentions, gestures, behaviours, opinions, or desires to be, through aggregating massive amounts of data and machine learning. She refers to this as "personalisation without subjects" and identifies the mistake of discussing concerns over personal data when what more crucially is at stake are the processes of subjectification through data mining and profiling. Under contemporary conditions, it is clear that governments exert forms of violence on their citizens in quite subtle ways that do not appear directly violent. The "violence of participation" (Meissen 2007), for instance, is a form of violence that doesn't appear violent at all and inherent antagonisms are hidden from view (that Schmitt would identify as essential to our understanding of politics).[19]

Therefore — and this is my point — it becomes necessary to produce paradoxes at the level of software in recognition of its central role in the structural logic of contemporary capitalism. The violence embodied in software is inherent to the way it prescribes and determines certain ethical decisions and actions as well as how subjectivation operates in societies of control. Like the myth of freedom of choice or participation, violence is demonstrated at multiple levels of execution, and exerted against information that wants to be free and code that wants to remain undead.

* * *

Benjamin's "Critique of Violence" described the potential for "pure immediate violence"—human action that neither makes nor preserves law, but is outside of the law altogether. The idea of pure violence does not apply to any violent action in itself, but in its relation to the conditions under which it is constituted. The concept is complex and draws together class violence with the theology of divine violence represented by Judaic Messianism[20]—where redemption is provided by pure divine violence. So rather than promote terrorist violence, Benjamin instead calls for "collective political action that is lethal not to human beings, but to the humanly created mythic powers that reign over them" (Buck-Morss 2003, 33).

The concept of pure violence is a violence that appears to come from nowhere—from beyond the law—in which "killing is neither a crime nor a sacrifice", because law applies only to the living: "Divine violence is an expression of pure drive, of the *undeadness*, the excess of life, which strikes the 'bare life' regulated by law" (Žižek 2008, 168). The explanation makes reference to Agamben's *Homo Sacer: Sovereign Power and Bare Life* (1998) that questions the nature of law and biopower (thus again extending Foucault). To explain briefly, under Roman law, someone who committed a certain kind of crime was banned from society and rights as a citizen revoked: "Homo sacer" (sacred life) was excluded from law itself, while being included at the same time. Agamben explains how this figure is the inverse of the sovereign who stands, on the one hand, within law and outside of the law—since they have the power to decide the state of exception where law is "suspended"—the exception. According to Agamben, biopower, which takes the bare lives of the citizens into its political calculations, may be more marked in the modern state, but has essentially existed since the beginnings of sovereignty in the West, since this structure of exception is essential to the core concept of sovereignty. Referring to Schmitt's view of sovereignty and the rule of exception, Agamben explains this as "the condition of being excluded through an inclusion, of being in relation to something from which one is excluded" (1998, 26-7). Because politics has been contaminated with law in the state of exception according to Agamben, and because only human action is able to cut the relationship between violence and law, it becomes increasingly difficult for humans to act effectively against sovereign power. Hence we get all kinds of desperate actions that are symptomatic of more general and paranoid aspects of contemporary culture—from suicide to mass killings (Berardi 2015; Cox 2013).

Agamben is drawing upon Benjamin's formulation of the necessity of a politics of pure means in order to develop an idea of life as pure immanence. His own formulation of this, in *Means without End*, emphasizes that: "Politics is the sphere of pure means, that is, of the absolute and complete gesturality of human beings" (Agamben 2000, 59). To Agamben, gesture (or pure means) is not action as a means in itself but a pure and endless mediality that disrupts the false distinction and presents means without end. The event of language, for instance, is political in as much as it relates to the free use of pure means. It can perhaps be seen how software operates in a similar manner, making means more apparent and thus opening up the political dimension of coding.

It is the *undeadness* of code that seems to allow for this, as action in excess of violence. Both the undeadness of information and the (undead) logic of programmability are attempts to reanimate dead materials, highlighting the potential to draw together instruction and execution across multiple layers of operation.[21] Think, for example, of a forkbomb,[22] a denial-of-service attack wherein a process continually replicates itself in an infinite loop to deplete available system resources, causing resource starvation and eventually *killing* the system. When there is no other choice, one might speculate further about how software might express pure means in such ways once directed at the sovereign technical infrastructures that already exert forms of violence upon us. This seems necessary to balance the ways in which life now operates under contemporary conditions and in order to introduce further and more ethical exceptions to sovereign rule.

:(){ :|:& };:

Notes

1. A version of this article was published in Spanish, "Crítica de la violencia software" (2015), itself based on an even earlier version, "Critique of Software Security" (2009, 27–39).

2. Butler is referring to Althusser's notion of interpellation (see Cox & McLean 2013).

3. See http://www.thefreedictionary.com/execution.

4. See Eric Snodgrass's "What is executing here?" in this volume for a more detailed description of Howse's *pain registers*.

5. I refer to the attacks in Brussels (22 March 2016) and the Charlie Hebdo shootings in Paris (7 Jan 2015) provoked by satiric images of Mohammad and their earlier re-publication of the *Jyllands-Posten* cartoons of Muhammad in 2006; and the shootings at the public event "Art, Blasphemy and Freedom of Expression" at the Krudttønden cultural centre, Copenhagen (14–15 Feb 2015), where Swedish artist Lars Vilks was in attendance and thought to have been the main target because of his drawings of Muhammad.

6. Much the same was said by Deleuze in "Postscript on the Societies of Control": "Computer piracy and viruses, for example, will replace strikes and what the nineteenth century called 'sabotage' ('clogging' the machinery)" (1992, 3–7).

7. In addition, the question of violence has been addressed by many others, such as: Hannah Arendt's "On Violence" (1969);
Pierre Clastres's "Archaeology of Violence" (1979); Frantz Fanon's *The Wretched of the Earth* (published in French as *Les damnés de la terre*, 1961) in which violence opposes the violence of colonialism; Georges Sorel's "Reflections on Violence" (1915); Irving Wohlfarth's "Critique of Violence" (2009), which charts the connections between Benjamin's essay and the Red Army Faction operating in Germany during the 1970s.

8. It is worth noting that although terrorism is a legitimate concern of course, it is Far-right terrorism, right wing extremism, we should really fear. It is a fact that "Right-wing extremists in the United States still kill more people than jihadis" (*Nettime* mailing list, 24 Nov 2015).

9. In response to 9/11, Agamben writes: "A state which has security as its sole task and source of legitimacy is a fragile organism; it can always be provoked by terrorism to become itself terroristic." (2001; Cox & Sützl 2009, 23–25).

10. A denial-of-service (DoS) attack is an attempt to make a machine or network resource unavailable to its intended users, such as to temporarily or indefinitely interrupt or suspend services of a host connected to the Internet. A distributed denial-of-service (DDoS) is where the attack source is more than one, and often thousands of unique IP addresses.

11. See http://en.wikipedia.org/wiki/Operation_Payback.

12. See http://thehackernews.com/2015/11/anonymous-hacker-isis.html.

13. Available at http://www.ccc.de/hackerethics?language=en. In general, hacker simply refers to a person who is capable of creating hacks, or demonstrating technical virtuosity. Hackers are generally understood as those who attempt to penetrate security systems on remote computers, but this is a pejorative use of the term. To clarify, a hacker is someone with proficiency and practical understanding of the structure and operations of computer networks and systems, whereas crackers or system intruders are hackers with malign intentions (likened to terrorists even).

14. The Electronic Disturbance Theater (EDT) initially executed FloodNet in April and December 1998 on Mexican and American government sites respectively. FloodNet can also be downloaded from http://www.thing.net/~rdom/ecd/floodnet.html. Also see Stalbaum (2002).

15. Tor is a web browser that prevents others from learning your location or browsing habits. See https://www.torproject.org/.

16. To be clear, I am referring to how the Free Software Foundation define freedom: "'Free software' is a matter of liberty, not price. To understand the concept, you should think of 'free' as in 'free speech', not as in free beer.") Also see Cox & McLean (2013), for an elaboration on this issue.

17. The Universal Declaration of Human Rights (adopted in 1948) is available at http://www.un.org/en/documents/udhr/.

18. The European Convention on Human Rights (adopted in 1950) is available at http://www.hri.org/docs/ECHR50.html.

19. Further evoking Carl Schmitt's notion of enmity, from *The Concept of the Political*, of 1927. Schmitt's critique of liberalism lies in its inability to recognize antagonism as inevitable in human societies, and the political differentiation of friend or enemy is at the centre of this. The foregrounding of 'friendship' in social media is arguably part of the same logic where the inherent antagonisms of software are made relatively invisible.

20. Discussion of Benjamin's essay and its rejection of the law for "messianic anarchy" appears in Wohlfarth's "Critique of Violence: the deposing of the law" (2009).

21. Wendy Chun refers to 'undeadness' in her comments on the time dimension of instruction and execution. Source code becomes a source only after the action has taken place. She is referring to Derrida: "Source code becomes a source only through its destruction, through its simultaneous nonpresence and presence. Code (both biological and technological), in other words, is "undead" writing, a writing that — even when it repeats itself — is never simply a deadly or living repetition of the same." (Chun 2011, 192)

22. The example that follows was written by Jaromil in 2002, available at https://jaromil.dyne.org/journal/forkbomb_art.html. The user executes the fork bomb by pasting the following 13 characters into a UNIX shell. Below is an explanation of how it executes:

```
:()   # define ':' -- whenever we say ':',
do this:
{     # beginning of what to do when
we say ':'
:     # load another copy of the ':'
function into memory...
|     # ...and pipe its output to...
:     # ...another copy of ':' function,
which has to be loaded into memory
# (therefore, ':|:' simply gets two
copies of ':' loaded whenever ':'
is called)
&     # disown the functions -- if the
first ':' is killed, all of the functions
# that it has started should NOT be
auto-killed
```

```
}       # end of what to do when we
say ':'
;       # Having defined ':', we should
now...
:       # ...call ':', initiating a chain-
reaction: each ':' will start two more.
```

References

Agamben, Giorgio. 1998. *Homo Sacer: Sovereign Power and Bare Life*. Stanford, CA: Stanford University Press.

——. 2000. *Means without End: Notes on Politics*. Minneapolis: University of Minnesota Press.

——. 2001. "On Security and Terror." In *Frankfurter Allgemeine Zeitung*, September, 20.

——. 2005. *State of Exception*. Chicago: University of Chicago Press.

Benjamin, Walter. (1921) 1996. "Critique of Violence." In *Walter Benjamin: Selected Writings, Volume 1, 1913–1926*, edited by Marcus Bullock & Michael W. Jennings, 236–252. Cambridge, MA: Harvard University Press.

Berardi, Franco. 2015. *Heroes: Mass Murder and Suicide*. London: Verso.

Buck-Morss, Susan. 2003. *Thinking Past Terror: Islamism and Critical Theory on the Left*. London: Verso.

Butler, Judith. 1997. *Excitable Speech: A Politics of the Performative*. London: Routledge.

Chun, Wendy Hui Kyong. 2011. *Programmed Visions: Software and Memory*. Cambridge, MA: MIT Press.

Coleman, Gabriella. 2014. *Hacker, Hoaxer, Whistleblower, Spy: The Many Faces of Anonymous*. London: Verso.

Cox, Geoff. 2012. "Virtual Suicide as Decisive Political Act." In *Activist Media and Biopolitics: Critical Media Interventions in the Age of Biopower*, edited by Wolfgang Sützl & Theo Hug, 105–118. Innsbruck: University of Innsbruck Press.

——. 2015. "Crítica de la violencia software." In *Concreta 05*, June, http://editorialconcreta.org/-CONCRETA-05-102-.

Cox, Geoff, and Martin Knahl. 2009. "Critique of Software Security." In *Creating Insecurity*, edited by Geoff Cox and Wolfgang Sützl. New York: Autonomedia.

Cox Geoff, and Alex McLean. 2013. *Speaking Code: Coding as Aesthetic and Political Expression*. Cambridge, MA: MIT Press.

Deleuze, Gilles. 1992. "Postscript on the Societies of Control." In *October* 59 (Winter): 3–7.

Dolar, Mladen. 2006. A Voice and Nothing More. Cambridge MA: MIT Press.

Galloway, Alexander R., and Eugene Thacker. 2007. *The Exploit: A Theory of Networks*. Electronic Mediations, 21. Minneapolis: University of Minnesota Press.

Howse, Martin. 2012. *pain registers*. Available at http://www.1010.co.uk/org/execution.html.

Ianelli, Nicholas, and Aaron Hackworth. 2005. "Botnets as a Vehicle for Online Crime." CERT Coordination Center, Carnegie Mellon University.

Miessen, Marcus. Ed. 2007. *The Violence of Participation*. Berlin: Sternberg Press.

Mitropoulos, Angela. 2007. "The Social Softwar." In *Web 2.0: Man's Best Friendster? Mute* 2: 4, January.

Plummer, Quinten. 2015. "Tor Attack Pits Anonymous Against Lizard Squad: PSN and Xbox Live Back Online." In *Tech Times*, January 1. Available at http://www.techtimes.com/articles/23334/20150101/tor-attack-pits-anonymous-against-lizard-squad-psn-and-xbox-live-recovering.htm.

Rouvroy, Antoinette. 2013. "Algorithmic Governmentalities and the End(s) of Critique." Lecture, *Society of the Query* #2, Institute for Network Cultures,

October 2013. Available at http://networkcultures.org/query/2013/11/13/algorithmic-governmentality-and-the-ends-of-critique-antoinette-rouvroy/.

Stalbaum, Brett. 2002. "The Zapatista Tactical FloodNet: A collaborative, activist and conceptual art work of the net." Available at http://www.thing.net/~rdom/ecd/ZapTact.html.

Trotsky, Leon. (1911) 1987. "Terrorism." In *What do we mean...?, Education for Socialists* 6, March, London Socialist Worker's Party. Available at http://www.marxists.de/theory/whatis/terror2.htm.

Wohlfarth, Irving. 2009. "Critique of Violence: the deposing of the law." In *Radical Philosophy* 153, January/February: 13–26.

Žizěk, Slavoj. 2008. *Violence: Six Sideways Reflections.* London: Picador.

The Battle of Algiers. 1966. Film directed by Gilles Pontecorvo.

On Commands and Executions: Tyrants, Spectres and Vagabonds

David Gauthier

It is difficult to address the notion of command and execution without addressing that of tyranny. The concept of execution is an eerie construct that at once implies a prescription and a proscription in its suggestion that a rule or command is imposed and enforced on an indeterminate substrate (subjects, objects, matter or otherwise). Thus, it also suggests a certain type of violence that is at once effected and effaced, or, differently put, execution insinuates a despotic foreclosure. In that sense, the problematics of execution are central to the notion of control, which speaks both to the order of reason that it imposes and by which it is assessed. It also points to moments and milieux of erasure where a given order vanishes in indeterminacy—intervals and gaps that the order itself creates and forbids, its necessary residual exterior.

While the software/hardware divide has been a recurrent topic of conversation within the field of Software Studies, I argue that the subject needs to be pushed forward to consider the under-theorised notions of command/execution. Moving from a conception of software as ideology to a conception of software as tyranny, this article shows how the symbolic order of the law, which underpins notions of command and instruction, leads to an impasse when confronted with the question of execution. In turn, rather than seeking an understanding of execution from the despotic perspective of commands and instructions, the current inquiry identifies the various loci where such a perspective collapses and it petitions for a practice of execution that conceives of it as an event in its own right rather than a mere afterthought.

Software as Ideology

In order to illustrate the problematic the notion of execution entails, I will first focus on a particular debate about source code and ideology that took place between Wendy Hui Kyong Chun (2005, 2008) and Alexander R. Galloway (2006). This debate was partly prompted by the nascent field of

Software Studies which elected "software" as the prime object of study of New Media discourse (Fuller 2006). In her articles, Chun warns that in divorcing software from hardware and in focusing on its discursive and semantic aspects, one effects an epistemological and political move since "software perpetuates certain notions of seeing as knowing ... creating an invisible system of visibility. The knowledge software offers is as obfuscatory as it is revealing" (2005, 27). To further grasp the arguments of the debate, it is worth highlighting how the advent of Computer Science, with its emphasis on symbolic programming languages, drastically changed the ways in which computing was conceived from the 1950s onwards. Programming and coding practices, prior to the advent of computing languages, were affairs of crafty local conventions and customs that were highly tailored for individual machines across various sites (Nofre et al. 2014, 49). With the growing commercialisation of computing machinery, the concept of programming languages came about as a means to standardise these local conventions and customs, encapsulating them into syntactic and semantic forms that would present traits of both mathematical notations and natural language:

> *The notion of a programming language, which is connected to the idea of universality, became central to this exercise of boundary work that sought to disengage the activity of programming from local conventions, and to transform it into a transcendent and universal body of knowledge. From this endeavour, programming languages and algorithms emerged as epistemic objects stripped of any marks that would associate them with specific hardware.* (Nofre et al. 2014, 66)

The consequence of the advent of "universal" languages was not only that programming acquired a type of "machine independence" (source code able to be built and executed on a variety of machines), but more importantly, it brought about an amassing of linguistic objects written in various "universal" programming languages, and which, in turn, developed an epistemic and discursive life of their own. Programming languages could thus carve out their own computing invariant—a transcendent "island of semantic stability" (66)—by rendering invisible the machine that was once literally in plain sight. It is clear, then, that the universalisation of programming *as* language produced a kind of stratification and disjunction of computing that cut off the tacit and innate relationship programming had, and indeed still has, with the material, processual and "crafty" aspects of hardware which, consequently, became an invisible and illegible "black box" (Brown and Carr qtd. in Nofre et al. 2014, 54).

Speaking of this disjunction between the legible symbolic programming language and the illegible "black box", Chun posits that, as a result, "software is a functional analog to ideology" (Chun 2005, 43). This analogy between software as an object in itself and as an ideology stems from the fact that software instantiates a strict division and upholds an illusory dialectical logic of cause and effects (input and output) between infrastructure—the obscure and illegible "black box"—and superstructure—manifest and legible programming languages. This rupture speaks to the foreclosure of language over the matter of computing, an operation that totalises the linguistic regime of programming by concealing the totality of its material substrate. Inevitably, then, questions of operations and meaning are (re)claimed by this linguistic regime alone in that it is the only regime capable of lending itself to "objective" interpretations and, in so doing, legitimatises itself. By locating the birth of symbolic programming languages at the grave of material hardware, Computer Science put forth a type of "source" (code) reading of computer programs solely based on human-readability, as opposed to machine-readability, for instance. Addressing this divide, Chun concludes by noting that "because of the histories and gazes [it] erase[s]; and because of the future [it] points toward[s] … [s]oftware has become a commonsense shorthand for culture and hardware a shorthand for nature" (46).

To grasp the potency of Chun's warning, it is important to turn to Galloway's intervention and show how his framings, according to Chun, further highlight the illusory conflation of code (software) and execution (hardware). In his article "Language Wants To Be Overlooked", Galloway (2006) acknowledges that code necessitates a hardware infrastructure in order to function; he writes, "code exists first and foremost as commands issued to a machine. Code essentially has no other reason for being than instructing some machine how to act" (326). We can clearly see how Galloway's concept of code sustains this split between infrastructure (the machine) and superstructure (code as written commands issued to control the machine) when he famously declares that "code is the only language that is executable" (325). The paramount problem with this conception of command and control, instruction and execution, code and machine is that, as Chun rightly puts it, "[in making] the argument that code is automatically executable, the process of execution itself must not only be erased, but source code also must be conflated with its executable version" (2008, 305). This erasure of execution, by conflating linguistic commands and machine operations, has the corollary of reducing notions of contingent computing events and processes solely to written instructions which command them. In other words, in conflating code and execution one conflates logos with action, explicitly erasing all the problematics, discrepancies and variations action entails (303). Going further with her analysis, as I will discuss in the next section, Chun posits that symbolic code thus becomes law wherein executive, legislative and juridical power coincide to establish a pure state of exception—"code as law as police", where the gap between word and force, and logic and praxis is effectively effaced (2011, 101).

Leaving aside Chun's discussion of the law for now, I would like to emphasise that Galloway's concept of software as language or machine (2006, 327) is solely concerned with the manipulation of symbols. The symbolic order of the command, to put it this way, is put in a prescriptive relationship with its physical "support". The processual and temporal gap existing between the issuing of a command and the return of results is denied any agency whatsoever as the logic of symbols and codes supersedes the one of their entropic medium, a non-processual or eventless notion of execution that seems to be symptomatic of some software oriented media theories. In this regard, both Galloway's and Lev Manovich's (2001) notions of transcoding are worth examining. For Manovich, "to 'transcode' something is to translate it into another format" (47). Similarly, for Galloway, software is a prime exemplar of "technical transcoding without figuration" (2006, 319), where the various "lower level" layers composing the subsystems of the machine (logic gates, registers, etc.) are put into a relation of pure equivalence. As Galloway notes, "one of the outcomes of this perspective is that each layer is technologically related, if not entirely equivalent, to all the other layers" (327).[1]
We thus can clearly see that for both theorists the temporal

and material process by which the machine codes and decodes is completely bracketed since their concept of transcoding solely privileges the outcome of this process, that is, the resulting written format or data structure (323). For Galloway, "there is a privileged moment in which the written becomes purely machinic and back again" (319), for which, then, everything that is machinic ought to be equivalent. While Galloway does not develop his notion of "machinic" further than simply alluding to a complex aggregate of "'lower' symbolic interactions of voltages through logic gates" (319), he does differentiate between conceiving of software as language and conceiving of software as machine (327) in positing that "code is machinic first and linguistic second" (326). While it can be argued that software commands differ from "illocutionary" commands and that software is dissimilar to "speech acts", the point of the current inquiry is to examine the notion of command as such. It aims at problematising how this notion relies on a given symbolic order (arithmetical, logical, algorithmic, legal, machinic, etc.) that substitutes itself for the event that is execution, which, I argue, has nothing to do with symbols alone but rather points elsewhere.

Software as Tyranny

While arguments depicting software as being the "machinic turn" of ideology, in the case of Chun's earlier essays (2005, 2008), or allegory, in the case of Galloway (2006), seem convincing, I intend to look elsewhere to account for the tension between command and execution, word and action. I find it peculiar, to say the least, that the Church-Turing thesis in its physical form, which I believe lurks underneath these discussions about symbolic algorithms and their physical instantiation, is framed in terms of ideology or allegory. Therefore, in what could be considered a bold move, I follow the conviction that "ideology has no importance: what matters is not ideology … but the organisation of power" (Guattari and Lotringer 2009, 37). Thus, rather than seeking inspiration from a critique of ideology, as do Chun and Galloway, I turn to critiques of violence and theories of law and authority that address how concepts of law are enforced through rules, instructions and commands. While Chun's later essay (2011) does turn to a critique of violence, in which she develops the notion of software as law, or code as law, she does not address and focus on the intricacy of the tandem command-execution in the manner I am suggesting here.[2] To be clear, my aim is not to reify a false idea that symbols are immaterial constructs and thus unreal, or to reduce software to hard-ware, or to argue that infrastructure supersedes superstructure, but rather to theoretically look at how symbolic commands are made to operate in the first place.

According to the mathematical form of the Church-Turing thesis, which is mainly concerned with effective procedures, executability and reliability can be defined as such:

> *Executability: the procedure consists of a finite number of deterministic instructions (i.e. instructions determining a unique next step in the procedure), which have finite and unambiguous specifications commanding the execution of a finite number of primitive operations.*
>
> *Reliability: when the procedure terminates, the procedure generates the correct value of the function for each argument after a finite number of primitive operations are performed.* (Piccinini 2011, 737)

From these informal descriptions, it is worth examining how a command (instruction) is necessarily active in the sense that it is prescriptive: it requests and constrains action to fulfil the promise of its execution which, in turn, should shed expected effects. Yet the command itself does not act per se, but rather prescribes an action that it, in turn, assesses or judges ("correct value"). A distinction must thus be made between what Jacques Derrida calls "performative" and "constative" (1990, 969), where the former denotes the act of execution and the latter the part of judgement that assesses the effects of the former in light of its initial commanding. In short, the constative, which both definitions of executability and reliability speak to, forms a hermeneutic loop (interpretation, action/execution, interpretation), where the central moment of action—the primitive operation—is at once effected and effaced by interpretation itself.[3] Hence, the constative always presumes the performative, "that is to say [its] essential precipitation, which never proceeds without a certain dissymmetry and some quality of violence" (969).

According to the aforementioned definitions, to do justice to an instruction, a primitive operation has to generate a correct output. However, as Derrida points out, there is no justice of the performative as such, but only just-ness, that is, performing according to prior conventions, methods, or protocols; the performative, he writes, "cannot be just, in the sense of justice ... it always maintains within itself some irruptive violence, it no longer responds to the demands of theoretical rationality" (969). The implicitness and precipitateness of the performative buried within the constative hermeneutic loop speaks, in more general terms, of the conflation of command and execution as discussed in the previous section. What this conflation does, I argue, is to veil the "irrational" violence of the performative that still, necessarily, constitutes the core of the constative. While there may be rules, methods and protocols prescribed by a given command or instruction, the urgency and precipitateness of the performative make it act, nonetheless, "in the night of non-knowledge and non-rule" (967). What the notion of execution harbours then is an act that is at once a "non-knowledge", a "non-rule", a "non-protocol", a "non-method". In other words, the concept of execution points to the reverse side of the law, that is, its necessary primitive exterior.

The rapport between the interior and exterior of the law begs further nuancing. For Derrida, "violence is not exterior to the order of *droit* [law]. It threatens it from within" (989). Yet, as I argued above, the violence of execution stands as a primitive outside to the symbolic order of law; it operates in an inordinately different register as "non-knowledge" and ultimately as "non-law" or "out-law". The order of law, the hermeneutic loop of the constative, as I discussed above, may well comprise a certain placeholder for the moment of action/execution, but it nonetheless is articulated by a totally different language (if actual language there is), which at once prompts execution as such only to efface it after the fact by substituting it with an interpretation of its deciphered effects: a correct instruction for a correct value. Yet the moment of action/execution still remains illegible from the perspective of the constative. The problematic of the symbolic order is its despotic attempt to codify, and therefore foreclose everything by means of substitution, giving it the grounds and monopoly to justify itself as a righteous transcendental order capable of "decreeing to be violent, this time in the sense of an outlaw, anyone who does not recognize it" (987).

There are thus two types of outlaws I want to unearth here: (1) the heretic outlaw that has been judged as such for not recognising the law's order (not following conventions, method, protocol, etc.) and consequently ruled "outside" by decree— an error or "miscomputation" (Piccinini 2007, 505) — and (2) the "autochthon" outlaw that executes and hence founds the constative loop outright, and who therefore stands "outside" the law by necessity — primitive operations. Both vouch for, from the perspective of the law, a sense of legible illegibility, or "foreignness", since they both imply a passage to action as a moment of non-law, a transgression of order.

For Derrida, the moments of action/execution are, by themselves, moments of "mystique". He writes, "[these] moments supposing we can isolate them, are terrifying moments ... [They] are themselves, and in their very violence, uninterpretable or indecipherable. That is what I am calling 'mystique'" (1990, 991). What Derrida points to with "uninterpretable" and "indecipherable" is the limit of interpretation as such. Derrida's "mystique" speaks to the event that is execution and how symbolic instructions feign "that of which is in progress" during the event; he writes "[i]t is precisely in this ignorance that the eventness of the event consists, what we naively call its presence" (991). This ignorance [*non-savoir*] as a moment of deferring or drifting of interpretation, as a suspension of the law, is paradoxically equated to its own presence and fosters its own becoming. Law is a spectre during the moment of execution, it is a presence in absence. As a result, execution always exceeds its interpretation or interpretation *tout court*: "[it] is the moment in which the foundation of law remains suspended in the void or over the abyss, suspended by a pure performative act that would not have to answer to or before anyone" (991–3). Thus, the first aforementioned outlaw may well be condemned as heretic — the position of the error or miscomputation — but it nonetheless harbours an eccentricity that exceeds the law and its instruction, an eccentricity that has to answer to or before no one.

Unpacking the term heresy sheds light on what the becoming of the law entails at the moment of action/execution. Etymologically, heresy is derived from the greek αἱρετικός [hairetikos], which, accor-ding to Thayer's Greek-English lexicon, denotes at once "fitted or able to take or choose" and "schismatic, factious, a follower of the false doctrine". The former sense of the term designates an action (taking or choosing) that, as mentioned above, exceeds interpretation, while the latter denotes an interpretation or judgement as such, which takes place after the fact/action. Both senses thus speak to the becoming of heresy from action to its judgment. As a result, at the moment of action/execution, the becoming of the law coincides with the becoming of heresy. In fact, Derrida tells us, these two becomings are exactly the same. The moment of conservation of the law, by which the hermeneutic loop is instantiated and heretic positions are decreed as such, is the same as the moment of the founding the law. Any position before the law, such as the heretic position, calls for a potential repetition of itself: "[a] position is already iterability, a call for self-conserving repetition" (997). In other words, a position before the law permits and promises, it defies and puts forward a vow to repeat and iterate.

Thus what I have termed the heretic outlaw above is in fact the same conceptual personage as the autochthon outlaw. The figure of the outlaw, then, "would no longer be before the law, rather [it] would be before a law not yet determined, before the law as before a law not existing yet, a law yet to come" (993). Put differently, law's transgression is before the law in the sense that it is an infringement of an existing law yet, at the same time, it points to the potential commencement of another: a proscription becoming prescription. There is no pure founding position of the law as such, only iterations of it, as "conservation in its turn refounds, so that it can conserve what it claims to found" (997). Hence, the heretic position is at once a position of commencement and commandment, a promise of a new order; and "even if the promise is not kept in fact, iterability inscribes the promise as guard in the most irruptive instant of foundation" (997). In this way, the law threatens outlaws, always necessarily, as much as outlaws threaten the law from within, always necessarily. Besides, isn't the heretic position a key position in that it allows for a critique of violence and the law in the first place?

What this amounts to, following Derrida's notion that there is no strict opposition between the conservation and foundation of the law, no position before the law that does not necessarily imply its own iteration, and vice versa, is that the position of the heretic is as forcible as the one of the police, which, by decree, is supposed to enforce the law. In fact, the terms heretic and police are metonyms that refer to mere positions during the moment of action/execution. As stated above, during this event, the whole order of the law is suspended, interpretation deferred, and "that of which is in progress" during this interval equates to a symbolic void, a moment of "non-law". There can only be symbolic substitutes for what amounts to mere positional acts during execution. At this level of reality, betrayal and enforcement are both in states of becoming, that is, not yet individuated or, rather, judged as such. This is precisely the paradox of law: the insurmountable distance it creates between its prescriptive instructions and its actual "presence-in-action", or, rather, "absence-in-action".

In light of this, Chun's insight of conceiving code as law can be thought of anew. In equating code to law and law to police, thus producing a triad of code as law as police, she writes, "[code] as law as police, like the state of exception, makes executive, legislative and juridical powers coincide. Code as law as police erases the gap between force and writing ... in a complementary fashion to the state of exception" (2011, 101). I beg to differ from this perspective and keep the moment of execution as a moment of suspension of the law, a moment of "non-law", a moment of "non-writing", yet a moment of force and intensity, as I argue in the next section. What Derrida shows us, by equating law's conservation and foundation, is that the legislative and executive powers already coincide, albeit in a strange way, and thus, that the state of exception is no exception after all. Yet, the strangeness and clandestinity of the coinciding of the legal and executive comes not from their coinciding as such but more from the fact that law is always necessarily non-present at the moment of action/execution. Derrida talks about the spectre of the law to account for this non-presence, or absence. Thus, Chun's motto of code as law as police can be refactored as code as law as spectre. A position of law is a promise at the moment of execution, a becoming yet to shed the iteration that will "conserve what it claims to found" (Derrida 1990, 997).

Outlaws, Itinerants, and Vagabonds

So far, I have shown that the notion of execution from the perspective of the law merely points to its primitive exterior. What if this perspec-tive were to be reversed? What would a practice of execution then entail, rather than producing a sequence of instructions? It is not because the law loses its ground and becomes phantom-like that "that of which is in progress" during the moment of execution amounts to nothing, a pure void. There is nothing particularly profound in effecting this reversal of perspective, taking the viewpoint of the heretic outlaw, so to speak. In a sense, that is precisely what Gilbert Simondon's critique of hylomorphism is all about.

To be rather brief at this point, the hylomorphic scheme conceives of both organic or inorganic individuals as engendered by the conjugate of form and matter. One of the classic examples used to illustrate the form-matter dynamic is that of a brick. Simply put, according to the hylomorphic scheme, the production of a brick would be as follows: give a passive lump of clay (potential) a parallelepiped form (actualisation). In other words, a pure form—the parallelepiped—is applied to an indeterminate raw lump of material—the clay—so the lump itself undergoes a transformation and takes the shape of a parallelepiped and, in turn, sheds an individual brick. In this scheme, the form itself is of prime importance since it directs matter in its process of transformation from an undetermined shape to a determined one; put differently, form actualises matter's latent potential. Form is thus the sole source of actualisation that governs the transformation of the lump of raw clay—it determines the indeterminate.

Simondon acknowledges that there is a notion of a genesis, or more precisely of an ontogenesis, involved in hylomorphism, yet it is an "ontogenesis in reverse" (2013, 23).[4] What Simondon does is to reverse this reverse, so to speak, by devising concepts that allow for "knowing the individual through individuation rather than [knowing] individuation from the individual" (24). Instead of conceiving of ontogenesis as a restricted and narrow concept denoting the genesis of a given individual (as hylomorphism does), Simondon conceives of it as a "partial and relative resolution manifesting itself in a system containing potentials and involving a certain incompatibility in relation to itself, incompatibility composed of forces and tension" (25). In a sense, Simondon's notion of individuation stands against the telos of hylomorphism, that is, against erecting the Individual as a privileged origin (form) and finality (brick). The individual he puts forth is thus grasped as a relative reality, never fully realised, and the process of individuation perpetual rather than transitive.

The tension and contrasts between the form-matter couple of hylomorphism are even more clearly and vividly exposed by the discourse on the instruction-execution divide I have critiqued. As argued earlier, positions before the law are always mere potentials at the moment of action/execution, and thus the law itself is always in a process of becoming rather than final, as it can never truly be founded once and for all. Because of this problem of origin and finality of the law—its incompatibility in relation to itself—a rapport can be drawn here with Simondon's critique of hylomorphism. For Simondon, the technical operation that "imposes a form to a passive and indeterminate material" is not only a phantom-like operation, but more importantly is tyrannical. He writes:

> *[It] is not only an abstract operation considered by the spectator that sees what comes in and out of the workshop without knowing what the actual elaboration is. It is essentially an operation commanded by a free man [of the Republic] and executed by the slave ... The true passivity of matter is its abstract availability under the given order that others will execute.* (51)

Simondon's image of the spectator (or should I say spectre) who remains outside of the workshop is most evocative here: the workshop is hylomorphism's own "outside"—"[t]he hylomorphic scheme corresponds to the knowledge of a man who remains outside of the workshop and only considers what comes in and what comes out of it" (46). The same outside perspective could be said of a programmer who considers digital execution solely from his computer's command line. His remark of the situation of the slave can be linked to the one of the outlaws and the heretics depicted in the previous section. The hylomorphic scheme, like that of the law, is necessarily founded on primitive external entities that it appropriates by despotic means. Yet, in his treatise, Simondon argues that to truly grasp the process of form-taking, such as the moulding of a brick, "it is not enough to enter the workshop and work with the artisan: one should enter the mould itself to follow the operation of form taking at different levels of magnitude of physical reality" (2013, 46).

Moving from question of law to questions of science, Gilles Deleuze and Félix Guattari engage with notions of interiority and exteriority of the law, and frame the aforementioned

perspectival reverses in these terms:
> *A distinction must be made between two types of science, or scientific procedures: one consists in "reproducing," the other in "following." The first involves reproduction, iteration and reiteration; the other, involving itineration, is the sum of the itinerant, ambulant sciences ... following is not at all the same thing as reproducing, and one never follows in order to reproduce ... Reproducing implies the permanence of a fixed point of view that is external to what is reproduced: watching the flow from the bank. But following is something different from the ideal of reproduction. Not better, just different. One is obliged to follow when one is in search of the "singularities" of a matter, or rather of a material, and not out to discover a form.* (Deleuze and Guattari 1987, 372)

What thus becomes clear is how software as law institutes this transcendental fixed point of view—the aforementioned constative loop—by isolating, stratifying, discretising, categorising and foreclosing the spatiotemporal continuum the process of execution articulates. Computer Science, as the science that legislates, is thus responsible for abstracting moments and locales from this continuum and structuring logical concepts and categories out of these abstractions. Yet the theorematic coordinates such a science puts forth are based on various spatiotemporal cuts and erasures; in other words, from a spatiotemporal continuum a logical series is extracted that, as a result, features as many forbidden zones or vanishing points as there are terms in the series. The theorematic power of Computer Science comes from its given authority in decreeing laws and concepts that produce the sacrosanct apodictic apparatus of empty repetition—that is, the repetition of the same and the similar. Without this apodictic apparatus, Computer Science would be destined to follow the progression of a given spatiotemporal phenomenon at ground zero and thus lose its transcendental, and fixed, point of view.

Execution asks to be followed, not iterated. Practices of execution entice an itineration within the residual outside of software, that is, an itineration at ground level where the theorematic coordinates of software are projected on the ground. In order to account for the spatiotemporal individuation of the event of execution proper, one has to step out of

Computer Science's apodictic apparatus of categorisation and traverse the zones of indeterminacy this apparatus constructs. To follow is to cross the interstice's in-between states, in-between commands and in-between rules and laws. It is to traverse these moments of non-law, non-knowledge, non-rule, non-protocol, non-method; in short, to follow is to transgress the imposed dominant order and, in so doing, to problematise the rationale behind its disposition of minoring an outside. The reason I have, in the previous section, focused on the notion of outlaw and positions of heresy before the law is to call attention to power relations inherent in this process of minoring. The problem of execution concerns the domain of epistemology as well as that of work and labour, be it human or non-human. Not only does the creation of a residual outside raise questions of legibility and illegibility in terms of knowledge, but further, it promulgates certain types of social practices and work hierarchies that perpetuate types of despotism and tyranny based on certain valuations of work and systems of visibility and invisibility based on this very outside.[5]

While one may be lured into looking for notions of execution in Computer Science books or to practice execution from his/her computer's command line, I suggest one has to look elsewhere and engage differently with code and circuitry to truly grasp and follow the event that is execution. As short concluding remark, I would like to suggest that luckily, another type of heretic "science" of execution, or rather a practice, already exists that is not usually featured in Computer Science literature per se but is, nonetheless, always and necessarily performed when producing a piece of hardware or a piece of software—that is the practice of *debugging*. True "occult science", debugging requires one to follow the thread of execution of a given program, that is, to follow the itineration and vagabonding of signs and signals within the architecture of a given machine at a given time. A bug, error, failure, or miscomputation necessarily begs to be followed. It is an event itself, or, rather, speaks to the individuation of execution in and for itself. It requires that the illusory disjunction or stratification of instruction and execution, signs and matter, and the discretised dynamics this disjunction puts forth be suspended and problematised. What the practice of debugging highlights is the fragile conjunction of signs and signals in focusing on the technical operations that mediates them in time and space.

To debug is to open bare the foreclosure of the aforementioned symbolic order of the law and enter Simondon's mould, so to speak: to observe and intervene during the event that links the two technological half-chains of the sign and the signals, the opcode and the dipole.

Debugging, as liminal and vagabond science, as well as an effective practice of execution, is potent in problematising and debunking the tyrannic minoring of an outside some Computer Science concepts necessarily produce, and, in turn, that some Software Studies discourses reproduce. After all, debugging is about problems and problematisation, may it be of a piece of machinery or a piece of theory. In fact, problematics is its only mode of operation. There are no software stacks nor interfaces along the path of the vagabond outlaw, only curious spectres.

Notes

1. The same emphasis on the symbolic outcome of an execution can be said of Galloway's equating two quadratic equations written in a "high-level" and "low-level" programming languages (2006, 319). Surely both equations, expressed differently, shed the same numerical solution, yet their respective technical unfolding during execution are nothing but equal, as Chun points out (2008, 306–7).

2. See the present collection's contribution "RuntimeException()—Critique of Software Violence" by Geoff Cox, who also discusses software in terms of violence, in a different, albeit complementary, way to this chapter.

3. The notion of interpretation here does not necessarily denotes a semantic interpretation as a comprehension of the meaning of a command or result in a mathematical or linguistic sense. The loop structure I am describing here holds for purely mechanistic conceptions of computing such as the one put forth by Piccinini (2008, 2007). Interpretation, in this case, thus relates to notions of internal semantics rather than external ones (Piccinini 2008, 214–5).

4. All citations from Simondon are my translations.

5. See Linda Hilfling Ritasdatter's contribution "BUGS IN THE WAR ROOM—Economies and /of Execution" in the present collection, where she addresses on question software maintenance and labour in terms of neo-colonial hegemony.

References

Chun, Wendy Hui Kyong. 2005. "On Software, or the Persistence of Visual Knowledge." *Grey Room* 18: 26–51.

———. 2008. "On 'Sourcery,' or Code as Fetish." *Configurations* 16 (3): 299–324.

———. 2011. "Crisis, Crisis, Crisis, or Sovereignty and Networks." *Theory, Culture & Society* 28 (6): 91–112.

Deleuze, Gilles, and Félix Guattari. 1987. *A Thousand Plateaus: Capitalism and Schizophrenia*. Minneapolis: University of Minnesota Press.

Derrida, Jacques. 1989. "Force De Loi: Le Fondement Mystique De L'Autorité / Deconstruction and the Possibility of Justice." *Cardozo Law Review* 11: 920–1046.

Fuller, Matthew. 2006. "Software Studies Workshop." Piet Zwart Institute — Software Studies Workshop. http://web.archive.org/web/20100327185154/http://pzwart.wdka.hro.nl/mdr/Seminars2/softstudworkshop.

Galloway, Alexander R. 2006. "Language Wants To Be Overlooked: On Software and Ideology." *Journal of Visual Culture* 5 (3): 315–31.

Guattari, Félix, and Sylvère Lotringer. 2009. *Chaosophy: Texts and Interviews 1972-1977*. Semiotext(e) Foreign Agents Series. Los Angeles, CA: Semiotext(e).

Manovich, Lev. 2002. *The Language of New Media*. MIT Press ed. Leonardo. Cambridge, MA: MIT Press.

Nofre, David, Mark Priestley, and Gerard Alberts. 2014. "When Technology Became Language: The Origins of the Linguistic Conception of Computer Programming, 1950–1960." *Technology and Culture* 55 (1): 40–75.

Piccinini, Gualtiero. 2007. "Computing Mechanisms." *Philosophy of Science* 74 (4): 501–26.

———. 2008. "Computation without Representation." *Philosophical Studies* 137 (2): 205–41.

———. 2011. "The Physical Church—Turing Thesis: Modest or Bold?" *The British Journal for the Philosophy of Science* 62 (4): 733–69.

Simondon, Gilbert. 2005. *L'individuation à la lumière des notions de forme et d'information*. Krisis. Grenoble: Millon.

Deadly Algorithms: Can Legal Codes Hold Software Accountable for Code that Kills?

Susan Schuppli

Algorithms have long-adjudicated over vital processes that help to ensure our wellbeing and survival, from pacemakers that maintain the natural rhythms of the heart, genetic algorithms that optimise emergency response times by cross-referencing ambulance locations with demographic data, to early warning systems that track approaching storms, detect seismic activity, and even prevent genocide by monitoring ethnic conflict with orbiting satellites.[1] However algorithms are also increasingly being tasked with instructions to kill: executing coding sequences that quite literally execute.

Computing Terror

Guided by the Obama Presidency's conviction that the war on terror can be won by "out-computing" its enemies and pre-empting terrorists threats using predictive software — no doubt bolstered by the President's reliance on big data and social media to return him to office in 2012 — a new generation of deadly algorithms is being designed that will both control and manage the "kill-list," and along with it decisions to strike (Crider 2014).[2] It is noteworthy to recall that the language of computation is already deeply informed by the history of certain legal processes, such that the term "execute", as in "to execute a coding script", heralds from the fourteenth-century legal reference to carry out or accomplish a course of action: to prosecute, to issue a warrant, or to sentence. Within the context of this essay the term "execute" gains yet further meanings: it is only by executive decision that the US President can execute the kill order, which in turn executes a coding script that operates the remote-controlled drone, that is itself engaged in acts of summary execution. Indeed, the now terminated practice of "signature strikes", which employed data-analytics to determine emblematic patterns of "terrorist" behaviour which in turn were used to identify potential targets on the ground already points to a future in which intelligence gathering, assessment, and military action, including the calculation of who can legally be killed, will largely be performed by machines based upon an ever-expanding database of aggregated information. However this transition to execution by algorithm is not simply a continuation of killing at ever-greater distances inaugurated by the invention of the bow that separated warrior and foe, as many have suggested.[3] It is also a consequence of the ongoing automation of warfare, which can be traced back to the cybernetic coupling of Claude Shannon's mathematical theory of information with Norbert Wiener's wartime research into feedback loops and communication control systems.[4] As this new era of intelligent weapons systems progresses, operational control and decision-making will increasingly be out-sourced to machines.

In 2011 the US Department of Defence (DOD) released its "roadmap" forecasting the expanded use of unmanned technologies, of which unmanned aircraft systems — drones — are but one aspect of an overall strategy towards the implementation of fully autonomous Intelligent Agents. It projects its future as follows:

> *The Department of Defense's vision for unmanned systems is the seamless integration of diverse unmanned capabilities that provide flexible options for Joint Warfighters while exploiting the inherent advantages of unmanned technologies, including persistence, size, speed, maneuverability, and reduced risk to human life. DOD envisions unmanned systems seamlessly operating with manned systems while gradually reducing the degree of human control and decision making required for the unmanned portion of the force structure.*
> (DOD 2001, 3)

The document is a strange mix of cold-war caricature and Fordism set against the backdrop of contemporary geopolitical anxieties, as it sketches out two imaginary vignettes to provide "visionary" examples of the ways in which autonomy can improve efficiencies through inter-operability across military domains, aimed at enhancing capacities and flexibility between manned and unmanned sectors of the Army, Air Force and Navy. In these future-scenarios the scripting and casting are familiar, pitting the security of hydrocarbon energy supplies against rogue actors equipped with Russian technology. One concerns an aging Russian nuclear submarine deployed by a radicalised Islamic nation-state that is beset by an earthquake in the Pacific, thus contaminating the coastal waters of Alaska and threatening its oil energy reserves. The other involves the sabotaging of an underwater oil pipeline in the Gulf of Guinea off the coast of Africa, complicated by the approach of a hostile surface vessel capable of launching a Russian short-range air-to-surface missile (1–10). These action-film vignettes—fully elaborated across five pages of the report—stand in perplexing counterpart to the claims being made throughout as to the sober science, political prudence and economic rationalisations that guide the move towards fully unmanned systems. On what grounds are we to be convinced by the vision and strategies being advanced? On the basis of a collective cultural imaginary that finds its politics within the CGI labs of the infotainment industry or via an evidence-based approach to solving the complex problems posed by changing global contexts? Not surprisingly, the level of detail (and techno-fetishism) used to describe unmanned responses to these risk scenarios is far more exhaustive than the three primary challenges the report identifies as specific to the growing reliance and deployment of automated and autonomous systems. Implementing a higher degree of autonomy faces the following challenges, the report suggests:

> *1. Investment in science and technology (S&T) to enable more capable autonomous operations.*
> *2. Development of policies and guidelines on what decisions can be safely and ethically delegated and under what conditions.*
> *3. Development of new Verification and Validation (V&V) and T&E techniques to enable verifiable 'trust' in autonomy.* (DOD 2011, 27)

The delegation of decision-making to computational regimes is of crucial consideration in so far as it poses significant ethical dilemmas but also raises urgent legal concerns as to whether existing juridical frameworks are even capable of attending to the emergence of these new algorithmic actors and their machine-executable formats. This is especially concerning given that the logic of precedent which organises much legal decision-making (within common law systems) has operated according to the same logic that organised the drone programme in the first place: namely the justification of an action based upon a pattern of behaviour that was established by prior events. This legal aporia intersects with a parallel discourse around moral responsibility; a much broader debate that has tended to structure arguments around the deployment of armed drones as an antagonism between humans and machines. As the author of the entry on "Computing and Moral Responsibility" in the *Stanford Encyclopedia of Philosophy* put it:

> *Traditionally philosophical discussions on moral responsibility have focused on the human components in moral action. Accounts of how to ascribe moral responsibility usually describe human agents performing actions that have well-defined, direct consequences. In today's increasingly technological society, however, human activity cannot be properly understood without making reference to technological artifacts, which complicates the ascription of moral responsibility.* (Noorman 2012)

When one poses the question, under what conditions is it morally acceptable to deliberately kill a human being, one is not asking whether the law would permit such an act for reasons of imminent threat, self-defence or even empathy for someone who is in extreme pain or in a non-responsive vegetative state. The moral register around the decision-to-kill operates according to a different ethical framework that doesn't necessarily bind the individual to a contract enacted between the citizen and the state. Moral positions can thus be specific to individual values and beliefs whereas legal frameworks permit actions in our collective name as citizens contracted to a democratically elected body that acts on our behalf but with which we might be in political disagreement. While it is much easier to take a moral stance towards events that we might oppose—US drone strikes in Pakistan—than to justify a claim as to their specific illegality given the anti-terror legislation that has been put in place since 9/11, assigning moral responsibility, proving criminal negligence or demonstrating legal liability for the outcomes of deadly events becomes even more challenging when humans and machines interact to make decisions together, a complication that will intensify as unmanned systems become more sophisticated and act as independent legal agents. In addition, the outsourcing of decision-making to the judiciary as regards the validity of scientific evidence since the 1993 *Daubert* ruling—in a case brought against Merrell

Dow Pharmaceuticals—has also made it difficult for the law to take an activist stance when confronted with the limitations of its own scientific understandings of technical innovation. At present it would be unreasonable to take an algorithm to court when things go awry, let alone when they are executed perfectly, as in the case of a lethal drone strike. By focusing upon the legal dimension of algorithmic liability as opposed to more wide-ranging moral questions I do not want to suggest that morality and law should be consigned to separate spheres. However, it is worth making a preliminary effort to think about the ways in which algorithms are not simply re-ordering the fundamental principles that govern our lives, but might also be asked to provide alternate ethical arrangements derived out of mathematical axioms.

Algorithmic Accountability

It is my contention that law, which has already expanded the category of "legal personhood" to include non-human actors such as corporations, also offers ways to think about questions of algorithmic accountability (Dewey 1926, 656, 669). Of course many would argue that legal methods are not the best frameworks for resolving moral dilemmas, but then again nor are the objectives of counter-terrorism necessarily best serviced by algorithmic oversight. Shifting the emphasis towards a juridical account of algorithmic reasoning might prove useful when confronted with the real possibility that the kill list and other emergent matrices for managing the war on terror will be algorithmically derived as part of a techno-social assemblage in which it becomes impossible to isolate human from non-human agents. It does however raise the "bar" for what we now need to ask the law to do. The degree to which legal codes can maintain their momentum alongside rapid technological change and submit "complicated algorithmic systems to the usual process of checks-and-balances that is generally imposed on powerful items that affect society on a large scale" is of considerable concern (Data & Society Research Institute 2014). Nonetheless, the stage has already been set for the arrival of a new cast of juridical actors endowed perhaps not so much with freewill in the classical sense (that would provide the conditions for criminal liability), but intelligent systems which are wilfully free in the sense that they have been programmed to make decisions based upon their own algorithmic logic (Teubner 2006).

While armed combat drones are the most publically visible of the automated military systems that the DOD is rolling out, they are but one of the many remote-controlled assets that will gather, manage, analyse and act on the data that they acquire and process.

Proponents of algorithmic decision-making laud the near instantaneous response-time that allows such Intelligent Agents — what some have called "moral predators" — to make micro-second adjustments to avert a lethal drone strike should, for example, children suddenly emerge out of a house that is being targeted as a militant hideout (Strawser 2010). Indeed robotic systems have long been argued to decrease the error-margin of civilian casualties that are often the consequence of actions made by tired soldiers in the field. Nor are machines overly concerned with their own self-preservation, which might likewise cloud judgement under conditions of duress. Yet, as Sabine Gless and Herbert Zech ask, if these "Intelligent Agents are often used in areas where the risk of failure and error can be reduced by relying on machines rather than humans … everywhere, the question arises: Who is liable if things go wrong?" (2014)

Typically when injury and death occurs to humans, the legal debate focuses upon the degree to which such an outcome was foreseeable and thus adjudicates on the basis of whether all reasonable efforts and preemptive protocols had been built into the system to mitigate against such an unlikely occurrence. However, programmers cannot of course run all the variables that combine to produce machinic decisions, especially when the degree of uncertainty as to conditions and knowledge of events on the ground is as variable as the shifting contexts of conflict and counter-terrorism. Werner Dahm, Chief Scientist at USAF, stresses the difficulty of designing error-free systems: "You have to be able to show that the system is not going to go awry — you have to disprove a negative" (Agence-France Presse 2012, 2). Given that highly automated decision-making processes involve complex and rapidly changing contexts mediated by multiple technologies, can we reasonably expect to build a form of ethical decision-making into these unmanned systems? And would an algorithmic approach to managing the ethical dimensions of drone warfare — for example, whether to strike sixteen-year old Abdulrahman al-Awlaki in Yemen because his father was a radicalised cleric;

a fate that he might inherit—entail the same logics that characterised signature strikes, namely that of proximity to militant-like behaviour or activity?[5] The euphemistically rebranded kill list known as the "disposition matrix" suggests that such determinations can indeed be arrived at computationally. As Greg Miller notes: "The matrix contains the names of terrorism suspects arrayed against an accounting of the resources being marshaled to track them down, including sealed indictments and clandestine operations" (2012).

Intelligent systems are arguably legal agents but not as-of-yet legal persons, although precedents pointing to this possibility have been set in motion. The idea that an actual human being or "legal person" stands behind the invention of every machine who might ultimately be found responsible when things go wrong, or even when they go right, is no longer tenable and obfuscates the fact that complex systems are rarely, if ever, the product of single authorship, nor do humans and machines operate in autonomous realms. Indeed, both are so thoroughly entangled with each other that the notion of a sovereign human agent functioning outside the realm of machinic mediation seems wholly improbable. Consider for a moment only one aspect of conducting drone warfare in Pakistan—that of US flight logistics—in which we find that upwards of 165 people are required just to keep a Predator drone in the air for 24 hours, the half-life of an average mission. These personnel requirements are themselves embedded in multiple techno-social systems composed of military contractors, intelligence officers, data-analysts, lawyers, engineers, programmers, as well as hardware, software, satellite communication, operation centres (CAOC), and so on. This does not take into account the R&D infrastructure that engineered the unmanned system, designed its operating procedures and beta-tested it. Nor does it acknowledge the administrative apparatus that brought all of these actors together to create the event we call a drone strike.[6]

In the case of a fully automated system, decision-making is reliant upon feedback loops that continually pump new information into the system in order to recalibrate it. But perhaps more significantly in terms of legal liability, decision-making is also governed by the system's innate ability to self-educate: the capacity of algorithms to learn and modify their coding sequences independent of human oversight. Isolating the singular agent who is directly responsible—legally—for the production of a deadly harm (as currently required by criminal law) suggests, then, that no one entity beyond the Executive Office of the President might ultimately be held accountable for the aggregate conditions that conspire to produce a drone strike and with it the possibility of civilian casualties. However, given that the US doesn't accept the jurisdiction of the International Criminal Court and Article 25 of the Rome Statute governing individual criminal responsibility, what new legal formulations could, then, be created that are able to account for indirect and aggregate causality born out of a complex chain of events including so called digital perpetrators? American tort law, which adjudicates over civil wrongs, might be one such place to look for instructive models. In particular, legal claims regarding the use of environmental toxins, which are highly distributed events whose lethal effects often take decades to appear, and involve an equally complex array of human and non-human agents, have been making their way into court, although not typically with successful outcomes for the plaintiffs. The most notable of these litigations are the mass toxic tort regarding the use of Agent Orange as a defoliant in Vietnam and the Bhopal disaster in India.[7] Ultimately, however, the efficacy of such an approach has to be considered in light of the intended outcome of assigning liability, which in the cases mentioned was not so much deterrence or punishment, but, rather, compensation for damages.

Recoding the Law

While machines can be designed with a high degree of intentional behaviour and will out-perform humans in many instances, the development of unmanned systems will need to take into account a far greater range of variables, including shifting geopolitical contexts and murky legal frameworks when making the calculation that conditions have been met to execute someone. Building in fail-safe procedures that abort when human subjects of a specific size (children) or age and gender (males under the age of 18) appear, sets the stage for a proto-moral decision making regime. But is the design of ethical constraints really where we wish to push back politically when it comes to the potential for execution by algorithm? Or can we work to complicate the impunity that certain techno-social assemblages currently enjoy? As a 2009 report by the

Royal Academy of Engineering on Autonomous Systems argues,

> Legal and regulatory models based on systems with human operators may not transfer well to the governance of autonomous systems. In addition, the law currently distinguishes between human operators and technical systems and requires a human agent to be responsible for an automated or autonomous system. However, technologies which are used to extend human capabilities or compensate for cognitive or motor impairment may give rise to hybrid agents ... Without a legal framework for autonomous technologies, there is a risk that such essentially human agents could not be held legally responsible for their actions—so who should be responsible? (Royal Academy of Engineering 2009)

Implicating a larger set of agents including algorithmic ones who aid and abet such an act might well be a more effective legal strategy, even if expanding the limits of criminal liability proves unwieldy. As the 2009 ECCHR *Study on Criminal Accountability* in Sri Lanka put it: "Individuals, who exercise the power to organise the pattern of crimes that were later committed, can be held criminally liable as perpetrators. These perpetrators can usually be found in civil ministries such as the ministry of defense or the office of the president" (ECCHR 2010, 88). Moving down the chain of command and focusing upon those who participate in the production violence by carrying out orders has been effective in some cases (Sri Lanka), but also problematic in others (Abu Ghraib) where the indictment of low-level officers severed the chain of causal relations that could implicate more powerful actors. Of course, prosecuting an algorithm alone for executing lethal orders that the system is in fact designed to make is fairly nonsensical if the objective is punishment. The move must rather be part of an overall strategy aimed at expanding the field of causality and thus broadening the reach of legal responsibility.

My work as a researcher on the *Forensic Architecture* project, alongside Eyal Weizman and many others, in developing new methods of spatial and visual investigation for the UN enquiry into the use of armed drones, provides one specific vantage point for considering how machinic capacities are reordering the field of political action and thus calling forth new legal strategies.[8] In taking seriously the agency of things, we must also take seriously the agency of things whose productive capacities are enlisted in the decision to kill. Computational regimes, in operating largely beyond the thresholds of human perception, have produced informatic conjunctions that have redistributed and transformed the spaces in which action occurs, as well as the nature of such consequential actions themselves. When algorithms are being enlisted to out-compute terrorism and calculate who can and should be killed, do we not need to produce a politics appropriate to these radical modes of calculation and a legal framework that is sufficiently agile to deliberate over such events?

Decision-making by automated systems will produce new relations of power for which we have as of yet inadequate legal frameworks or modes of political resistance—and, perhaps even more importantly, insufficient collective understanding as to how such decisions will actually be made and upon what grounds. Scientific knowledge about technical processes does not belong to the domain of science alone, as the *Daubert* ruling implies. However, demands for public accountability and oversight will require much greater participation in the epistemological frameworks that organise and manage these new techno-social systems and that may be a formidable challenge for all of us. What sort of public assembly will be able to prevent the pre-mature closure of a certain "epistemology of facts" as Bruno Latour would say, that are at present cloaked under a veil of secrecy called "national security interests"—the same order of facts that scripts the current DOD roadmap for unmanned systems?

In an ABC radio interview titled "The Future of drone strikes could see execution by algorithm", Sarah Knuckey, Director of the Project on Extrajudicial Executions at New York University Law School, emphasised the degree to which drone warfare has strained the limits of international legal conventions and with it the protection of civilians.[9] The "rules of warfare" are "already hopelessly out-dated", she says, and will require "new rules of engagement to be drawn up". "There is an enormous amount of concern about the practices the US is conducting right now and the policies that underlie those practices. But from a much longer-term perspective and certainly from lawyers outside the US there is real concern about not just what's happening now but what it might mean

10, 15, 20 years down the track" (Quince 2013, 2–3). Could these new rules of engagement — new legal codes — assume a similarly preemptive character to the software codes and technologies that are being evolved — what I would characterise as a projective sense of the law? Might they take their lead from the spirit of the Geneva Conventions protecting the rights of non-combatants, rather than from those protocols (the Hague Conventions of 1899, 1907) that govern the use of weapons of war and are thus reactive in their formulation and event-based? In short, a set of legal frameworks that is not determined by precedent — by what has happened in the past — but, instead, by what may arguably take place in the future.

Notes

This article first appeared in *Radical Philosophy* (187, Sept/Oct 2014, Commentary 2–8), and appears here with permission. It has been updated in response to issues discussed within this edited collection.

1. See, for example, the satellite monitoring and atrocity evidence programmes: "Eyes on Darfur" (http://www.eyesondarfur.org) and "The Sentinel Project for Genocide Prevention" (http://thesentinelproject.org).

2. See also the flow chart "How Obama Decides Your Fate if He Thinks You're a Terrorist" (in Byman and Wittes 2013).

3. For a recent account of the multiple and compound geographies through which drone operations are executed, see Derek Gregory's "Drone Geographies" (2014).

4. Contemporary information theorists would argue that the second-order cybernetic model of feedback and control, in which external data is used to adjust the system, doesn't take into account the unpredictability of evolutive data internal to the system resulting from crunching ever-larger datasets (Luciana Parisi 2013, Introduction). For a discussion of Wiener's cybernetics see Reinhold Martin's "The Organizational Complex: Cybernetics, Space, Discourse" (1998, 110).

5. When questioned about the drone strike that killed sixteen-year old American-born Abdulrahman al-Awlaki, teenage son of radicalized cleric Anwar Al-Awlaki in Yemen in 2011, Robert Gibbs, former White House Press Secretary and senior adviser to President Obama's re-election campaign, replied that the boy should have had "a more responsible father".

6. "While it might seem counterintuitive, it takes significantly more people to operate unmanned aircraft than it does to fly traditional warplanes. According to the Air Force, it takes a jaw-dropping 168 people to keep just one Predator aloft for twenty-four hours! For the larger Global Hawk surveillance drone, that number jumps to 300 people. In contrast, an F-16 fighter aircraft needs fewer than one hundred people per mission." Medea Benjamin, *Drone Warfare: Killing by Remote Control* (2013, 21).

7. See Peter H. Schuck, Agent Orange on Trial: Mass Toxic Disasters in the Courts (1987). See also: www.bhopal.com/bhopal-litigation.

8. Notable members of the Forensic Architecture drone

investigative team also included Jacob Burns, Steffen Kraemer, Francesco Sebregondi and SITU Research. http://www.forensic-architecture.org/case/drone-strikes/.

9. See Bureau of Investigative Journalism, "Get the Data: Drone Wars". www.thebureauinvestigates.com/category/projects/drones/drones-graphs.

References

Agence-France Presse. 2012. "The Next Wave in U.S. Robotic War: Drones on Their Own." *Defense News*, 28 September. Available: www.defensenews.com/article/20120928/DEFREG02/309280004/The-Next-Wave-U-S-Robotic-War-Drones-Their-Own.

Benjamin, Medea. 2013. *Drone Warfare: Killing by Remote Control*. London and New York: Verso Books.

Byman, Daniel and Wittes, Benjamin. 2013. "How Obama Decides Your Fate If He Thinks You're a Terrorist." *The Atlantic*, 3 January.

Crider, Cori. 2014. "Killing in the Name of Algorithms: How Big Data Enables the Obama Administration's Drone War." *Al Jazeera America*, 18 May. Available: http://america.aljazeera.com/opinions/2014/3/drones-big-data-waronterrorobama.html.

Data & Society Research Institute. 2014. "Workshop Primer: Algorithmic Accountability." The Social, Cultural & Ethical Dimensions of 'Big Data' workshop.

DOD. 2011. *Unmanned Systems Integrated Roadmap FY2011-2036*. Washington, DC 20301: Office of the Undersecretary of Defense for Acquisition, Technology, & Logistics.

Dewey, John. 1926. "The Historic Background of Corporate Legal Personality." *Yale Law Journal* 35.6.

ECCHR. 2010. *Study on Criminal Accountability in Sri Lanka as of January 2009*. Berlin: European Center for Constitutional and Human Rights.

Gless, Sabine and Zech, Herbert. 2014. "Intelligent Agents: International Perspectives on New Challenges for Traditional Concepts of Criminal, Civil Law and Data Protection." Text for 'Intelligent Agents' workshop, 7–8 February, University of Basel, Faculty of Law, www.snis.ch/sites/default/files/workshop_intelligent_agents.pdf.

Gregory, Derek. 2014. "Drone Geographies." *Radical Philosophy* 183 (January/February): 7–19.

Martin, Reinhold. 1998. "The Organiza-tional Complex: Cybernetics, Space, Discourse." *Assemblage* 37.

Miller, Greg. 2012. "Plan for Hunting Terrorists Signals U.S. Intends to Keep Adding Names to Kill Lists." *Washington Post*, 23 October, www.washingtonpost.com/world/national-security/plan-for-hunting-terrorists-signals-us-intends-to-keep-adding-names-to-kill-lists/2012/10/23/4789b2ae-18b3-11e2-a55c-39408fbe6a4b_story.html.

Noorman, Merel. 2012. "Computing and Moral Responsibility." *The Stanford Encyclopedia*, 18 July. Available: https://plato.stanford.edu/entries/computing-responsibility/.

Parisi, Luciana. 2013. *Contagious Architecture: Computation, Aesthetics, and Space*. Cambridge, MA: The MIT Press.

Quince, Annabelle. 2013. "Future of Drone Strikes Could See Execution by Algorithm." *Rear Vision*. Ed. Transcript, 2–3.

Royal Academy of Engineering. 2009. *Autonomous Systems: Social, Legal and Ethical Issues*. London: RAE.

Available: www.raeng.org.uk/societygov/engineeringethics/pdf/Autonomous_Systems_Report_09.pdf.

Schuck, Peter H. 1987. *Agent Orange on Trial: Mass Toxic Disasters in the Courts*. Cambridge, MA: Belknap Press of Harvard University Press.

Strawser, Bradley Jay. 2010. "Moral Predators: The Duty to Employ Uninhabited Aerial Vehicles." *Journal of Military Ethics*, vol. 9, no. 4: 342–68.

Teubner, Gunther. 2006. "Rights of Non-Humans? Electronic Agents and Animals as New Actors in Politics and Law." *Journal of Law & Society* 33 (4): 497–521.

Executing Micro-temporality

Winnie Soon

Loading webpages, waiting for social media feeds, streaming videos and content, are mundane activities in contemporary culture. Such mundane activity includes network-connected devices that transmit and distribute data across multiple sites—referred to as data. In these scenes, data are constantly perceived as a stream (Berry 2011, 3; 2012, 388; 2013, n.p; Fuller 2003, 52), indicating characteristics of vast volume, speed of update, continuous flow and delivery. The concept of streams characterises the Internet rather than web pages (Berry 2011, 143). The web is a dynamic stream of information in which users can participate and follow. It is fast-changing and generative, data records are continuously updated and executed in a manner in which an end cannot be foreseen. There is a temporal dimension to the data stream and in today's networked communication data streams indicate events that are regarded as instantaneous in capitalised economies. The *now* that we are experiencing through perceptible streams is entangled with computational logic.

From social media feeds to playback video to mobile applications, users encounter a distinctive spinning icon during the loading, waiting and streaming of data content. This spinning icon represents an unstable streaming of the *now*. A graphical animation known as throbber tells users something is loading-in-progress, but nothing more. A similar yet very different form of a process indicator, such as a progress bar, expresses more information than a throbber. In contrast to a progress bar, which is more linear in form, a throbber does not indicate any completed or finished status and progress. It does not explain processual tasks in any specific detail when compared with a progress bar.[1] With a throbber, all that is presented is a spinning icon, perceived as repeatedly spinning under constant speed, as well as indicating invisible background activities for an indeterminate and unforeseeable timespan. If one looks up the dictionary definition of the verb "throb",[2] it is defined as a strong and regular pulse rhythm that resonates with a throbber's design and in regards to how it performs on the Internet today. But such design can be seen to oversimplify the micro-operations of networked technology, making one believe that the network is working with a certain regularity and that all data are queuing underway, thus rendering the network conditions of the *now*.

This chapter investigates data processing that takes place behind a running throbber. In particular, it examines the temporal complexity of data streams, in which data processing and code inter-actions are operated in real-time. The notion of inter-actions references computer science's understanding of "interaction" (Beaudouin-Lafon 2008; Bentley 2003; Murtaugh 2008; Wegner 1997) as well as the notion of "intra-actions" from philosophy (Barad 2003, 2007). The term I develop here, code inter-actions, highlights the operational process of things happening within and across machines through different technical substrates, interacting with each other via running code. In contrast to the understanding of technical interaction, process emerges through "entangled agencies" (Barad 2007, 33). Barad's notion of intra-actions refers to the entanglements of material relations that are not only technically and scientifically specific, but also with mixed factors and domains of operations that are regarded as social, political, economical and cultural (2007, 232–233).

In the following session, I will illustrate how a cultural and operative reading of an abstracted form of throbber allows an examination of data streams in contemporary computational culture. This chapter will first unfold a cultural reading of a throbber, then continue with a detailed discussion and analysis of the underlying operative and technical processes. It opens up the cultural and computational logics that are constantly rendering the pervasive and networked conditions of the *now*.

A (brief) cultural reading of a throbber

With its distinct design characteristic of a spinning behaviour hinting at background processing, the throbber icon acts as an interface between computational processes and visual communication. One of the earliest uses of the throbber can be found in the menu bar of a Mosaic web browser in the early 1990s, developed by the National Center for Supercomputing Applications (NCSA), with the browser interface designed by scientist Colleen Bushell (Albers 1996; Roebuck 2011, 348–349). This throbber[3] contains a letter "S" and a globe that spins when loading a web page. This kind of a spinning throbber with the company's graphical logo can also be witnessed in subsequent software browsers, such as Netscape and Internet Explorer. While the throbber spins, it visually indicates actions are in progress. These actions, from a user's point of view, could be interpreted as the loading of web data or connecting to a website by a software browser. From a technical perspective, it involves Internet data transmission and a browser that renders the inter-actions of code. The spinning behaviour stops when a webpage is finished loading within a browser. A web browser is software able to render and display requested content, making network calls and requests, and storing data locally (Garsiel and Irish 2011). In this respect, the spinning throbber icon represents complex inter-actions of code under network conditions. A throbber, with its spinning characteristic, can therefore be said to be rooted in, and specific to, Internet culture.

More recently, the throbber icon is no longer only attached to software browsers, appearing also on different web and mobile applications, including social media platforms in particular. The contemporary throbber transforms into a spinning wheel[4] that consists of lines or circles that are arranged in radial and circular form, moving in a clockwise direction. A throbber is animated and spun, or throbbed, with a constant rate, demonstrating a regular tempo. Each individual element of a wheel[5] sequentially fades in and out repeatedly to create a sense of animated motion. These spinning wheels appear after a user has triggered an action, such as swiping a screen with feeds in order to request the latest information. They also appear after a user has confirmed an online payment or is waiting for a transaction to complete. Perhaps most commonly of all, a throbber is seen when a user cannot watch a video clip loading smoothly over an Internet connection. As a result, an animated throbber appears as a spinning wheel on a black colour background, occupying the whole video screen while the video is buffering.

Figure 1. Throbber in the form of circles and lines, used with permission 2016.[6]

A throbber represents the speed of network traffic that is also tied to our affective states and perception of time. Emotionally, it can be frustrating to encounter buffering, as it involves interruption. Things do not flow smoothly and users become impatient in waiting for an unknown period of time or for something yet to come. Taiwanese artist Lai Chih-Sheng exhibits his throbber animated icon, titled *Instant*[7] (2013), with a minimalistic presentation, expressing the relation between waiting and time. This waiting is considered as unproductive, in that it consumes time. As artist-researcher James Charlton describes it: "It is a gaze that goes beyond the screen to an event not yet here" (2014, 171). The loading time of the throbber appears wasted and unproductive, as it is often associated with the perception of slowness of a network.

On September 10, 2014, a campaign called "Internet Slowdown day"[8] was launched as part of the "Battle for the Net", promoting net neutrality and Internet freedom. Customised loading icons, similar to a throbber, were put up on different websites, symbolising the potential impact of controlled traffic that would be implemented by Internet Service Providers in the name of increasing profit. In other words, the campaign argued for Internet speed equality across all websites and that no unequal conditions, such as fast-lane traffic, should be given to any prioritised website. More than 10,000 corporations showed support by putting up self-designed throbber icons. As is evident in this context, the throbber has a significant and symbolic meaning within cultural and political realms.

In contemporary art,[9] the throbber as cultural icon is remade by artist Aristarkh Chernyshev, showing the spinning behaviour through customised LEDs in a physical installation. The LEDs formulate the word "loading", circulating in a motion directly reminiscent of a spinning throbber. Chernyshev's artwork *LOADING* (2007)[10] aims to present this icon and its data exchange process as cultural phenomena, with the cultural icon of a throbber expressing various dimensions of time—from the loading time of a browser to the regular tempo of a spinning throbber to the slowness of the Internet network—in understanding data streams. Beyond different cultural instances, however, the operative and technical dimensions of a running throbber should not be undermined, as they can provide a specific perspective for further understanding how the now is being organised computationally as streams.

Drawing from a method proposed by Wolfgang Ernst in the field of Media Archaeology, the meaning of data streams can be analysed and understood via an application of a "cold gaze" upon data streams. Ernst's approach is used to engage with the mechanical and operational logic of computation, and the method of "cold gaze" aims to describe cold facts in a distinctly material-oriented, as opposed to narrative-based, approach (Parikka 2011, 2012; Ernst 2013). In taking into consideration the operative and technical perspectives of network transmission, Florian Sprenger provocatively argues that the concept of stream is a metaphor. He says:

> *The network structure of today's communication channels and of their information stream is often understood as providing a direct connection between users and services or between two communication partners, even though there cannot be any direct connections on digital networks. The metaphor of the flow conceals the fact that, technically, what is taking place is quite the opposite. There is no stream in digital networks.* (Sprenger 2015, 88–89)

Sprenger highlights the possible misconception of a flow or a stream, suggesting that there is a gap between the experienced and operative streams. He reminds us that two widely used concepts—flow and stream—in digital media are metaphors that potentially mislead anyone looking to understand the actual technical processes that take place beneath a stream. Drawing upon Ernst's (2013, 186–189) notion of micro-temporality, the focus of such approaches is with the nature and operation of signals and communications, mathematics and digital computation within its deep internal and operational structures. The added prefix "micro", therefore, addresses the micro-operative processes that are not apparent within an immediate human register. Ernst's notion of micro-temporality draws (after Foucault) on the concept of discontinuity (2006, 105). In Foucault (1972, 3), discontinuity offers an alternative perspective to understanding knowledge beyond its stable form of narration and representation. Both Foucault and Ernst use discontinuity as a means to examine the gaps and ruptures of things that go beyond signs or representational discourses.

To bring together concepts of discontinuity and micro-temporality is to offer an alternative perspective in examining streams behind a planetary scale global economy which renders the *now*. Streams can be understood as highly capitalised and as operating in massive scales under globalised processes that disseminate into every part of the world as cultural and economic phenomena. In the words of Peter Osborne, the *now* "is primarily a global or a planetary fiction" (2013, 26). Thus, the notion of discontinuous micro-temporality highlights the micro-processes and gaps of a stream that is manifested within networked presence-oriented feeds and their regular interruptions by a throbber. The concept of discontinuous micro-temporality points towards the temporal dimension of streams that present the *now*. The following section will take a micro-temporal analysis to foreground the notion of discontinuous micro-temporality that takes into account operative processes.

Micro-temporal analysis

Following the Von Neumann Architecture that was first initiated in 1945, mathematician and physicist John von Neumann designed a computer architecture consisting of a processing unit that contains an arithmetic logic unit, a control unit and a memory unit for performing arithmetic operations, operational sequence control and data and instruction storage respectively, also known as a stored-program computer (von Neumann 1945, 1–2). In this setup, a central clock[11] coordinates these units, executing computer instructions in a precise manner.

The appearance and disappearance of a graphical throbber is rendered by code, instructing when a throbber should be displayed on a screen. However, computer instruction is more than source code. In Computer Science and Engineering, the "Fetch-Execute cycle" is used to describe how a Central Processing Unit (CPU) performs code instructions through a series of steps that are executed within clock cycles (Burrell 2004, 135; Frabetti 2015, 153). The high-level instruction breaks into many micro-instructions by fetching and executing values from and in the memory space. The micro-instructions are highly ordered. The instruction pointer (also known as program counter) is used to keep track of the instruction sequence. This pointer is incremented after fetching an instruction and storing the memory address of the next instruction to be executed. The computer will continue repeating the cycles that fetch instructions and data from memory and then execute them one after another in sequence until the final instruction is reached (see also Frabetti 2015, 150–159). In short, executing code instructions involves the reading and writing of memory,[12] generating a sequence of micro-operational steps and the actual computation. The appearance or disappearance of a throbber on a screen is not an exception. All of the code instructions are operated across on/off states, generally known as "flip-flops" and logic gates used to store and control data flow. Underneath a graphical throbber is the inter-action of data, code and micro-instructions. The micro-temporality of instructions is driven by the internal clock as there are things that have to be done exactly at a specific time. Importantly, the machine clock forms a basic infrastructural activity of contemporary technology, organising and maintaining the sequences and components of computation that are essential in performing operational tasks. This microperspective allows us to be attentive to how time is structured and organised computationally and differently.

Packet switching and data buffering

Networked data are streamed over a technological network. This also relates to how data transfers and operates geopolitically across devices that are constrained by structures, infrastructures and "micro-decisions" (Sprenger 2015) along a transmission process. The following discussion will focus on the processes of packet switching and data buffering that are operated behind a running throbber.

In the late 1960s, the world's first packet switching network, called the ARPANET, was introduced, laying the groundwork that led to the development of the Internet as it has developed today. The concept of packet switching was fundamental to understanding how data are organised and flow. A data stream was chopped into smaller blocks as "packets", which were then sent via a communications channel in and through different routes, rates and sequences, known as packet switching (Baran 2002). Between the two connection points—sender and receiver—data, indeed, does not have a direct connection. According to Paul Baran, one of the inventors of the packet switched computer network, real-time connections between sender (transmitting end) and user (receiving end) are an illusion. Instead, the fast-enough data rate gives only a *sense* of real-time connection between a sender and receiver. Fundamentally, the routing of a data packet transmits through different sites. Although a selected path is based on "adaptive learning of past traffic" (44), there are real-time decisions that have to be made to locate the shortest path[13] due to the dynamics of network conditions. In other words, data travels "via highly circuitous paths that could not be determined in advance" (43).

It is worth noting that data packets pass through intermediate devices like gateways, switches and routers in their journey. According to the Protocol specifications (RFC 793 and RFC 791), there is a field called "Time to Live" (TTL) that limits the lifespan of data within a connection (Postel 1981b, 51, 1981a, 14). Data packet routing means that a connection between sender and receiver contains multiple switching computers and a route is made up of multiple "hops".[14] TTL is defined as the number of hops that a packet has to pass through before reaching its destination. This also means that if a packet passes through more than a defined number of hops, that particular packet is being discarded, alluding to the time to die, as opposed to live. Therefore, each packet has its own lifespan. The idea behind having the TTL field is to prevent any instances of endless circulating of data packets within the network. These decisions are monitored and executed in real-time. This real-time execution is similar to what Wendy Hui Kyong Chun describes within the context of hardware and software systems in which computation responds to the live condition. She says,

> *[H]ard and software real-time systems are subject to a 'real-time' constraint—that is, they need to respond, in a forced duration, to actions predefined as events. The measure of real time, in computer systems, is its reaction to the live—its liveness.* (Chun 2008, 316)

The notion of liveness can be understood as the decisions and reactions that are required to execute beneath various real-time constraints. To Chun, liveness is expressed at the temporal level in which a system is required to react and respond according to its user input and output. But in the case of technological networks, the response may not include direct human intervention, and machines take charge of decisions and in real-time and responses in a forced duration. The micro-temporality of a stream involves "micro-decisions" (Sprenger 2015) as well as interruptions in real-time. Every micro-decision, the routing decision via multiple hops for example, takes time. Decisions are made not only in real-time but also in a micro-temporal interval. This also applies to the process of data buffering; we normally understand this by seeing a throbber that interrupts a stream. What then are the micro-decisions involved in data buffering?

A buffer is understood as a temporal storage that usually stores a small amount of data in physical memory. While some data are stored in a buffer, other segments of data are being read and processed. This also means that software applications are not required to wait for the entire media file to be downloaded. "Just in Time" (JIT) delivery is used in streaming media, allowing for the playback of partially received data temporarily stored in the client's buffer (Pereira and Ebrahimi 2002, 260). In this sense, both the playback of buffer data and the receiving of the remaining data can be made simultaneously (and, in addition to the case of video and audio, this is also commonly experienced in loading any relatively large size file, such as a PDF or an image within a browser). The buffer is where software applications, such as a browser or media player, access the input data and process it as output data. In other words, the processing of data consists not only of the transferring part, but rather, as Ernst reminds us, through "a coupling of storage and transfer in realtime". He continues, "[w]hile we see one part of the video on screen, the next part is already loaded in the background" (Ernst 2006, 108). More precisely, the viewer is not watching the content as data arrives, instead, the viewer is watching the processed data that has arrived and stored in the buffer. This process of temporal storage and playback gives us an understanding of the relation between buffer and streams, in which there is latency between data arrival (from the network), data storage (within internal memory) and data processing (inside a machine) at micro-time intervals. Streaming is essentially "achieved by buffering the transmitted data before the actual display" (Meinel and Sack 2013, 780). A throbber is entangled with this latency, interacting with different pieces of data in different ways.

Ideally, the "buffer empties itself at one end just as quickly as it fills up at the other end", as described by Christoph Meinel and Harald Sack (783). If there is transmission delay that is within a threshold time t, it is regarded as unnoticeable in playback. However, if the delay of the individual segment exceeds the threshold time t, a throbber will then display.
A program performs to read and process the buffer but the data

has not arrived yet, and this gap and rupture will lead to the appearance of a throbber. This is the instance in which we can perceive and experience the discontinuous micro-temporality.

Normally, a throbber is seen when loading a big chunk of data, which is commonly seen in video sites, mostly due to the instability or low bandwidth of a network that causes the delay of data segment arrival (exceeds the threshold time t). Buffering is highly related to time as it allows different rates to occur simultaneously, decoupling "time dependencies" between the input and output of data (55). As a result, data can be consumed and processed at a different rate by program applications. Data, in the case of streaming, is actively and constantly being stored (written) and removed (read) in the buffer at different speeds and rhythms, oscillating between the invisible and visible. The micro-temporality of buffering transforms the space of a buffer that works with both internal and external data. This buffer space, as a site of inter-actions, contingently and temporally performs variations. Although what has been written in the buffer will be automatically read and processed, technology does not guarantee that all the data are written in the buffer.

The absence of data

Dropped frames (frames of video that are dropped during playout) are a relatively common experience in real-time communications and video streaming. Dropped frames impact upon the user's viewing experience because of frames that disappear within a perceivable continuous stream. When an audio-visual is played back at the receiver's side, this introduces gaps in the stream and it is able to produce glitches or jittery audible effects. This is different from displaying a throbber on a screen, where nothing can be seen on a screen despite the animated graphic. When experiencing dropped frames, one can still see or hear something, but just not necessarily in good quality.

In some situations, the issue of dropped frames is seamless because it does not create significant quality degradation. Such visible and invisible dropped frames are caused by packet loss, the absence of certain parts of data during data transmission across nodes throughout the journey. Indeed, packet loss is highly relevant to the notion of micro-temporality. According to James F. Kurose and Keith W. Ross, the delay time for transmitting data does not only include "store-and-forward" in each buffer nodes, but also "queuing delays" that are subjected to network congestion and are not predictable in advance (2013, 25). Packets are required to queue up and wait for the transfer while the network is congested. Under streaming conditions, data are continuously transmitted across multiple sites. However, the amount of buffer space is limited at each site, which means a newly arriving packet potentially has no space to be stored in while the stored packet is still queuing for its next routing. In this situation, "packet loss will occur—either the arriving packet or one of the already—queued packets will be dropped" (25).

The robust design of network protocols consists of an automatic mechanism to detect and trigger retransmission for packet loss. However, for real-time conversational applications and media streaming platforms for live concerts, such as Skype and YouTube, delay time for each packet is a critical issue as the transmission demands to be continuous. Both conversations and live concerts are unceasing. On the one hand, the absence of data is crucial as packet loss is related to the degradation of quality, and it could immediately impact the visual or audio quality in a live environment. On the other hand, if data arrives with significant delay, the application design at the receiver's end is then required to determine if such data will still make sense in playback, in particular where conversation and data are constantly played-back as a stream. In deciding whether the data should be played-back or ignored, acceptable latency becomes a decision that is inscribed in the software and platform design. During streaming conditions, a throbber will be seen for a weak connection (as for the case of Skype conversation). A serious data loss may even result in the automatic termination of a connection—which also means the tolerance is unacceptable from the point of view of software design. The technical consequences of data loss is nothing new if one has used Skype or other communication applications like what's app, weChat or Line, in which it is not uncommon to have the experience of glitches or jitter effects, as well as a throbber display on a screen. But what is of concern here is rather the cultural implications of these absent data, or the potentiality of packet loss at any moment of time.

Here the absent data requires our attention. Firstly, the absence of data might be caused by a voluntary condition. It is possible for an application to discard late-arriving data that are within acceptable latency because it is insignificant to the entire user experience. Secondly, due to the buffer capacity, data loss can occur anytime and at any sites during the entire journey of a data transmission. Last, but not least, when the network bandwidth cannot match the application's processing rate, there will be data loss.[15] As a result, not all data are treated equally and able to arrive at the destination and take a perceptible form. Even though the presence of a stream is mediatised as audio and visuals through a screen, there is still the possibility of absent data. The absence, although it cannot be mediatised in its perceptible form at the receiver's end, is implied in the presence of streams, in which conversation or video playback is kept running. The point is that the mundane activity that we wait and stream through a screen is loaded with unperceivable gaps.

To explain further, the logic of buffering and data processing are constantly performed through the presence and absence of data. A display of a throbber presents another reality, a reality that is conflated with an invisible material infrastructure and the absence of material substrates. Furthermore, a throbber and its underlying data buffering involve discrete-time signaling—the milliseconds of time lost and the absence of data-presenting multiple realities which lie at the heart of time-dependent logics. Therefore, reality is not only a matter of continuous flow and the immediacy of a stream. Taking account of materiality, such a notion of reality refers neither to the symbolic meaning of content, the feeling of presence or the immediacy of data delivery, but rather a tension is expressed between continuity and discontinuity through the performativity of code. That is to say, when taking into account packet loss, the liveness or *nowness* of a stream is about an absent present. The notion of discontinuous microtemporality explicates the invisibility of computational culture by shifting our attention from the cultural understanding of a throbber and what is visible on a screen to invisible microevents that are running in the background, events that are not separated but entangled as absent present.

Absent data are rarely mentioned in the commercial products that frame contemporary digital culture, inasmuch as it possibly relates to quality degradation or may be regarded as not noticeable. Within a stream, there are these discontinuous forces that constitute the continuous presence. Sometimes the forces appear to be strong, yet at other times they are weak; in some cases more visible, and at other times unnoticeable. The notion of discontinuity pays attention to the gaps, ruptures and pauses that are interwoven within the continuous flow of a data stream. From the display of a running throbber to its disappearance while a stream is presented, *discontinuous micro-temporality* highlights the forces and presence of micro-decisions and micro-interruptions that reconfigure the nowness or liveness of a stream.

Conclusion

A stream is manifested into continuously updating feeds, passing through hops and sites, which in part defines the now. The mundane throbber calls for a critical attention towards mediated processes not only at a planetary scale, but also at the micro-temporal level of operations, including clock cycles, instructions execution, packet switching and data buffering, which exhibit micro-decisions and micro-interruptions. The notion of discontinuous micro-temporality takes into account the micro-processes, gaps and ruptures and, more importantly, the absence of data that renders present realities. This sheds light on the understanding of streams in computational culture, in particular, on how time is processed and organised to present the *now* under live conditions.

The existence of a throbber is a by-product of a commercial application that informs users to wait for an unknown period of time. Through the use of a throbber in developing various services — such as live streaming, social media platforms, data and transactional applications — this cultural icon offers a critical space for understanding how the *now* is being made operative. A throbber is a cultural phenomenon that appears in almost every application that operates within a live computational environment. A throbber is not only a technical or functional object but also entangled with other cultural and micro-processes. This chapter explicates the computational logic behind a throbber as well as the real-time dynamics of computational networks and, hence, the rendering of the pervasive and networked conditionings of *nowness*.

Acknowledgements

The concept of this paper was developed through the seminars and conferences on 'execution' in 2015 and 2016. I am thankful to the team of Critical Software Thing and the team of respondents, including Geoff Cox, Christian Ulrik Andersen and Femke Snelting, as well as the participants of the execution conference for their comments on the earlier concept of this paper. I am especially grateful to the editors of this book, providing insightful and constructive feedback. Finally, an earlier version of this chapter has been published in ISEA2016 Conference Proceedings, and I thank the reviewers and Jane Prophet in providing their comments.

Notes

1. Computer operations are usually explained in conjunction with the use of a progress bar, for example, the transferring and copying of specific files and directories, or illustrating installation procedures.

2. See: http://www.oxforddictionaries.com/definition/english/throb.

3. The mosaic throbber also allows user to click on it to stop loading a webpage (Roebuck 2011, 348).

4. The use of lines that indicates the progress activity of a computer can be found in the early operating system of Unix that consists of few string characters as '[', '—', '\', '|', '/', ']' (Roebuck 2011, 349).

5. Coincidently, the visual design of a throbber is similar to the design of early wristwatches (with crystal guards) that were made for soldiers in World War I. Both include the concept of a wheel in the form of circles or lines of petal shape. See: http://www.oobject.com/category/earliest-wrist-watches/.

6. Source: "18 CSS3 and jQuery Loading Animations Solution." Design Modo, May 30, 2015, http://designmodo.com/css3-jquery-loading-animations.

7. See: https://www.facebook.com/ESLITE.PROJECTONE/photos/?tab=album&album_id=437623016346200.

8. For more details, see: https://www.battleforthenet.com/sept10th/.

9. Other artists have also explored this throbber icon. For example, artist Gordan Savičić explores the perception of time through his work *Loading* (2009), that turns an ordinary windowpane into a screen (Savičić 2009). Alongside this chapter, I have also developed a project called *The Spinning Wheel of Life* (2016) that explores the micro-temporality of computation (Soon 2016).

10. See: https://festivalenter.wordpress.com/2009/04/09/electroboutique-by-alexei-shulgin-roman-minaev-aristarkh-chernyshev/.

11. Thanks to Brian House who first introduced the concept of computer clock to me in the *.exe (ver0.1) workshop (House 2015).

12. Memory is used here in a broad sense that includes computer main memory, instruction register and memory buffer register, etc.

13. For more details about the determination of the shortest path, see Meinel and Sack (2013, 350–352).

14. A hop refers to "the leg of a route from one end system to the nearest switching computer, or between two adjacent switching computers, or from the switching computer to a connected end system" (Meinel and Sack 2013, 451).

15. For example, a 50% data loss is encountered when a network has only a maximum bandwidth of 5 Mbps and the application requires 10 Mbps.

References

Albers, Michael C. 1996. "Auditory cues for browsing, surfing, and navigating." In Frysinger, S.P. and

G. Kramer (eds), *Proceedings of the 3rd International Conference on Auditory Display (ICAD 1996)*. Palo Alto, California: ICAD.

Barad, Karen. 2003. "Posthumanist Performativity: Toward an Understanding of How Matter Comes to Matter." *Journal of Women in Culture and Society*, 28(3).

———. 2007. *Meeting the Universe Halfway: Quantum Physics and the Entanglement of Matter and Meaning*. Reprint. Durham: Duke University Press.

Baran, Paul. 2002. "The Beginnings of Packet Switching: Some Underlying Concepts." *IEEE Communications Magazine* 40 (7): 42–48.

Beaudouin-Lafon, Michel. 2008. "Interaction Is the Future of Compu-ting." In *HCI Remixed: Reflections on Works That Have Influenced the HCI Community*, edited by Thomas Erickson and David W. McDonald, 263–266. Cambridge, MA, London: The MIT Press.

Bentley, Peter. 2011. "The Meaning of Code." In *Code: The Language of our Time*, edited by Gerfried Stocker and Christine Schöpf, 33–36. Linz: Hatje Cantz, 2003.

Berry, David M. *The Philosophy of Software Code and Mediation in the Digital Age*. Basingstoke: Palgrave Macmillan.

———. 2012. "The Social Epistemologies of Software." *Social Epistemology* 26 (3–4): 379–398.

———. 2013. "Introduction: What is code and software?" In *Life in Code and Software: Mediated Life in a Complex Computational Ecology*. Open Humanities Press.

Burrell, Mark. 2004. *Fundamentals of Cmputer Architecture*. New York: Palgrave Macmillan.

Charlton, James. 2014. "Post Screen Not Displayed." In *Post-Screen: Device, Medium and Concept*, edited by Helena Ferreira and Ana Vicente, 170–182. Lisbon: CIEBA-FBAUL.

Chun, Wendy Hui Kyong. 2008. "On 'Sourcery,' or Code as Fetish." *Configurations* 16 (3): 299-324.

Ernst, Wolfgang. 2006. "Dis/continuities: Does the Archive Become Metaphorical in Multi-Media Space?" In *New Media, Old Media: A History and Theory Reader*, edited by Wendy Hui Kyong Chun and Thomas Keenan. New York, London: Routledge.

———. 2013. *Media Archaeology: Method and Machine Versus History and Narrative of Media*. Edited by Jussi Parikka, Digital Memory and the Archive. Minneapolis: University of Minnesota Press.

Foucault, Michel. 1972. *The Archaeology of Knowledge and the Discourse on Language*. New York: Pantheon Books.

Frabetti, Federica. 2015. *Software Theory: A Cultural and Philosophical Study (media philosophy)*. London: Rowman & Littlefield International.

Fuller, Matthew. 2013. *Behind the Blip: Essays on the Culture of Software*. New York, London: Autonomedia.

Garsiel, Tali, and Paul Irish. 2011. "How Browsers Work: Behind the Scenes of Modern Web Browsers." Last modified August 5. http://www.html5rocks.com/en/tutorials/internals/howbrowserswork.

House, Brian. 2015. "Sound and The Heat of The Cut." http://softwarestudies.projects.cavi.au.dk/index.php/Exe0.1_Brian_House.

Kurose, James F., and Keith W. Ross. 2013. *Computer Networking: A Top-Down Approach*. Pearson Education.

Laplante, Philip A. 2000. *Dictionary of Computer Science, Engineering and Technology*. CRC Press.

Meinel, Christoph, and Harald Sack. 2013. *Internetworking: Technological Foundations and Applications*. Berlin: Springer.

Murtaugh, Michael. 2008. "Interaction." In *Software Studies: A Lexicon*, edited by Matthew Fuller, 143-148. Cambridge, MA: The MIT Press.

Osborne, Peter. 2013. *Anywhere Or Not At All: Philosophy of Contemporary Art*. London: Verso.

Parikka, Jussi. 2011. "Operative Media Archaeology: Wolfgang Ernst's Materialist Media Diagrammatics." *Theory, Culture & Society* 28 (5):52-74.

———. 2012. *What is Media Archaeology*. Cambridge: Polity Press.

Pereira, Fernando, and Touradj Ebrahimi. 2002. *The MPEG-4 book*. Prentice Hall.

Postel, Jonathan. 1981a. Internet Protocol - Darpa Internet Program Protocol Specification (RFC 793). Information Sciences Institute.

———. 1981b. Transmission Control Protocol—Darpa Internet Program Protocol Specification (RFC 791). Information Sciences Institute.

Roebuck, Kevin. 2011. *Virtual Desktops: High-Impact Strategies—What You Need to Know: Definitions, Adoptions, Impact, Benefits, Maturity, Vendors*. Dayboro: Emereo Publishing.

Savičić, Gordan. *Gordan Savicic— fleshgordo vs. frescogamba*, http://www.yugo.at/processing/?what=loading.

Soon, Winnie. 2016. "The Spinning Wheel of Life (work-in-progress)." *Digital Art and Technology*. http://siusoon.net/home/?p=1407.

Sprenger, Florian. 2015. *The Politics of Micro-Decisions: Edward Snowden, Net Neutrality, and the Architectures of the Internet*. Lüneburg: Meson Press.

Von Neumann, John. 1945. "First Draft of a Report on the EDVAC."

Wegner, Peter. 1997. "Why Interaction is More Powerful than Algorithms." *Commmunications of the ACM* 40 (5): 80-91.

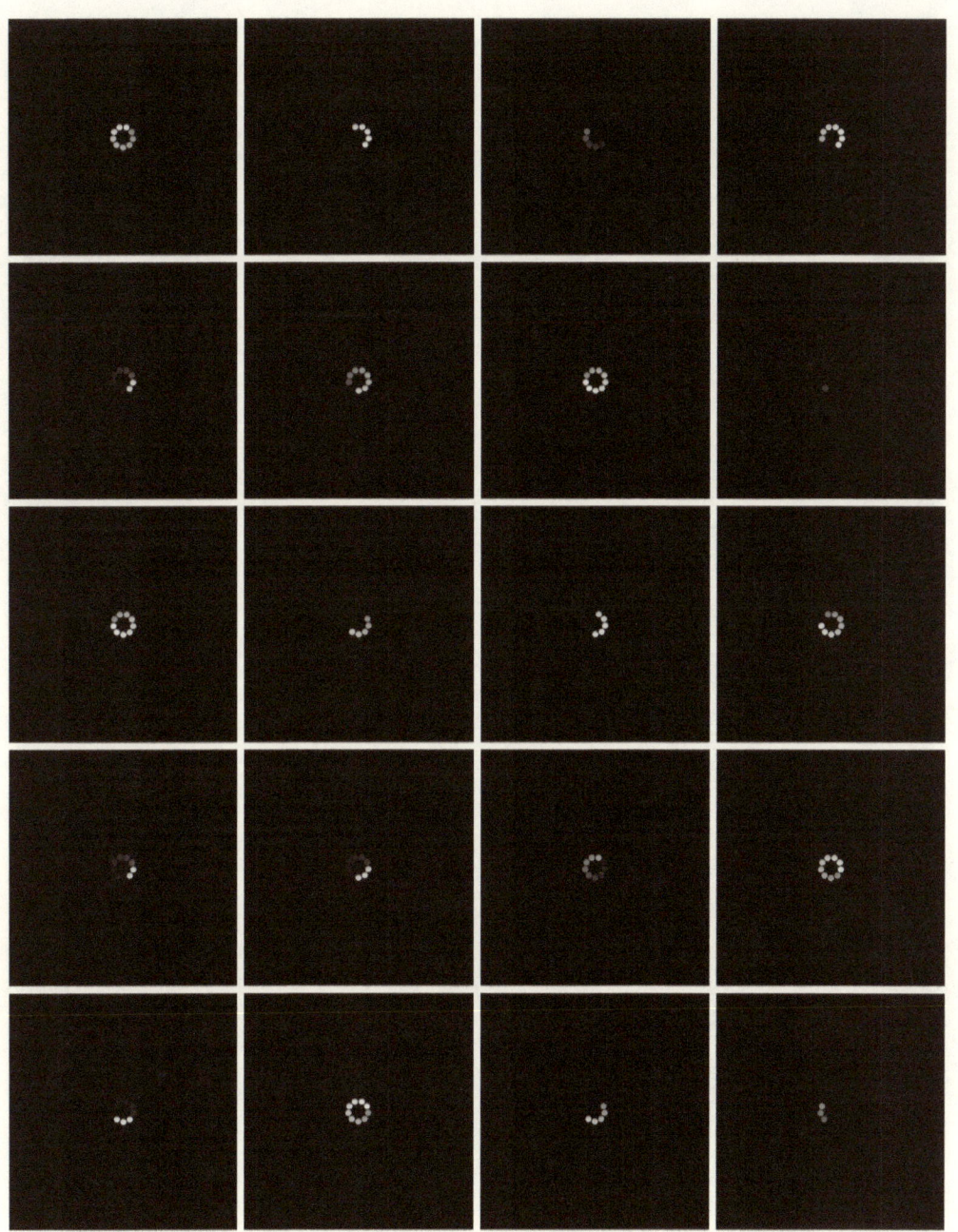

Winnie Soon, *The Spinning Wheel of Life* (2016)

Synchronising Uncertainty: Google's Spanner and Cartographic Time

Brian House

Introduction

In the following text, I discuss contemporary, large-scale, network-distributed databases, exemplified by the largest of all, Google's Spanner—so named because it circumscribes the entire planet. Though largely unknown to the public, Spanner is the infrastructure behind Google search, Google's advertising platform, and applica-tions like Gmail that billions of people use every day.

To operate at such scale, Spanner must synchronize time over the extent of the globe, and I situate this endeavour within a genealogy of Western timekeeping strategies extending from astronomical observations in the age of maritime navigation to the various electromagnetic media that have coordinated the clocks of railroads and satellites. This lineage demonstrates how evolving notions of temporality are inexorably bound to geography and to the material practice of cartography.

I argue that *random access*, a fundamental property of individual hard drives, is already cartographic by virtue of how it encapsulates the contingencies of time—this is what maps aspire to do. By physically extending this principle across the planet, Spanner explicitly links such data cartography with geographic mapmaking.

Further, random access also marks a shift in the evolution of time synchronisation. With Spanner, the ambition to establish an absolute measure of time itself is superseded by the need for synchronic slices—time is executed as "logical snapshots" of globally consistent data. By negotiating a contingent sense of time in order to posit a discrete one, Google extends strategic modes of knowledge that are inseparable from histories of industrialisation, colonialism, and militarism to our everyday interactions with its products.

"Cartographology"

I would like to begin with the hard drive which sits inside every internet server and on which, arguably, contemporary network culture is predicated. Jacques Derrida famously noted that writing is not secondary to spoken language, but that the means of inscription produces its own meaning (Derrida 1980). In an essay entitled "Extreme Inscription: Towards a Grammatology of the Hard Drive", Matthew Kirschenbaum extends this notion by articulating the material characteristics of the disk as a writing technology. Briefly, those are that the drive is

- a *signal processor* that converts between digital and analog signals
- *differential*, in that it both depends on the measurement of difference in the physical media, and, by extension, that it represents difference
- *chronographic* because the physical act of reading and writing data takes time
- *volumetric* since the disk platters take up space
- *rationalized* because every part of the disk has an address
- *motion-dependent* as the read/write head mechanically moves
- *planographic* because "the surface of the disk, in order to fly scant nanometers beneath the air bearings, must be absolutely smooth"
- and *non-volatile* because a disk does not forget anything when it is turned off

Some of these properties may be more or less relevant with newer technologies (solid state drives, for example, have no moving parts, so the idea of motion-dependency has to be loosened). But it is significant that most of these properties describe temporal processes inherent in the operation of the device—it is precisely these material contingencies in time that the hard drive encapsulates and attempts to conceal.

Such encapsulation is exemplified by *random access*[1] —another of Kirschenbaum's properties that more or less incorporates all the rest. The term refers to how the data of a storage medium can be accessed without regard to the order in which the data have been written. This differs fundamentally from sequential storage media such as magnetic tape in which information is arranged linearly and order is directly related to access time (imagine fast-forwarding and rewinding a cassette to get to your favourite song). To quibble, in any given situation certain data may in fact be quicker to access than others. But the goal of random access is to minimize the average time taken for a program to read or write an unpredictable sequence of data. In effect, this abstracts the details of the storage mechanism so that access time can be treated as a constant by the software that uses the disk. "Random" as "unpredictable" thus sits alongside its colloquial usage as "irrelevant"—constant time means everything in the data space is treated the same.

This planer, addressable, timeless surface functions in a way analogous to a geographic map. As Michel de Certeau beautifully puts it, maps transform

> *the* temporal articulation *of places into a spatial sequence of points. A graph takes the place of an operation. A reversible sign is substituted for a practice indissociable from particular moments and "opportunities" ... it is thus a mark* in place of *acts.*
> (Certeau 1984, 35)

The map gains its power from this atemporality—that the flow of time has been deferred elsewhere means it can be "seized as a whole by the eye in a single moment" (Certeau 1984, 35), and it is this that enables strategic planning. This is not so different from how we think of data as a field of knowledge laid out before us. Us, or an algorithm—both the search routine that interprets the past and the artificially intelligent program that predicts the future depend on a static, map-like representation on which they can operate. Therefore, what I'm proposing is that what's at stake with storage technology is not only a matter of grammatology, as in the study of writing, but of what might be called *cartograph-ology* and the equally inscriptive cultural practice of mapmaking. If Kirschenbaum has elucidated the cartographic techniques of the hard drive, what are those of a distributed database such as Spanner?

Consistency

Random access is technically straightforward to achieve when it comes to an individual disk within a single computer. But consider that Spanner is, as Google says, "designed to scale up to millions of machines across hundreds of datacenters and trillions of database rows" (Corbett 2012, 1). Further, these machines are not in the same place—there are data centers on six continents. Data in such a distributed system are *sharded*, which means that a single database must be coordinated across a network of storage devices. Sharding allows the system to scale—it abstracts the database from the disk in order to overcome the inherent size and speed limitations of individual pieces of hardware. This means that unlike Kirschenbaum's grammatology of a hard drive, a *cartographology* of a distributed database cannot be done purely on a mechanical level. Rather, it must account for the software architecture and processual techniques whereby that hardware is organised.

In that regard, we have to consider the big problem for any distributed database—maintaining *consistency*. A consistent database is one that is always in a valid state—that is, all information across the network is up-to-date, and at any given time all applications and users are accessing the same information. This is a necessary prerequisite if it is going to function as a map. Again, that is easy for a single disk, but transfer time across the distributed network, especially under global circumstances, makes this extremely difficult.

To address it, Google starts with the idea of the *logical snapshot*, whereby the data across all machines, in all data centres, across every continent, is known to be consistent at a given point in time in the past. To be able to do that, you need to know the order in which the data have been written, irrespective of which shards they have been written on. This is easier said than done—techniques developed prior to Spanner rely on "complicated coordination protocols" (Metz 2012) to let each other know about each write—but such complexity limits the scalability of the system and its capability to act as a truly unified whole.

Google's innovation at first seems almost banal—to determine the order of the data, simply record the time at which each was written. Assuming a "global wall-clock", a logical snapshot is just a temporal slice at some point in the near past—far enough *in the past* to account for the communication delay between all the shards. However, the existence of such a clock turns out to be a big assumption. Google's Andrew Fikes declares, "as a distributed systems developer, you're taught from—I want to say childhood—not to trust time" (Metz 2012). Fikes could also mean any given *representation* of time, but the conflation is revealing. It situates Google's drive to establish a global wall-clock, which is the central ambition of Spanner, within a genealogy of Western timekeeping strategies concerned with synchronization over expanding geographic areas.

A brief history of time(keeping)

Peter Galison has written a persuasive history tracing the relationship between geography, media, and synchronicity (Galison 2003). He explains how the emergence of the mechanical clock in Europe in the sixteenth century permitted the unbinding of time from location—that is, a clock, propelled by its own internal mechanism, may indicate what time it is somewhere else. As Galison discusses, this was a critical, if incrementally achieved, innovation for navigation and cartography. Consider that in order to understand the globe as a grid of latitude and longitude coordinates, one's position on the grid has to be observable. Navigation by star position provides a relatively straightforward way to determine latitude via the night sky—the star Polaris aligns with the north pole, and the Southern Cross can be used to triangulate the south. But because of the rotation of the earth, longitude can only be reliably fixed given the time of a known location. For example, if it is midnight in London and the stars where I am are shifted ninety degrees from what I would expect in the London sky, then I am a quarter way around the globe. Hence the rationalised sense of time as a constant, independent dimension that is the same everywhere also marks the birth of contemporary cartography. This continues to resonate in culture: time and space are separately thought, but practically bound.

Galison goes on to trace the progression whereby train routes maintained a unified "train time" which gradually reconciled the divergent timekeeping of regional metropolitan centres. This process was predicated by the emergence of electromagnetic media in the form of the telegraph and later the radio that allowed time synchronisation to happen over greater distances—the infrastructure that is the direct antecedent of the fiber optics and undersea cables that carry data today. Progressively, the observatory hubs anchoring clocks to local astronomical measurements surrendered to the international standard of Greenwich Mean Time and modern discrete time zones. And at each step, this was a political negotiation, from the municipal level all the way up to the empire-building of Britain, industrial expansion in the

US, and the extension of French Revolutionary values seeking rationalised standards. As Galison puts it, "beating overhead in church spires, observatories, and satellites, synchronized clocks have never stood far from the political order" (Galison 2003, 143).[2]

While Greenwich Mean Time was originally directly tied to measurements at the Royal Observatory in the UK, it turns out that the Earth's rotation is not constant—tidal friction and changes in the Earth's mass due to melting glaciers cause it to vary. Subsequently, a more accurate reference was needed. Decoupling the notion of the day from the transit of the sun, which happened on January 1, 1972, is a profoundly modernist gesture. 9,192,631,770 cycles of radiation from the caesium-133 atom is the current international standard for one second, and the atomic clock is the basis for Universal Coordinated Time, or UTC.

Atomic clocks are also the foundation of contemporary map-making. Each of the satellites that make up the Global Positioning Service, or GPS, contains an atomic clock within it. In many ways, GPS—originally deployed by the US military—culminates the narrative of terrestrial time synchronization by literally rising above the earth. The system broadcasts clock signals to the ground, where receivers, ubiquitously embedded in things like mobile devices, triangulate their position—minute differences between the received times indicate varying distances to the known location of each satellite. This temporal negotiation smooths geographic space into the Cartesian grid postulated by post-Enlightenment thought—it is exemplified by the gesture of looking down at GPS-powered Google Maps on your iPhone in order to see the earth from above.[3]

True time

How does that iPhone keep time? Computing devices generally make use of a *real-time clock*, or RTC, which is based on a cheap crystal oscillator. An RTC will inevitably drift out of synchrony with other clocks due to temperature fluctuations and other physical factors. However, with systems connected to the internet, the RTC synchronizes with a *time server* using the Network Time Protocol, or NTP. Such servers are maintained by governments (time.nist.gov), independent foundations (pool.ntp.org), and large corporations (time.apple.com). In this case, synchronization happens via internet packets, and as such it is subject to network latency. For most systems, though, NTP is good enough.

However, when a Google engineer doesn't "trust time", it reflects practical experience that much can go wrong with NTP synchronization procedures. Communication may fail due to network variability, and, critically, machines distributed around the world will experience uneven latency in relation to a central time server. Clocks may or may not line up, and worse, there is no way to verify after the fact if this has happened.

Hence Spanner. First, Spanner eschews NTP and is linked explicitly to GPS — every data centre has a "time master" unit that is always receiving GPS time. There are also "Armageddon masters" within the system that have their own atomic clocks, in the extreme case that GPS should ever fail. Each machine continually updates its RTC by continuously polling a variety of these master clocks, both in the local data center and from across the network. The slightly differing times received from all the masters are combined to produce an optimal time estimation, an emergent consensus that is uniform across the globally-distributed database. This uniformity, however, comes with a level of calculated uncertainty, an artifact of all the aggregated network latency together with clock drift on individual machines.

This negotiated uncertainty is represented by what Google calls the TrueTime API. An API, or Application Programming Interface, is an essential programming concept based on obfuscation. Software components need not — and in fact, should not — know the implementation details of other components. Rather, an API provides stable terms through which software can reliably communicate while hiding the underlying, and potentially variable, mess. Application code that uses Spanner does so through the TrueTime API, which "explicitly represents time as ... an interval" that indicates the earliest and latest points that an event could possibly have happened. In other words, the brilliance of the TrueTime API is that it "reif[ies] clock uncertainty" (Hsieh 2012).

Google describes this strategy as being Rumsfeldian — that is, "known unknowns are better than unknown unknowns." They abandon the naïve hope that fast is fast enough — instead, Spanner leverages statistical knowledge about its own vast hardware to gauge how confident it can be about time. In an industry obsessed with making things faster, a counter-intuitive feature of the system is that "if the uncertainty is large, Spanner *slows down* to wait out that uncertainty" (Hsieh 2012). All of this is done in service to having a global wall-clock that Google can depend on—it is what makes those logical snapshots possible.

Random access geography

Finally we can return to Kirschenbaum. Does the scale achieved with Spanner exceed the qualities of the individual hard drive? This is undeniably the case. Yet, in many ways, such a geographically totalising database infrastructure aspires to function as a single disk. Revisiting and reformulating Kirschenbaum's grammatology, or our cartographology, elucidates the comparison.

Spanner is certainly a *signal processor*, but that analog-to-digital conversion now happens multiple times across the network switches and undersea cables of distributed infrastructure. It is still as *differential* as its individual disks. TrueTime itself clearly marks Spanner as *chronographic*. If the hard drive is volumetric, Spanner's data centers are extremely so. It is a *rationalised* system, because any data across the space may be addressed, and, significantly, that location *is also a geographical place*. Is Spanner *motion dependent*? If the hard drive has the spinning disk, Spanner adds the orbit of GPS satellites, the oscillation of the caesium atom, and the packets traversing the network. *Non-volatility* maps to Spanner's robustness and those Armageddon masters. And *planographic* speaks to the data centers spread out over the surface of the earth. We can therefore construct an analog between how Kirschenbaum enumerates the technology of inscription that is the hard drive and this far larger system, supplementing purely mechanical elements with software and geographic processes.

What about *random access*? Spanner's logical snapshots accomplish the same thing—they render the notion of time itself secondary to a consistent plane of stable data. It is the felt quality experienced by the individual or application that is able to call up any piece of information from the database at will, regardless of the material conditions of its storage. This is Spanner's goal, for all data to be available from any point and time, at a geographic scale.

Spanner makes the isomorphism of a hard drive to a map quite literal. This is even reflected by certain representations that Google puts forth, namely, Google Earth and Google Maps. The effortlessly spinning globe that one floats above in Earth might well serve as a metonym for the random access space coordinated by Spanner, as "Google Earth ... can be understood as the aesthetic rendering ... of the logic of Google search" (Munster 2013, 63). Search is, of course, the paradigmatic operation of random access and is inseparable from the rationalised qualities of the distributed database beneath it. A plain link is thus established between representation and infrastructure.

Conclusion

Clearly, though, there is a "sense" here, that is missing. Anna Munster's work on how we experience networks and data is particularly compelling in this respect. She explains how there is a difference between recognising something that is already within the parameters of what is knowable, as one does when pointing something out on a map, and the active, contingent process of experiencing some unknown potential unfold in time (Munster 2013, 43). The latter is, in short, the uncertainty that is exactly what Spanner urgently seeks to obfuscate. Where has the time gone? The TrueTime API extends the techniques of timekeeping in Galison's history — it is a synchronization procedure. But with Spanner, the quest to chase uncertainty down to ever finer intervals — even to the oscillations of the atom — is superseded by a concern with a sequence of logical snapshots that bypasses that uncertainty. Potential is abstracted away by an engineered lag behind the "now".

That the human experience of time is irreducible to modes of timekeeping should be self-evident — otherwise we would never have to check the clock. Consequently, as a totalising project, Spanner is aspirational. We are well acquainted with the "spinning beach ball of death" and other aesthetic ruptures we experience when technology can't quite keep up (see Winnie Soon's contribution in this volume) — the unresponsive hard drive, the stutter in the video stream, even the tone-deaf targeted ad — these moments reveal material contingencies that resist representation. In Spanner's case, "network lag" is a kind of shorthand for the physical resources and social structures required to build, connect, and maintain millions of computers across vast distances. They are left out of the map even as they are essential to the cartographic act. But when Spanner slows down the world to make it conform to its strategic view, that elision manifests in the micro-experiences of billions of users.

To "keep time" is to mark temporal experience, but to "keep" is also to withhold or suspend. To the extent that maps—whether of data, geography, or both—accomplish this, they reserve extraordinary power. But by understanding the practices of timekeeping that make such abstraction possible, we can rethink them as a particular construction of lived time and modulate our participation accordingly. After all, "keeping time" is also what drummers do in musical performance, and a distributed database, too, is a matter of temporal aesthetics rather than absolute measure.

Notes

1. Not to be confused with Random Access Memory.

2. Galison reprints a map of a French plan for synchronizing South America, with telegraph lines reaching Rio from Europe and encircling the continent, passing through Lima, and continuing north to the United States. It bears a remarkable similarity to an image in Wired accompanying its article on Spanner, an isomorphism which evinces similar ambitions.

3. See the work of Johnathan Hanahan, http://www.hanahan.works/pixel_posters.html.

References

Brewer, Eric. 2000. "Towards Robust Distributed Systems." PODC Keynote, July 19. http://www.cs.berkeley.edu/~brewer/cs262b-2004/PODC-keynote.pdf.

De Certeau, Michel. 1984. *The Practice of Everyday Life*. Trans. by Steven F. Rendall. Berkeley: University of California Press.

Derrida, Jacques. 1980. *Of Grammatology*. Trans. by Gayatri Spivak. Baltimore: Johns Hopkins University Press.

Galison, Peter. 2003. *Einstein's Clocks, Poincaré's Maps*. New York: W. W. Norton.

Hsieh, Wilson. 2012. "Google's Globally-Distributed Database." Paper presentation. See http://new.livestream.com/accounts/1545775/osdi12/videos/4646642 and also James C. Corbett et al (2012), *OSDI: Tenth Symposium on Operating System Design and Implementation Proceedings*.

Kirschenbaum, Matthew. 2008. "Extreme Inscription: A Grammatology of the Hard Drive" reedited from *Mechanisms: New Media and the Forensic Imagination*. Cambridge MA: MIT Press.

Marzullo, K. A. 1984. *Maintaining the Time in a Distributed System: An Example of a Loosely-Coupled Distributed Service*. Palo Alto: Stanford University.

Metz, Cade. 2012. "Google Spans Entire Planet With GPS-Powered Database." *Wired*, September 19. http://www.wired.com/2012/09/google-spanner/all/.

Munster, Anna. 2013. *An Aesthesia of Networks*. Cambridge MA: MIT Press.

Loading... 800% Slower

David Gauthier

Loading... 800% Slower addresses modern deceits and their latest scripts. It is concerned with the détournement of web pages' "critical rendering paths" so that browsers can render what they really are: timely designed assaults. The project disinters contemporary third party algorithmic oddments (http://cdn.krxd.net/controltag?confid=JQqG5SW9) that lurk deep in the murkiness of your web browser's script interpreter and which, as non-visual techniques of entrapment, act as conduits of a new kind of imperceptible propaganda that does away with our too slow affective registers. While some may be enticed to believe that the toneless term "data" mainly denotes bytes that primarily compose images, texts and, sometimes, sounds, it is rather predominantly in the form of machine-interpretable code that these bytes are queued and reassembled from end-to-end. Contemporary networks are not networks of perceptible images and texts but rather ones of ambulant and rampant code and scripts that do not warrant direct recourse, let alone signalling, to human sense or perception.

Loading... 800% Slower foregrounds how this non-human computational acceleration and automation work towards creating zones of felonious interactivity where the automated agency of browsers and servers directly supersedes and substitutes itself for intentional actions of their sacrosanct users. As human trans-actions are now being bolstered by machine-to-machine executions, which occur at timescales that completely bypass human consciousness, *Loading... 800% Slower* amplifies this temporal asymmetry between machine deliberation time and human deliberation time.

By slowing down to an excessive degree the bitrate of an internet connection while a browser plugin renders audible the various invisible and dubious scripts and DOM elements composing a given web page, this project feeds forward the uncanny temporality of human consciousness in rendering almost still (and loud) the temporal signals of the machine. While a given page is protractedly loading, it is prepared by *Loadingμ... 800% Slower*'s plugin which injects purpose-built software oscillators into its document object model.

scaffolds for web-sites

Site Optimization:
These apps provide
a serious means to

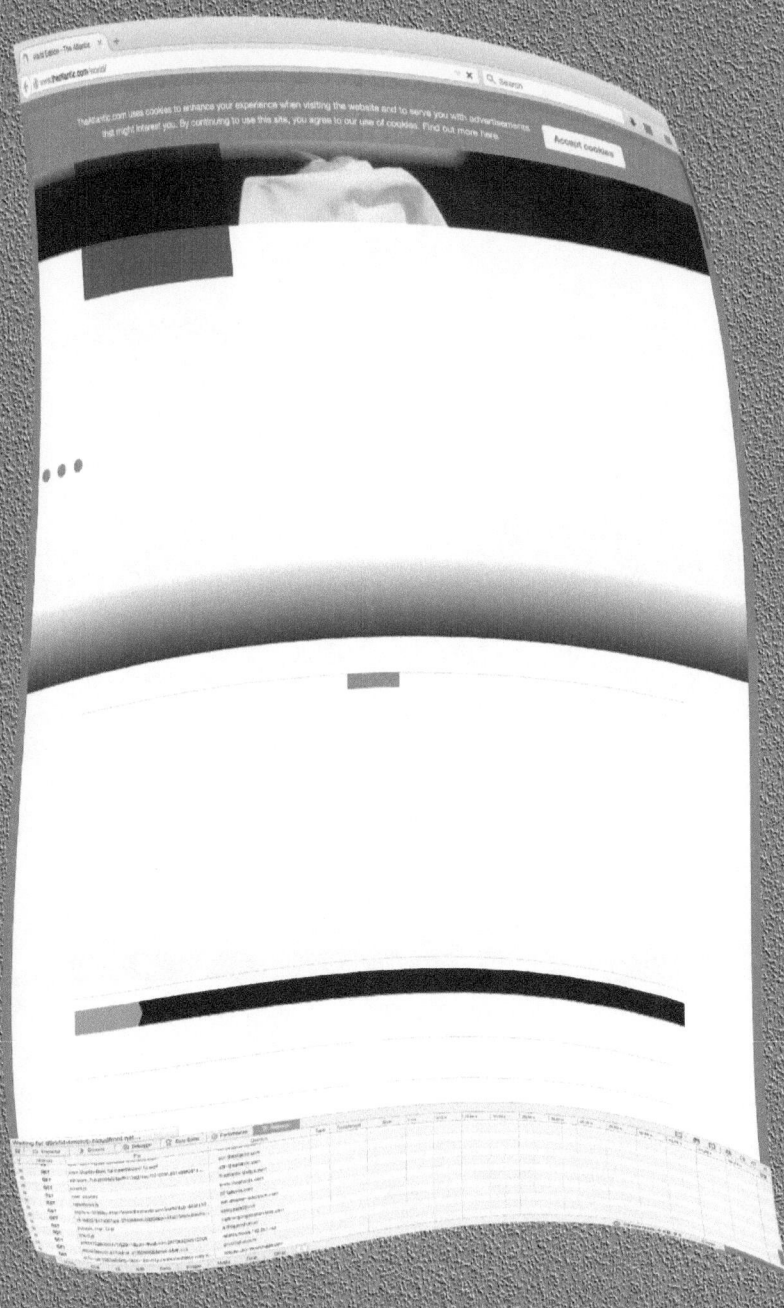

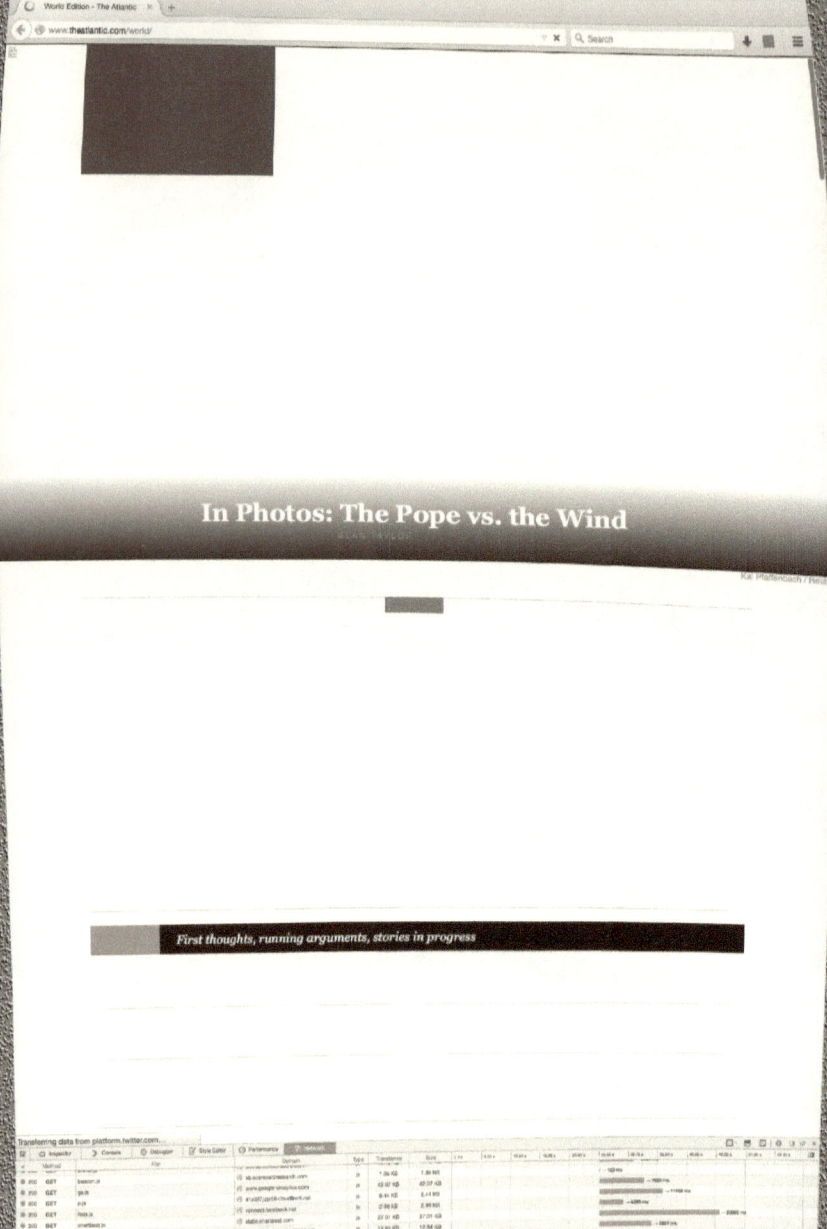

In Photos: The Pope vs. the Wind

First thoughts, running arguments, stories in progress

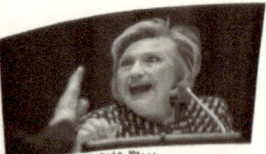

Clinton Horror Deja Vu...
No Bridge-Rumors of Campaign Implosion...
Biden ruling nothing out...
She lost every demo except 65+...
? BERNIE
DICK MORRIS: Falling Apart...
'Nixon panic'...
HEART: She May Never Recover...
GEARY: 'Horrible Campaigner Living in Different Era'...
Online fundraising juggernaut boosts Bernie as he plows ahead...
RESULTS: MAP
Republicans shatter turnout record; Dems lag behind...
Media Winners & Losers

CORRUPTION: CLINTON HAS EQUAL DELEGATES TO SANDERS

DRUDGE REPORT

Weekend Arctic Outbreak Could Break Records...

There are now 260,000 robots working in American factories...

Couple arrested for having sex on Las Vegas Ferris wheel...

CLAPPER: Gene Editing a WMD Threat...

Navy calls on researchers to create humanoid to fight fires, perform maintenance...

US Spy Satellite Begins Secret Mission...

Like in China...

USA soccer star says she wouldn't go to Rio Olympics because virus...

CDC expects transmission via mosquitoes in USA...

Jury convicts drunk driver who claimed he only consumed beer-battered fish...

UPDATE: Nurses recognize human emotion...

India police eye new weapon: Chilli-loaded slingshots!

Master forger arrested in Thailand over fake passports for migrants to Europe...

Feeling mystical? Brain's 'God Spot' might be damaged...

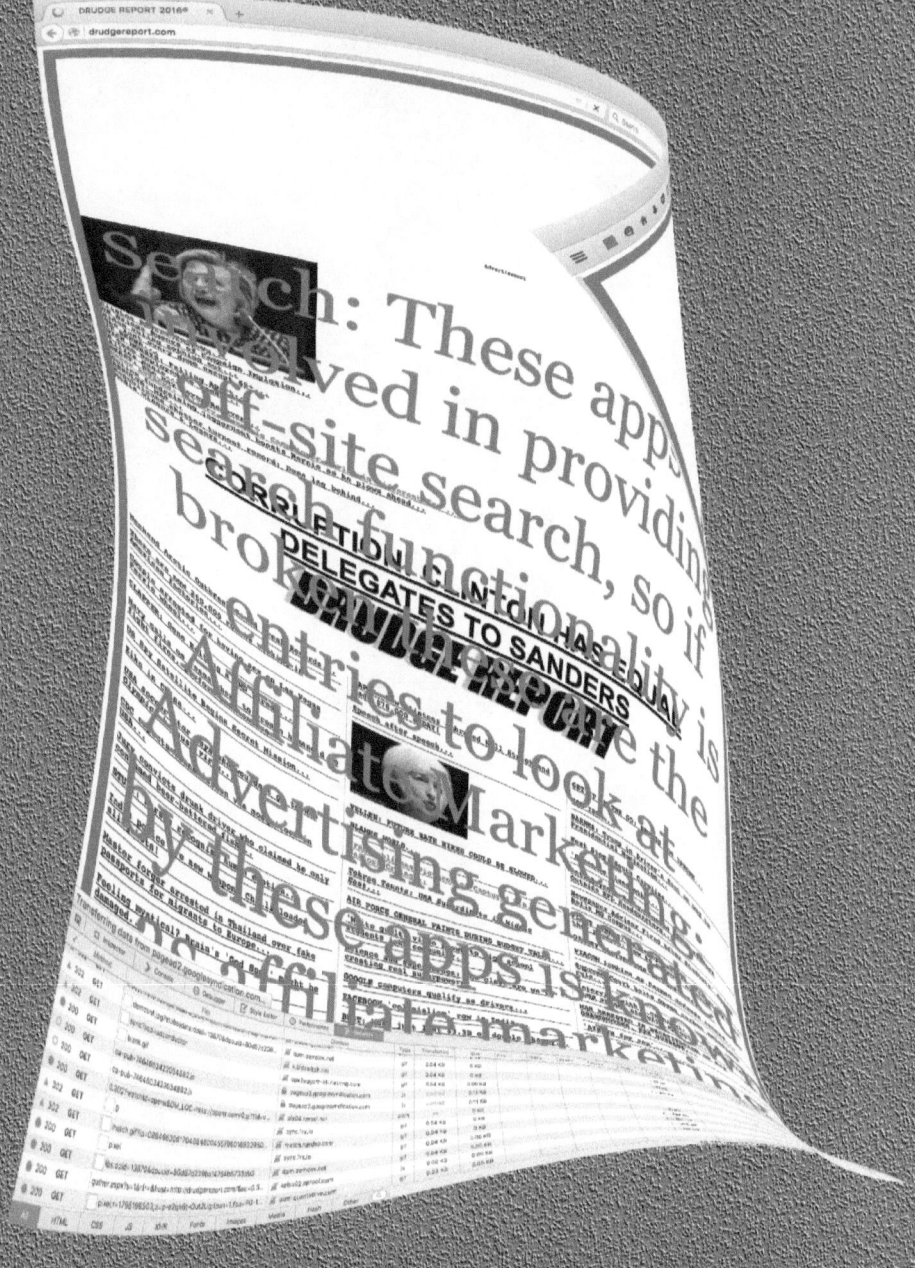

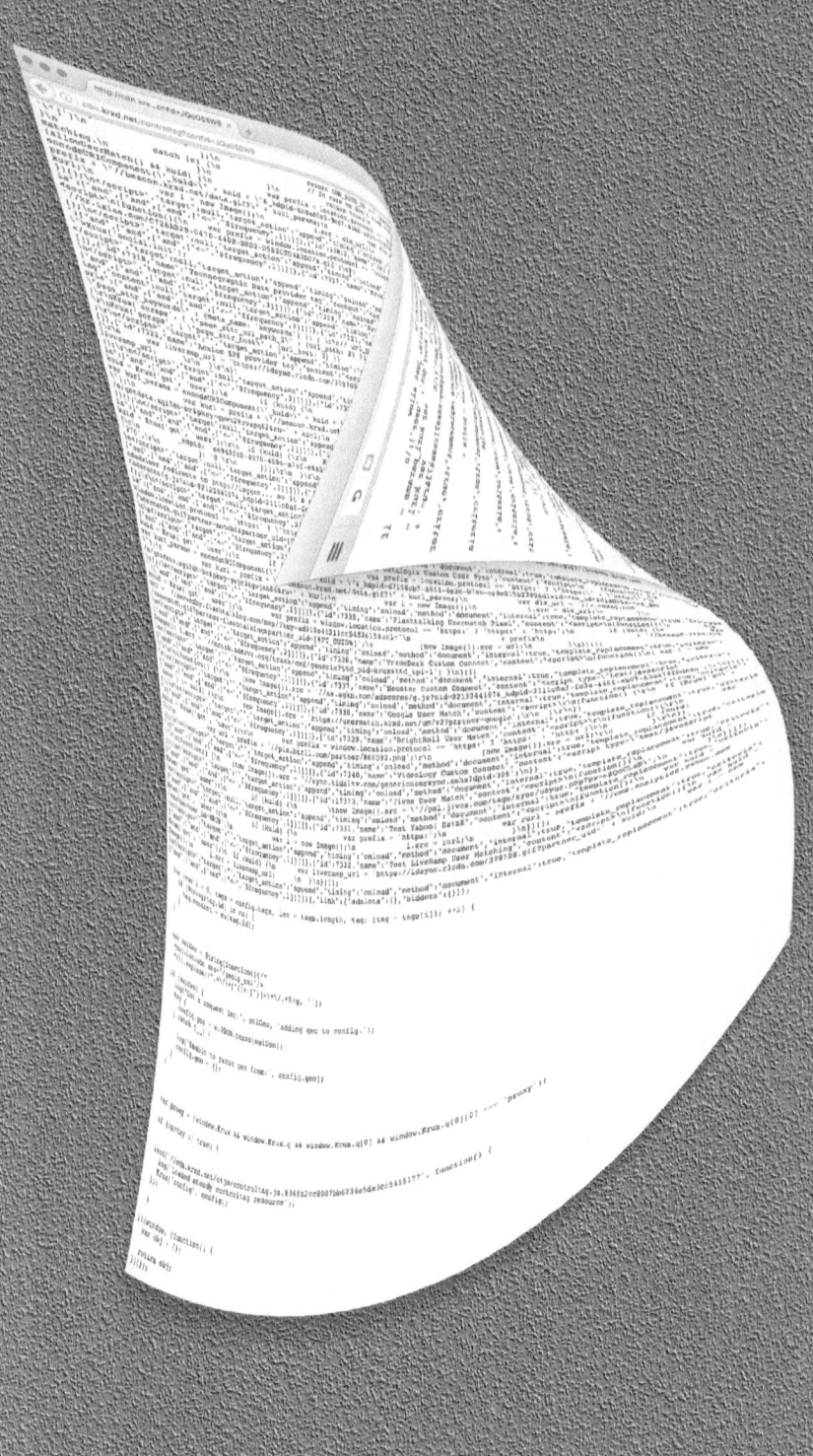

These various oscillators are then modulated by the type, provenance and amount of incoming bytes requested at various times during the temporal resolution/execution of the page. This parasitic rendering works towards orchestrating a noise composition that climaxes coincidently upon the transmission and execution of deceitful codes.

Medium: browser plug-in and web proxy server.
URL: http://gauthiier.info/loading-800p-slower/.

Special thanks to Michael Dieter.

The Editor
EndTime Magazine
PO Box 940729
Plano, TX 75094

Spring, 1999

Dear Editor,

If we let A=6, B=12, C=18, etc. all the way through Z=156. If you take the word

COMPUTER

and apply these values to the letters...

C = 18
O = 90
M = 78
P = 96
U = 126
T = 120
E = 30
R = 108

You will find that they add up to 666.

In Revelation 13:18: 'Let him that hath understanding count the number of the beast; for it is the number of a man; and his number is six hundred threescoreand six.'

I don't believe that this is a coincidence ... We have speculated that 'COMPUTER' will be the Mark.

Now we have proof!

Yours sincerely,
O. J. Briant

Excerpt: "666 new letters to the editor", *Bugs in the War Room*, Linda Hilfling Ritasdatter (2016).

BUGS IN THE WAR ROOM
—Economies and/of Execution

Linda Hilfling Ritasdatter

Chennai, South India. I am sitting in the office of a senior engineer of one of India's largest IT-companies. It is autumn 2014, but our conversation brings us to the years prior to the turn of the Millennium. She recalls her experiences of working within one of the many teams busy fixing the Y2K bug. The senior engineer describes the "war room", a space in which together with her colleagues over a duration of twenty-four hours she observed the world making the transition from the 31st of December 1999 to the 1st of January 2000. "Well, they thought that on January 1st, 12 AM in the morning all planes will stop, all towers will stop, all trains will stop, all the clocks would stop, and all systems will come to a standstill..." she says.

What follows is a close reading of the Y2K bug, which towards the turn of the millennium caused a world-wide crisis of computer systems, and thus stirred up the global economy. I have been working with this crisis over the last years. Part of this work was exhibited in my solo exhibition *Bugs in the War Room* at Overgaden - Copenhagen Institute for Contemporary Art in 2016. In this text I wish to elaborate further on the reflections presented in the exhibition specifically in relation to the notion of execution. Execution is here understood as a continuous incomplete process always on the verge of breakdown. This emphasises maintenance as an important part of the execution process—after all, the algorithms and information architectures supporting global flows need to be maintained in order to execute/flow at all.

Bugs

In the mid 1990s, attention started to be directed towards the so-called Year 2000 problem, or Y2K bug, as it was primarily dubbed in the Western world. Since the early days of computation, it had been a routine as well as a technical standard to indicate year dates with two digits instead of four, leaving out the numbers specifying the millennium in order to save costly computer memory. But awareness around the potential implications of such a practice began to come to the fore: When reaching the year 2000, the computer would not be able to distinguish the 00 of 2000 from the 00 of 1900. It was assumed that "[u]nless reprogrammed, bypassed or replaced these systems will malfunction at the turn of the century, if not before, with wide ranging consequences" (Downing 1998, i). The Y2K bug was presumed to lead to failures within major financial institutions like banks or stock exchanges, payroll systems, telecommunications and power systems (Koskinen 2000).

The senior programmer explains: "We had set up something called the war room to monitor the systems' changeovers. Because we were working across all the verticals like banking, critical transaction, transportation, i. e. where the planes have to land — they thought that some planes might not even land because of the Y2K problem."

Bruno Latour suggests a notion of "reverse black-boxing" to illustrate how a bug, by making a system fail, is reverse-black-boxing the system, thereby directing the user's attention away from the system as an enclosed object and towards the different parts of which the system is composed (Latour 1994, 36). Latour suggests the example of an overhead projector, which, when working, appears as an integrated closed black-boxed object, but upon breakdown, brings forth a network of interconnected objects and actors: lens, lamp, cooler, cables and further socio-technical components are made visible. In a similar way, Heidegger states that technology only appears to us in its breaking down, when it goes from a relatively transparent mode of "readiness-to-hand" and being at one's disposal (Heidegger 1962, 98) to announcing itself through the break-down, and thus becoming "present-at-hand" (52).
In Latour's theory of black-boxing, the reversal is mainly about exposing the relations that make up the technical object. For Heidegger, however, there was a larger issue of the "essence" of technology making itself present as well, relating to the overall role of technology in culture and nature as a whole (Heidegger 1977, 23–24). Following these lines of thinking, the bug that terminates a running process — a process of execution — draws attention to the relations which the execution process is part of, as well as to the "essence" of the systems that they are formed in, which in this case includes neo-colonial divides within global flows.

"Excerpt: 666 new letters to the editor", *Bugs in the War Room*, Linda Hilfling Ritasdatter (2016).

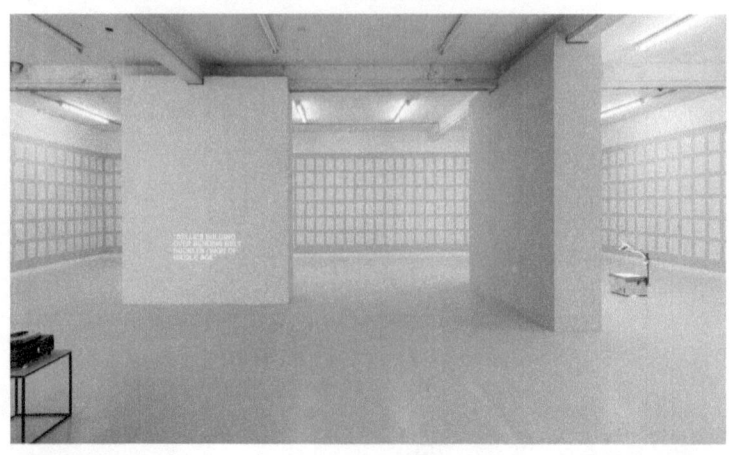
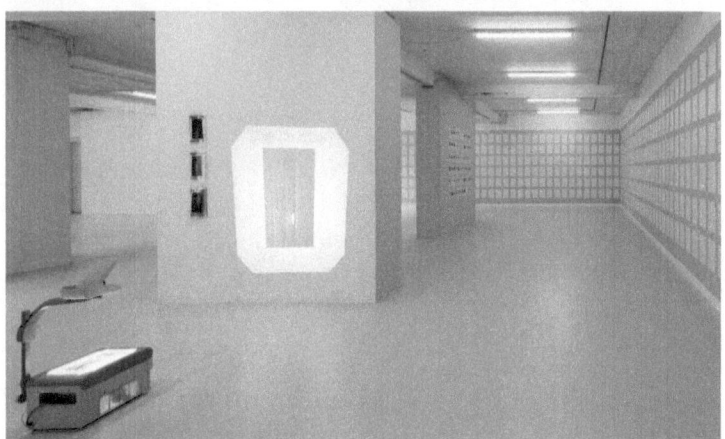
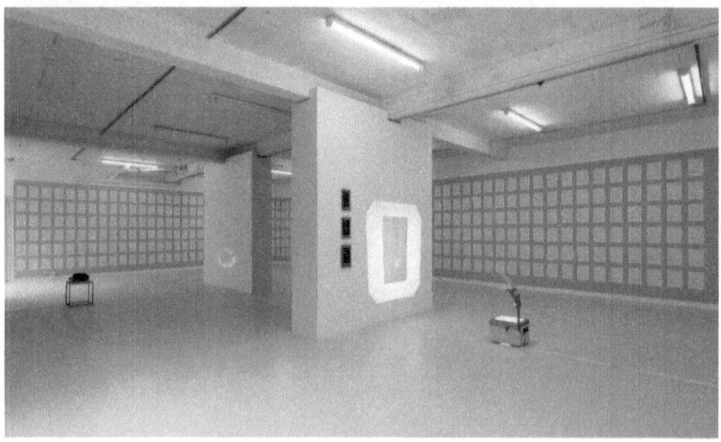

Bugs in the War Room at Overgaden—Institute for Contemporary Art, Copenhagen (2016). Photo: Anders Sune Berg.

At its core the Y2K Bug can be said to be caused due to a practice of executing as economically as possible. Leon A. Kappelman, the co-chairman of the Year 2000 working group for the Society for Information Management, estimated that the "use of two-digit years in a program written in the 1960's would have saved more than $1 million per billion bytes of data stored over the following 30 years" (Feder & Pollack 1998). The Y2K bug thus reflects the socio-economical development of three of the computer's core components: processor, memory and storage. The economic aspects of these three parts have evolved over different times and scales. The processor was quickly made capable of performing faster in relation to its price, i.e. it became cheaper to produce faster processors. The same was not true for memory, which remained expensive (storage became cheaper, but not reliable). Because memory was very expensive it became a practice (as well as a technological standard) to reduce the four digits of a given year into two digits or one byte, the so called "pack decimal", which at the turn of the Millennium would be labeled "Y2K bug". In other words, a supposedly technical error was initially a clever solution to a problem, which over time turned into a new problem. Consequently, the Y2K bug highlights socio-economic relations, including those of hardware, entangled within the process of execution. The Y2K bug reveals a dependency on external relations, departing from an understanding of execution as foremost enacted code.

War rooms

The senior programmer continues her recollection: "The war room was a 360 degree room where everybody was having a terminal to monitor the systems, talk to the clients. Then there were Maya phones, they thought even the phones would fail, even the phone companies, so there were alternative communication methodologies. There was a backup link. There was a fiber optic link", and, she notes, "There were not many people in the room. Only the key people, about 50 of us."

The engineer's description of the Y2K war room of the Indian IT corporation bears a resemblance to Ken Adam's set-design for the war room scenes in Stanley Kubrick's 1964 black comedy *Dr. Strangelove or: How I Learned to Stop Worrying and Love the Bomb*. It strikes me that Dr. Strangelove's war room equally was equipped with a 360 degree table.

It also had around 50 people gathered in the room—all with a terminal and a phone.

In "Lessons Learned from War Room Designs and Implementa-tions", US military consultant, Steven M. Shaker describes how war rooms play an important role in "developing tactics and grand strategies" within the US military (2002). Shaker traces the transformation of the war room from "rooms concentrated on maps, and on game tables with miniature flags and models representing force disposition and movement" (2002, 3), to how "[w]ith the advent of modern communications and near real-time reconnaissance and intelligence these rooms have refocused to concentrate on command and control rather than long range planning and strategy formulation" (3). War rooms are places of concentrated power, the site from which orders are given to be executed.

Adam's war room is indeed an iconic manifestation of such power. The story goes that when Ronald Reagan became president of the United States, he asked his "chief of staff to be shown the war room of Dr. Strangelove" (Adams 2009). Reagan assumed that this was a real room, placed within the Pentagon. This anecdote might tell more about Ronald Reagan's skewed relationship with war and reality.[1] Nevertheless, Adam's war room design with the 360 degree table in the centre of the triangular concrete bunker manifests an imaginary image of the epicentre of power and control in the Cold War era.

Dr. Strangelove, however, depicts disturbances within the straightforward hierarchy of the execution of top-down orders. The war room is the backdrop of desperate attempts to countermand an order issued by a mad general enforcing a nuclear air strike against the Soviet Union. But inherent discipline coupled with technological malfunctions makes it impossible to break the destiny of execution as presented in the film. The irony of the film is that the technology does not execute the orders perfectly, leaving the individuals committed to the system with the task of ultimately carrying out the execution. Eventually one plane attacks the USSR as requested, thus triggering the MAD (Mutual Assured Destruction) doctrine, presumably leading to complete annihilation of the Earth— with the exception of the group of men gathered in the war room, who are being moved to a safe place under ground.

Kubrick insisted that, despite the film being shot in black and white, the war room table should be covered with green

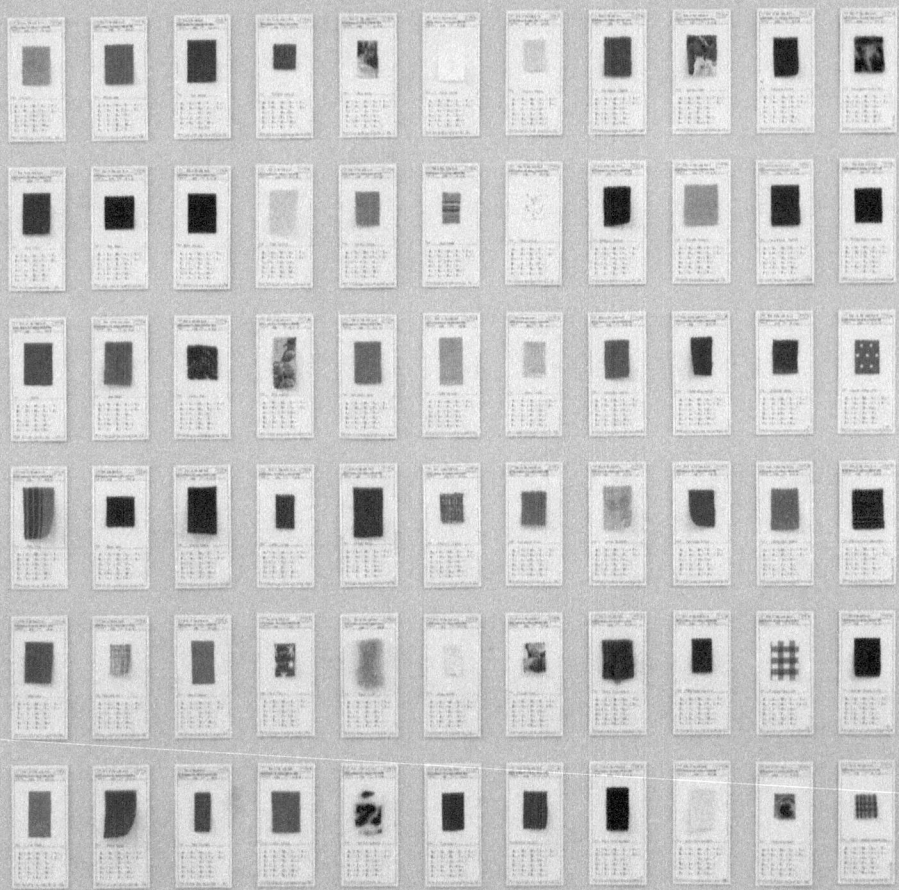

"66 tests of materials for covering a war room table", *Bugs in the War Room*, Linda Hilfling Ritasdatter (2016). Photo: Anders Sune Berg.

System	BUGS IN THE WAR ROOM	Sample 8 of 66
Program	TESTING MATERIALS FOR COVERING A WAR ROOM TABLE	Identification
Programmer LINDA	Date 23.11.15	

Type: NATURE'S HORSES

A/6 [1] G/42 [ ] M/78 [ ] S/114 [3] Y/150 [ ]
B/12 [ ] H/48 [1] N/84 [1] T/120 [1] Z/156 [ ]
C/18 [ ] I/54 [ ] O/90 [1] U/126 [1]
D/24 [ ] J/60 [ ] P/96 [ ] V/132 [ ]
E/30 [2] K/66 [ ] Q/102 [ ] W/138 [ ]
F/36 [ ] L/72 [ ] R/108 [2] X/144 [ ]

Result 6+2×30+48+84+90+2×108+3×114+120+126 = 1092

"66 tests of materials for covering a war room table", *Bugs in the War Room*, Linda Hilfling Ritasdatter (2016).

felt, as he wanted to give an impression of how the powerful men gathered around the table "were playing for the faith of the earth like a poker game" (Adams 2009). If Kubrick had made a film thirty years later depicting the paranoia of the Y2K bug, I wonder what material he would have chosen for the table of the Indian war room? The table of the Y2K war room did not assemble top leaders, or represent a top-down hierarchy of order and execution. On the contrary, it was a gathering as emergency-brigade, or the caretakers of global information architectures, ultimately calling for a different understanding of the war room's relation to power; away from top-down management, with orders followed by execution, towards a model of continuous executable maintenance and feedback. In this way, the Y2K war room turns out to be a crucial site for the understanding of execution's entanglement within a global economy: not because the Y2K war room is a focused centre of power and command, but rather on the contrary, because it is the site from which information architectures are being maintained and made to flow via a continuous maintenance of back end structures.

Anxious flows:

A letter to the editor of the Conservative Christian American magazine *End Time* in March/April 1999 read:

> *If we let A=6, B=12, C=18, etc. all the way through Z=156. If you take the word COMPUTER and apply these values to the letters, you will find that they add up to 666. In Revelation 13:18, "Let him that hath understanding count the number of the beast; for it is the number of a man; and his number is six hundred threescoreand six." I don't believe that this is a coincidence. We have speculated that the computerchip will be "the Mark" now we have proof! (Briant 1999, as cited in Tapia 2003, 493)*

The above letter points to the increasing paranoia around computers at the turn of the millennium. It was, however, not only apocalyptic Christians, but furthermore the Western business world, which towards the end of the 1990s reacted strongly to the increasing 'threat' of the Millennium bug and the potential economical losses related to it. As stated in the April, 1999 issue of *The Futurist* (as quoted by Fishman and Fosket 1999), "If you think your company will be okay because all your systems are Y2K compliant, guess again ... Just because you've worked out your Y2K bugs doesn't mean your suppliers have. If 5% of your suppliers go out on you, can your company survive?"

In "Revisiting the Y2K Bug: Language Wars over Networking the Global Order", Kirsty Best points out how the Y2K bug "illustrated the way in which the primacy of the individual within a global order is under threat from the contamination of others, the inability to seal one's borders" (Best 2003, 301). Such presumed omnipresence corresponds to Ulrich Beck's notion of the boomerang effect within what he calls "the Risk Society". Beck writes, "The multiplication of risks causes world society to contract into a *community of danger*" (Beck 1992, 44 — my emphasis). However, in March 1999, *The Financial Times* reported: "Federal officials have said that if they are not satisfied with other countries' plans for air traffic control, the Department of Transportation could ban flights between specified airports and the US or prevent US airlines and code sharers from flying over certain countries" (Fishman & Fosket 1998). In November of the same year, the semi-official private sector body of the UK, the so called Taskforce 2000, "advised travelers to avoid Italy, Germany, Switzerland and a number of other countries[2] for a five-week period around 1 January 2000" (Quiggin 2005, 49). Such divisions between "us" and "them" played out on micro as well as macro levels. For example, Kevin Quigley quotes a civil servant remarking on the process of correcting the Y2K bug within the British Government, saying that, "Given the consensus that 'it had to be done,' any opposition from within would have been the work of a troublemaker, not a team player ... becoming 'Y2K-compliant' was a badge of honour; it meant good corporate citizenship" (Quigley 2004, 818). This leads to a gap between those who are doing their duty, being "good citizens" and not asking any questions in opposition to a "few 'cynical' civil servants" reflecting critically on how Y2K-compliancy is being carried out (818). Hence the "us" will by all means attempt to continue the execution, whereas the "they" might not care about, be critical towards nor be capable of correcting the Y2K bug, and thus will have to be controlled by different means or symbolically excluded from the network.

At the same time, some developing countries spent enormous resources to become Y2K compliant, so as to avoid

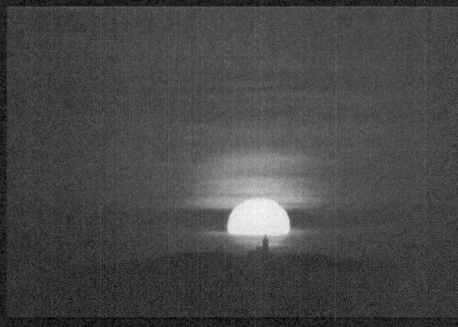

SUNRISE
2000-01-01

THE
INDIAN ENGINEER
SAYS:

"WE HAD SET UP SOMETHING CALLED THE WAR ROOM TO MONITOR THE SYSTEMS' CHANGE OVERS ...

... THE WAR ROOM WAS A 360° ROOM. EVERYBODY WAS HAVING A TERMINAL TO MONITOR THE SYSTEMS AND TALK TO THE CLIENTS ...

... THERE WERE NOT MANY PEOPLE IN THE ROOM. ONLY THE KEY PEOPLE. ABOUT FIFTY OF US."

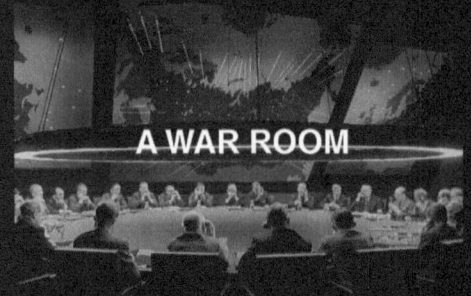

A WAR ROOM

THE PHOTOGRAPHER SAYS:

"SOMEHOW I MANAGED TO BE AWAKE AND IN THE RIGHT PLACE AT THE RIGHT TIME TO WATCH THE SUN RISE BEHIND MAY ISLAND ON THE FIRST OF JANUARY, 2000 ...

- IT WAS PERFECT!"

THE WESTERN Y2K EXPERT HAD SAID:

"I'M NOT WORRIED BY NEW ZEALAND OR AUSTRALIA, I'M A BIT MORE WORRIED BY JAPAN, BUT I AM MORE CONCERNED ABOUT THE REST OF THE FAR EAST ...

"... THE WORST PREPARED COME FIRST. I WISH THAT FOR ONE EVENING THE EARTH WOULD ROTATE THE OTHER WAY."

PETER DE JAGER AKA MR. MILLENNIUM BUG, 1999.

THE INDIAN ENGINEER SAYS:

"WE HAD TO MANAGE THE ENTIRE 24 HOURS - JUST FOLLOW THE SUN ON THAT DAY ..."

... VERY FEW CRITICAL PROBLEMS WERE THERE ...

... IT HAD NOTHING TO DO WITH THE DATE, JUST THE USUAL PRODUCTION SUPPORT PROBLEMS."

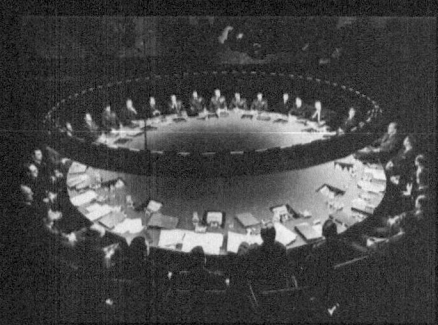

"80 slides for Kodak AV-2000 dia projector", *Bugs in the War Room*, Linda Hilfling Ritasdatter (2016).

exclusion on a macro level. Later, however, it was revealed that the "speculation that computers in developing countries would fail largely was based on anecdotal information" (researcher Matt Hotle from Gartner Group, as quoted by Hema Shukla 2000). Nevertheless, the enormous spendings were hardly scrutinised, but rather justified as a means to accelerated development, as for instance in Mexico, where the technical secretary of the National Commission for Y2K Information Conversion stated, "We've come out on top ... the quality of equipment and infrastructure has improved, and more companies are now using computers as a result of this experience" (Faiola 2000, as quoted in Best 2003, 303). Or in Southern Africa, where Stephen Mutul, in his analysis of the impact of the Y2K problem in a Southern African context, concludes by highlighting the benefits of the preparations for the Y2K bug (Mutula 2001, 26).[3] In this casting of the drive towards Y2K-compliancy in third world countries as yet another narrative of "catching up" with the West, a neo-colonial power structure comes to light. Even if the cause is a non-existent problem, the necessary compliancy is revealed as lying elsewhere: that of catching up with the reliance on networked IT infrastructures within global capitalism.

In the scrambling of nations to become Y2K compliant, the "risk" surrounding the Y2K bug took form as a discourse of the construction of the "other" (Best 2003, 302; Fishman & Fosket 1998), as well as anxious attempts of escaping such categorisation, rather than a "community of danger" as envisioned by Beck. Accordingly, the letter to the editor of *End Time* written in Spring 1999 (as referred to above), may read as a manifestation of such anxiety, where the problem of dealing with the contingency of the system transforms into a "paranoid cybernetics" (Cramer 2016). An absurd arbitrary system is created in order to maintain the otherwise sliding grip of control, thus allowing the letter writer to satisfyingly announce that "now we have proof!" on the basis of a home-invented numerological system in which letters of the word "computers" add up to 666. Despite the fact that this numerological system of course appears entirely arbitrary. Similarly, the Y2K problem was largely arbitrary for most developing countries, with the irony being that it was precisely workers in the outsourcing industries who ended up doing the main bulk of Y2K debugging and maintenance.

Economies and/of execution

Back in the office in Chennai, the engineer ends her account: "We had to manage the entire 24 hours. Just follow the sun on that day ... Very few critical problems were there. It had nothing to do with the date—the usual production support problems."

I keep thinking of the senior engineer's final remark that there were in reality very few problems out of the ordinary. There is a tendency to think of execution as an ongoing flow of running processes. But as Nathan Ensmenger (2009, 88) points out, "Software is not an end-product, but should rather be understood as a 'heterogeneous system' consisting of social as well as technological components". This means that since the world around the executed code is continuously being altered, the software itself has to be maintained and updated in order to be kept alive, i.e. to be executable at all. Thus the war room of the Y2K bug was not just a one off happening, conversely it is taking place all the time. In the senior engineer's company she and her colleagues are steadily making sure that the bugs in the war rooms — the usual production support problems — are found, corrected and enhanced in order for the networked global economy to continue executing.

Maintenance is about efficiency, and is thus a matter of economy and economising, and the Y2K problem could be said to manifest this as a problem of execution. Not as a relation between source code and executed object code, but in this case of execution as a matter of an economy of the hardware. For a brief moment, the mere scare of the potential breakdown made our global networked information architectures "present-at-hand", thus opening up for a comprehension of the complex internal relations between hardware, execution and the maintenance needed in order to make algorithms execute at all. But also, importantly, disclosing the role of execution as the main force upholding a networked global economy and the neo-colonial divides that are maintained and supported within such a drive.

COBOL Program Sheet

System: ENDLESS ENDTIME
Program: PROOF
Programmer: LNDA AKA L. HILFLING RITASDATTER Date: 22.05.16
Sheet: 4 of 4

```
004010    INSPECT CAPITAL-STRING TALLYING COUNTER-P FOR ALL "P".
004020    INSPECT CAPITAL-STRING TALLYING COUNTER-Q FOR ALL "Q".
004030    INSPECT CAPITAL-STRING TALLYING COUNTER-R FOR ALL "R".
004040    INSPECT CAPITAL-STRING TALLYING COUNTER-S FOR ALL "S".
004050    INSPECT CAPITAL-STRING TALLYING COUNTER-T FOR ALL "T".
004060    INSPECT CAPITAL-STRING TALLYING COUNTER-U FOR ALL "U".
004070    INSPECT CAPITAL-STRING TALLYING COUNTER-V FOR ALL "V".
004080    INSPECT CAPITAL-STRING TALLYING COUNTER-W FOR ALL "W".
004090    INSPECT CAPITAL-STRING TALLYING COUNTER-X FOR ALL "X".
004100    INSPECT CAPITAL-STRING TALLYING COUNTER-Y FOR ALL "Y".
004110    INSPECT CAPITAL-STRING TALLYING COUNTER-Z FOR ALL "Z".
004120    MULTIPLY COUNTER-A BY VALUE-A GIVING VALUE-A.
004130    MULTIPLY COUNTER-B BY VALUE-B GIVING VALUE-B.
004140    MULTIPLY COUNTER-C BY VALUE-C GIVING VALUE-C.
004150    MULTIPLY COUNTER-D BY VALUE-D GIVING VALUE-D.
004160    MULTIPLY COUNTER-E BY VALUE-E GIVING VALUE-E.
004170    MULTIPLY COUNTER-F BY VALUE-F GIVING VALUE-F.
004180    MULTIPLY COUNTER-G BY VALUE-G GIVING VALUE-G.
004190    MULTIPLY COUNTER-H BY VALUE-H GIVING VALUE-H.
004200    MULTIPLY COUNTER-I BY VALUE-I GIVING VALUE-I.
004210    MULTIPLY COUNTER-J BY VALUE-J GIVING VALUE-J.
004220    MULTIPLY COUNTER-K BY VALUE-K GIVING VALUE-K.
004230    MULTIPLY COUNTER-L BY VALUE-L GIVING VALUE-L.
004240    MULTIPLY COUNTER-M BY VALUE-M GIVING VALUE-M.
004250    MULTIPLY COUNTER-N BY VALUE-N GIVING VALUE-N.
004260    MULTIPLY COUNTER-O BY VALUE-O GIVING VALUE-O.
004270    MULTIPLY COUNTER-P BY VALUE-P GIVING VALUE-P.
004280    MULTIPLY COUNTER-Q BY VALUE-Q GIVING VALUE-Q.
004290    MULTIPLY COUNTER-R BY VALUE-R GIVING VALUE-R.
004300    MULTIPLY COUNTER-S BY VALUE-S GIVING VALUE-S.
004310    MULTIPLY COUNTER-T BY VALUE-T GIVING VALUE-T.
004320    MULTIPLY COUNTER-U BY VALUE-U GIVING VALUE-U.
004330    MULTIPLY COUNTER-V BY VALUE-V GIVING VALUE-V.
004340    MULTIPLY COUNTER-W BY VALUE-W GIVING VALUE-W.
004350    MULTIPLY COUNTER-X BY VALUE-X GIVING VALUE-X.
004360    MULTIPLY COUNTER-Y BY VALUE-Y GIVING VALUE-Y.
004370    MULTIPLY COUNTER-Z BY VALUE-Z GIVING VALUE-Z.
004380    ADD VALUE-A VALUE-B VALUE-C VALUE-D VALUE-E VALUE-F VALUE-G
004390        VALUE-H VALUE-I VALUE-J VALUE-K VALUE-L VALUE-M VALUE-N
004400        VALUE-O VALUE-P VALUE-Q VALUE-R VALUE-S VALUE-T VALUE-U
004410        VALUE-V VALUE-W VALUE-X VALUE-Y VALUE-Z GIVING RESULT.
004420    IF RESULT EQUAL THE-NUMBER-OF-THE-BEAST THEN
004430        DISPLAY INPUT-STRING "IS THE MARK - NOW WE HAVE PROOF!".
004440
004450
004460
```

Opposite: Excerpt of COBOL source code for *Endless Endtime:
a complete index of all elements leading to the end of the world, vol I of ∞*,
Linda Hilfling Ritasdatter, Förlag Rojal (2016).

FINISH FAST
verb.; To reach the end of (something) quickly; quick; swift; rapid.

L. Hilfling Ritasdatter
Atelieretage 5
Gerichtstraße 12-13
13347 Berlin
Germany

The Editor
EndTime Magazine
PO Box 940729
Plano, TX 75094
USA

Berlin, 08-11-2015

Dear Editor,

If we let A=6, B=12, C=18, etc. all the way through Z=156 and if you take:

FINISH FAST

and apply these values to the letters...

F = 36
I = 54
N = 84
I = 54
S = 114
H = 48
F = 36
A = 6
S = 114
T = 120

You will find that they add up to 666.

In Revelation 13:18: 'Let him that hath understanding count the number of the beast; for it is the number of a man; and his number is six hundred threescoreand six.'

I don't believe that this is a coincidence. We have speculated that 'FINISH FAST' will be 'the Mark' now we have proof!

Yours sincerely,

/lnd4

Endless Endtime: a complete index of all elements leading to the end of the world, vol I of ∞, Linda Hilfling Ritasdatter, Förlag Rojal (2016).

Notes

1. Or maybe the other way around: DARPA's skewed relation with reality and war. After Operation Desert Storm (and the wide critique of General Norman Schwarzkop's aperances live on TV in the tent, which were seen as an embarrassing representation of US military command), means were taken within DARPA to hire Herman Zimmerman, the set-designer of Star Trek, to develop a mobile war room called 'The Enterprise' based on his design for the USS Enterprise NCC 1701 Bridge (Shaker 2002, 3).

2. The full list of countries which should be avoided included: Czech Republic, Finland, Germany, Hungary, Italy, Poland, Portugal, Russia, Spain as well as Switzerland.

3. Please see my PhD thesis (forthcoming, Malmö University Press, 2018) for an extensive elaboration on the developing countries' role in relation to the notion of development and Y2K compatibility during the turn of the millennium.

References

Adams, Ken. 2009. *Ken Adams on design*. Video. Victoria and Albert Museum. https://www.youtube.com/watch?v=qplg-58r9hk.

Beck, Ulrich. 1992. *Risk Society: Towards a New Modernity*. London; Newbury Park, CA: Sage Publications.

Best, Kirsty. 2003. "Revisiting the Y2K Bug: Language Wars Over Networking the Global Order." *Television & New Media* 4 (3): 297–319.

Briant, O. J. 1999. "Letter to the Editor." *End Time Magazine*.

Cramer, Florian. 2016. Presented at Crisis Computing, Overgaden —Institute for Contemporary Art, Copenhagen, May 22.

Downing, Emma. 1998. "The Millennium Bug: Research Paper." Great Britain, Parliament, House of Commons.

Ensmenger, Nathan. 2009. "Software as History Embodied." *IEEE Annals of the History of Computing* 31 (1): 88–91.

Feder, Barnaby J., and Andrew Pollack. 1998. "TRILLION-DOLLAR DIGITS: A Special Report. Computers and 2000: Race for Security." *The New York Times*, December 27. http://www.nytimes.com/1998/12/27/us/trillion-dollar-digits-a-special-report-computers-and-2000-race-for-security.html.

Fosket, Jennifer Ruth, and Jennifer Fishman. 2015. "Constructing The Millennium Bug Trust, Risk, And Technological Uncertainty." *CTheory* 0 (0): 10–13/1999.

Heidegger, Martin. 1977. *The question concerning technology and other essays*. New York, NY: Garland Publishing Inc.

———. 2001. *Being and time*. Reprint. Oxford: Blackwell.

Koskinen, John. 2016. "What Happened to Y2K? Koskinen Speaks Out." http://www.co-intelligence.org/y2k_KoskinenJan2000.html.

Kubrick, Stanley. 1964. *Dr. Strangelove or: How I Learned to Stop Worrying and Love the Bomb*. Comedy.

Latour, Bruno. 1994. "On Technical Mediation—Philosophy, Sociology, Geneology." *Common Knowledge* 3 (2): 29–64.

Mutula, S. M. 2001. "The Impact of Y2K in Southern Africa." *Information Development* 17 (1): 19–28.

Quiggin, John. 2005. "The Y2K Scare: Causes, Costs and Cures." *Australian Journal of Public Administration* 64 (3): 46–55.

Quigley, Kevin. 2004. "The Emperor's New Computers: Y2K (Re)Visited." *Public Administration* 82 (4): 801–29.

Shaker, Steven M. 2002. "Lessons Learned from War Room Designs and Implementations."

Shukla, Hema. 2000. "Indonesia, India Sail Smoothly into New Millennium despite Y2K Fears." *Associated Press Archive*, January 1.

Tapia, Andrea H. 2003. "Technomillennialism: A Subcultural Response to the Technological Threat of Y2K." *Science, Technology, & Human Values* 28 (4): 483–512.

Erasure

Audrey Samson

What has been conquered for all has been redefined by categories that are addressed to whoever, categories that produced amnesia and which are then vulnerable to the infernal alternatives concocted by capitalism.
– Isabelle Stengers in *Catastrophic Times: Resisting the Coming Barbarism*

How does erasure *execute* knowledge production? The following is a tour through a collection of *erasure* that provides a glimpse into the many directions that this question may take us, through the lens of a series of artistic interventions, academic research, experiments and artefacts.

I present these items from a collector's point of view. For achieving completion of this collection of erasures would be, in the words of Jean Baudrillard, like *death*. That is to say that the desire to complete the series, to achieve the perfection of its imaginary ending, is that which creates the elusive object of desire. As such, in the same way that a collection can always extend itself laterally, or spark a new one ([1968] 1996, 113), I am presenting it as an object of desire, fuelled by the impetus of neoliberal growth, which can never be complete and will forever expand into new meanings of execution, always towards the elusive erasure of death.

The collection begins with the archetypal storyteller: memory. Human memory is a careful curation of erasure. Most of what is experienced is not actualised in long term memory (Kandel 2007). It is neither forgotten, nor is it remembered in the first place. Amongst the select few moments that are retained, that we call memory, the parsimonious organ intently and iteratively erases (Hadziselimovic et al. 2014). The work of Estefanía Peñafiel Loaiza repeats this gesture in *Sans titre (figurants)*. She deliberately effaces certain *personnages* from newspapers with an eraser. The perseverance of this task, the cadavers of erasure, are *collected* and categorised (Figure 1). This play on history, or what is remembered, emphasises the relation to how an individual defines herself and acts in the world, namely because we think of our future as anticipated memories. According to psychologist Daniel Kahneman (2011), one of the major motivations for global tourism, for example, is the desire to collect memories. Execution as collection.

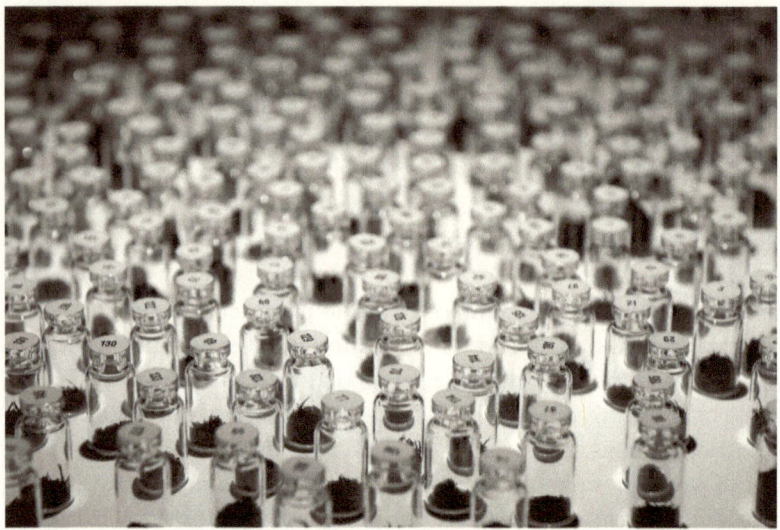

Figure 1. *Sans titre (figurants)* (2009–2011) by Estefanía Peñafiel Loaiza. Photo: © Marc Domage, courtesy of the artist.

The authoring power of memory is a notion that has been histori-cally capitalised upon by various regimes. The systematic erasure of peoples, national archives and artefacts have been used to strengthen specific notions of national (or religious) identity. In the same vein, such powers as the Chinese People's Party, Facebook and Google use erasure to obfuscate events that do not fit a certain political narrative or a set of private interests (Lim 2014; Travis 2013; Shaker 2006). Winnie Soon's *How to Get Mao Experience Through Internet…* (2014–15) is a monumentalising loop of obfuscations (Figure 2). The repeating, centred portrait of Mao blinds us from the surrounding landscape changes, itself a reminder of the vision curated by search engines such as Google, Flickr and Baidu. Obfuscation through repetition.

The politics of the archive are a powerful force driving knowledge production (Steyerl 2008; Brown & Davis-Brown 1998; Bowker & Star 1999; Derrida 1995). The Internet's inherent data transfer and storage redundancy model facilitates a sort of hyperthymesia[1] where the *execution* of social network sharing can construct fallacies or stain reputations. An emblematic case of this being that of the pepper spray incident at the University

ERASURE

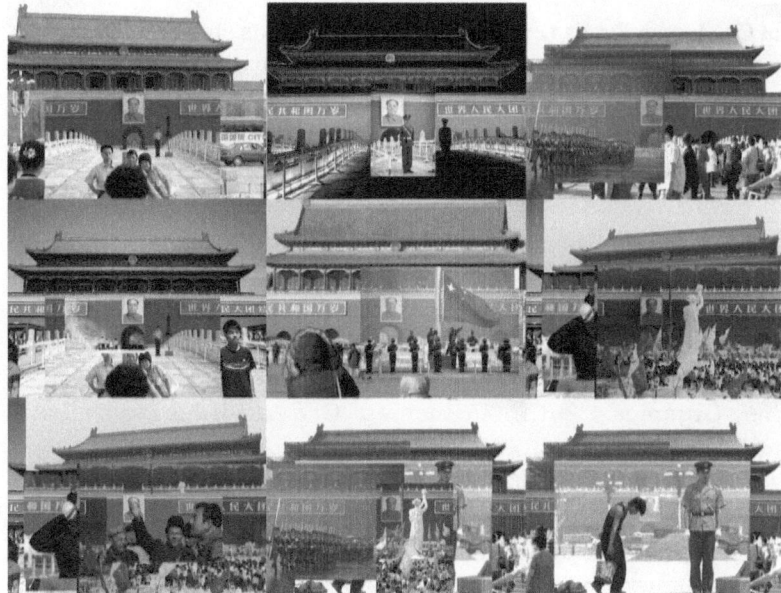

Figure 2. *How to get the Mao experience through Internet...* (2014–15) by Winnie Soon. The above are 9 collated screenshots of the animated GIF sequence.

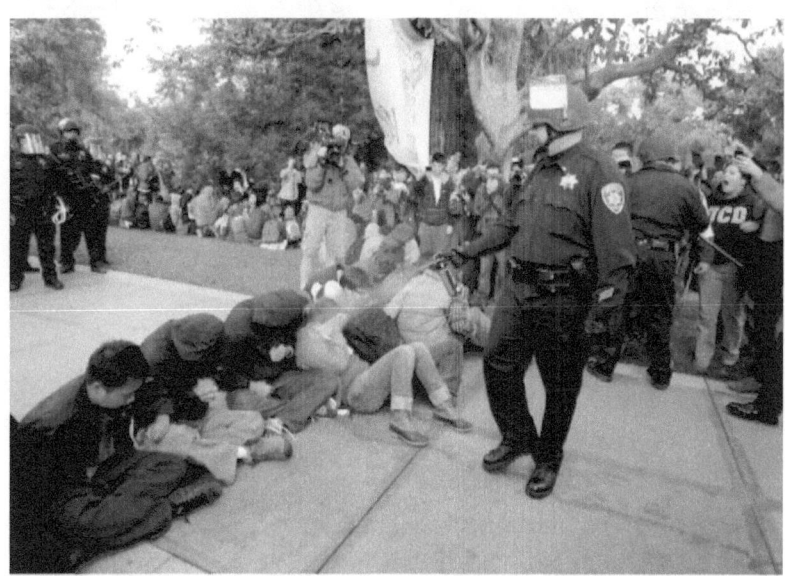

Figure 3. University of California Davis protest picture (2011).

of California Davis (Figure 3). The university's strategic communications office was later found to have employed "reputation management firms" to *delete* an incriminating photo from the Internet to avoid negative coverage of the events that took place in November 2011 (Jardin 2016). Brute force executio

As dissemination channels multiply, ecologies of power adapt by attempting to directly manage how representatives are perceived and evaluated by those they represent. Daniel Mayrit produced a series of photographs, *Imágenes Autorizadas* (Authorised Images), of Spanish police following the implementation of the Law on Protection of Public Safety (Ley Orgánica 4/2015). Nicknamed "Gag Law", this legislation makes it illegal to publish any images of forces of state security (Figures 4 and 5) (Miró 2016). In Mayrit's artwork the police are portrayed with pixelated faces, or without faces at all. The photographs exploit a legal loophole by making the police anonymous in the images. Nonetheless, Mayrit's exploit through anonymisation drew unexpected attention from the protagonists. Two police officers were noticed in the exhibition, engaged in trying to recognise their colleagues in the images. What has been erased in this instance is the visible and symbolic disagreement with the state (Urbinati 2000). *Pics or it didn't happen...*

Figure 4. Authorised Images (*Imágenes Autorizadas*), Untitled, by Daniel Mayrit (2016), courtesy of the artis

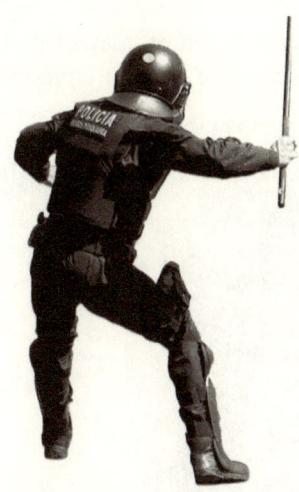

Figure 5. Authorised Images (*Imágenes Autorizadas*), Untitled, by Daniel Mayrit (2016), courtesy of the artist.

Such censorship has also masked the effacement of ecosystems for the extraction of raw material, such as the Alberta tar sands, under the guise of *national sacrifice zones* (Thomas-Muller 2010). These terraformed landscapes paradoxically become fodder to fuel the cultural machinery manufacturing hegemonic consent of the oil sands as *sustainable development* (Black et al. 2014). Species extinction results from the extensive landforming, a radical form of erasure that is both a material reality and a cultural discourse that legitimises inegalitarian social order (Dawson 2016). Such systems may in turn produce devastated landscapes of violence and trauma, such as the aerial photography of the Negev desert, depicted in Fazal Sheikh's *Memory Trace* (2015). Execution of epistemic and violent erasure

Meanwhile, deserts and forests are also making way for data centres. The materiality of data is terraforming the planet through extraction of resources and infrastructures to house data servers. *Crystal Computing (Google Inc., St. Ghislain)* is a video-based investigation by Ivar Veermäe into Google's data centre in Saint-Ghislain, Belgium, which in 2013 housed 296,960 servers (the second largest in the world). In his quest to visit the physical location of this monument, what might aptly be described by Shannon Mattern (2013) as *infrastructural tourism*, Veermäe finds that the location itself is blurred out of Google maps, and wrongly identified to be in Mons (Figure 6).[2] This means of erasure is reminiscent of "whiting outs" (Weizman and

Sheikh 2015), white spots left on maps by colonial cartographers that led to the wiping out of entire native cultures.

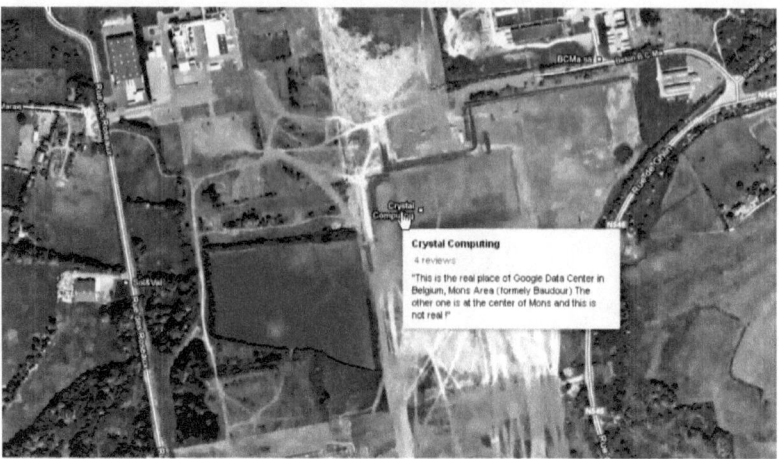

Figure 6. Still from *Crystal Computing (Google Inc., St. Ghislain)* (2014) by Ivar Veermäe, courtesy of the artist.

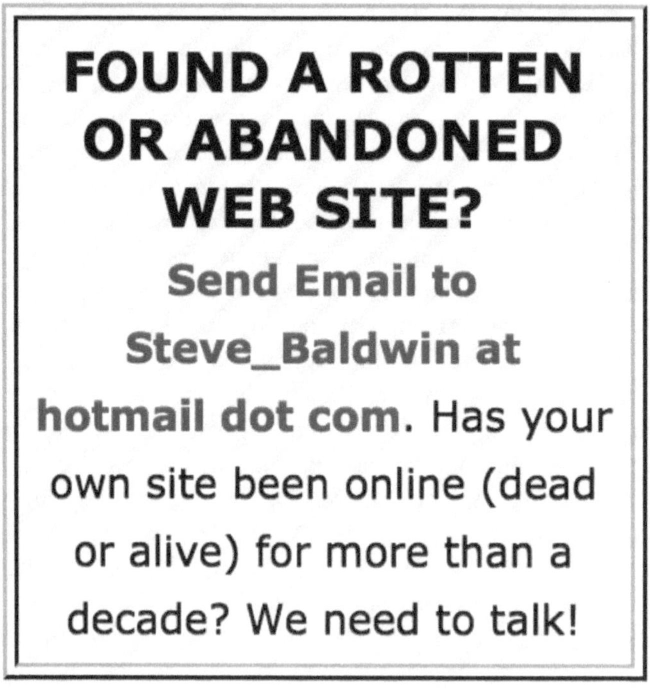

FOUND A ROTTEN OR ABANDONED WEB SITE?

Send Email to Steve_Baldwin at **hotmail dot com**. Has your own site been online (dead or alive) for more than a decade? We need to talk!

Figure 7. Screen capture from the *Ghost Sites of the Web* (n.d.). http://www.disobey.com/ghostsites/

The awe inspiring *technological sublime* (Nye 1996), monoliths that once attracted crowds, are now hidden away, fortresses of secrecy archiving our every move. Traces of these infrastructures are revealed through vestigial Internet lore, such as *Ghost Sites of the Web*, a collection of abandoned "Web 1.0 history" (Figure 7). Itself a deserted platform (its last post issued in 2008), *Ghost Sites of the Web* is described as a site for "forgotten web celebrities, old web sites, commentary, and news by Steve Baldwin. Published erratically since 1996."[3] Execution as haunting.

Erasure of data, or lack thereof, has important socio-political implications, ranging from refused entry to a country based on the grounds of decontextualised data that lives on in the network, to mass surveillance (Mayer-Schönberger 2009). *DEL?No, wait!REW* is an installation that prompts the visitor to make a decision about whether to *forever* delete or to publish a file publicly online (Figure 8). The files are recovered from hard drives "without the consent or the knowledge of the previous owners, who presume their content has been forever deleted".[4] The viewer literally initiates the execution of scripts that will either propagate or terminate an information set. Personal data is treated as an objet *trouvé*, fodder for junk art. Executing valuation.

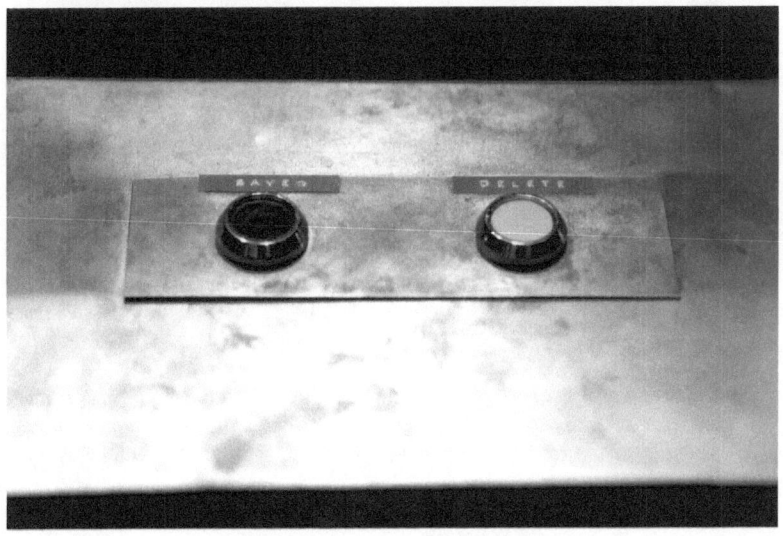

Figure 8. *DEL?No, wait!REW* (2014) by Michaela Lakova. (Photo: Michaela Lakova). Courtesy of the artist.

One of the proposed ethical solutions amidst this data amassing megalomania is "privacy sensitive" surveillance. An example of this is the Secure Erase Module (SEM), developed as part of an automated "suspicious" behaviour detection system, which deletes 95–99% of the footage collected (Neyland and Möllers 2016). The design includes auto-deletion algorithms that follow a similar logic as the detection algorithms. Moving objects are detected from the usual background and classified according to potentially suspicious parameters (i.e. if an object splits it might designate luggage left behind) (Figure 9). In practice, however, not all frames were gathered. Some frames were left behind undeleted, and the tool produced a continual output of partial failure. In addition, the deletion log generator, a sub-module of SEM, creates and records metadata, such as filenames of deleted objects. Privacy here is equated to the automated (failure prone) recognition and deletion of non-relevant data. Privacy as defective erasure.

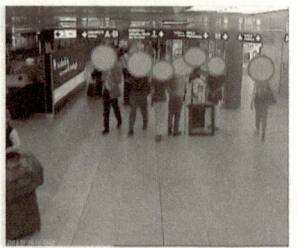
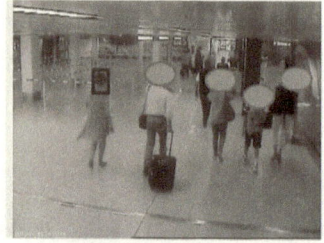
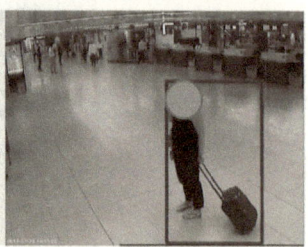
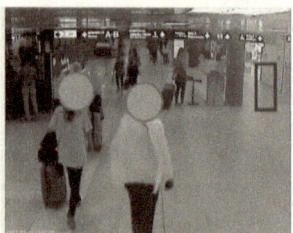

Figure 9. The image shows the failure of the software detection system, mistaking a body for the floor, a bag separated from its owner (though it is not), or the wall as a moving entity. Permission from Daniel Neyland.

The datafication of everything, which facilitates surveillance, is re-writing the landscape with ever expanding server farms and the extraction of resources to fuel data transfer and storage. My obsession with erasure was originally inspired by my desire to gain agency within these iterative inscription processes. I began by exploring the use of *blanking*, a term I borrow from Russell Thomsen (2015), which designates a form of withholding that transforms apprehension and communicates the presence of an absence. Thomsen coins this term in his description of a memorial design proposal for Auschwitz, an emergent ritual that is created through the experience of the absence of the site. Similarly, *ne.me.quitte(s).pas* is a digital data funeral that I originally developed with Jonathan Kemp that involves the degradation of memory chips with highly corrosive acid, of which the remains evoke the absence of the erased data (Figure 10). The material "data remnants" were given back to participants like cremation ashes. Erasure as memorialisation.

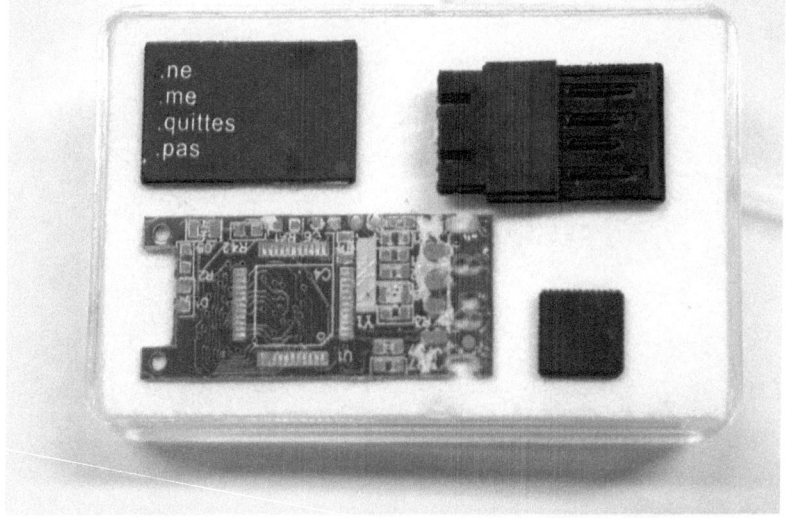

Figure 10. *ne.me.quitte(s).pas* (2014). The remains of the digital data funeral. All metal is corroded by the acid during a 90 min immersion in Aqua Regia (HNO3 + 3HCl).

The ruins of the erased data represent an agential force of erasure within the datafied landscape. Not unlike *subtraction*, which is defined by Keller Easterling (2014) as the disappearance of building that is itself a form of growth, a productive force managed by citizens, as opposed to the violent gentrification dictated by global financial industries.

From the public executions endemic to revolutionary propaganda to the use of erasure as an imaginative agency, this thought experiment acts as a tool for *thinking through* different forms of erasure and their relationship to knowledge production. It is through this survey of instantiations of *execution* portrayed by various practitioners that I hope to establish an ecology of practices of erasure that considers its potential for both destruction and cultural re-imaginings. A collection of *erasures* that embodies how execution, or the act of erasing, can categorise, divide, kill, heal and re-build systems such as memory, national identity, ideological frameworks, economy, ecology, networks and architecture.

Notes

1. A very rare condition also called Superior Autobiographical Memory, characterised by the ability to remember the events of any given day with accurate detail.

2. These statistics are dated from 2013. Interestingly, what was then blurred out has now been made visible. Tactics of erasure are shifting. See Crystal Computing (Google Inc., St. Ghislain) by Ivar Veermäe http://www.ivarveermae.com/CRYSTAL-COMPUTING/.

3. *Ghost Sites* of the Web. http://www.disobey.com/ghostsites.

4. See http://www.mlakova.org/works.html.

References

Baldwin, Steve. Ghost Sites of the Web. n.d. http://www.disobey.com/ghostsites.

Baudrillard, Jean. (1968) 1996. *The System of Objects*. Trans. J. Benedict. London and New York: Verso Books.

Black, Toban, Stephen D'Arcy, and Tony Weis, eds. 2014. *A Line in the Tar Sands: Struggles for Environmental Justice*. Oakland, CA: PM Press.

Bowker, Geoffrey C., and Susan Leigh Star. 2000. *Sorting Things Out: Classification and its Consequences*. Cambridge, MA: The MIT press.

Dawson, Ashley. 2016. *Extinction: A Radical History*. New York, NY and London: OR Books.

Derrida, Jacques. 1995. *Mal d'Archive: Une Impression Freudienne*. Paris: Éditions Galilée.

Easterling, Keller. 2014. *Critical Spatial Practice 4: Subtraction*. Berlin, Germany: Sternberg Press.

Hadziselimovic, Nils, Vanja Vukojevic, Fabian Peter, Annette Milnik, Matthias Fastenrath, Bank Gabor Fenyves, Petra Hieber et al. 2014. "Forgetting is Regulated Via Musashi-Mediated Translational Control of the Arp2/3 Complex." *Cell* 156 (6): 1153–1166.

Harvey Brown, R. & B. Davis-Brown. (1998). "The making of memory: the politics of archives, libraries and museums in the construction of national consciousness." *History of the Human Sciences*, 11(4): 17–32.

Jardin, Xenin. 2016. "UC Davis Paid $175,000 or More to Scrub Police Pepper Spray Incident from Web Searches". *Boing Boing*, April 13. http://boingboing.net/2016/04/13/uc-davis-spent-175000-to-scr.html.

Kandel, Eric R. 2007. *In Search of Memory: The Emergence of a New Science of Mind*. New York, NY: WW Norton & Company.

Kahneman, Daniel. 2011. *Thinking, Fast and Slow*. New York, NY: Farrar, Straus and Giroux.

Lakova, Michaela. n.d. http://www.mlakova.org/works.html.

Lim, Louisa. 2014. *The People's Republic of Amnesia: Tiananmen Revisited*. New York, NY: Oxford University Press.

Mattern, Shannon. 2013. "Infrastructural Tourism." *Places Journal*. https://placesjournal.org/article/infrastructural-tourism.

Mayer-Schönberger, Viktor. 2009. *Delete: The Virtue of Forgetting in the Digital Age*. New Jersey, NJ: Princeton University Press.

Miró, Francesc. 2016. Burlar la Ley Mordaza es Cuestión de Arte [Cheating the Gag Act is a Matter of Art]. *El Diario*, August 29. http://www.eldiario.es/cultura/arte/Poner-evidencia-Ley-Mordaza-exposicion_0_531946971.html.

Neyland, Daniel, and Norma Möllers. 2016. "Algorithmic IF... THEN rules and the conditions and consequences of power." *Information, Communication & Society* 1:1–18.

Nye, David E. 1996. *American Technological Sublime*. Cambridge, MA: The MIT Press.

Shaker, Lee. 2006. "In Google We Trust: Information Integrity in the Digital Age." *First Monday* 11 (4).

Sheikh, Fazal. 2015. *Erasure. Vol I Memory Trace*. Göttingen, Germany: Steidl.

Soon, Winnie. 2014. *How to get the Mao Experience through Internet*. http://siusoon.net/home/?p=1155.

Stengers, Isabelle. 2005. "Introductory Notes on an Ecology of Practices." *Cultural Studies Review* 11 (1): 183–196.

Steyerl, Hito. 2008. "Politics of the Archive: Translations in Film." *Transversal*. http://eipcp.net/transversal/0608/steyerl/en.

Thomas-Muller, Clayton. 2010. "The World's Biggest Climate Crime." *Left Turn*. July 14. http://endofcapitalism.com/2010/07/14/tar-sands-worlds-biggest-climate-crime.

Thomsen, Russell. 2015. "The Future of Auschwitz." In *Amnesia*, edited by Aaron Desben, Edward Hsu, Andrea Leung, Teo Quintana. *The Yale Architectural Journal*, Perspecta 48. Cambridge, MA: The MIT Press.

Travis, Hannibal. 2013. *Cyberspace Law: Censorship and Regulation of the Internet*. New York: Routledge.

Urbinati, Nadia. 2000. "Representation as Advocacy: a Study of Democratic Deliberation." *Political Theory* 28, 6: 758–786. http://www.jstor.org/stable/192219.

Veermäe, Ivar. 2014. *Crystal Computing (Google Inc., St. Ghislain)*. http://www.ivarveermae.com/CRYSTAL-COMPUTING.

Weizman, Eyal and Fazal Sheikh. 2015. *The Conflict Shoreline: Colonialism as Climate Change in the Negev Desert*. Göttingen, Germany: Steidl.

Posthuman Curating and its Biopolitical Executions: The Case of Curating Content

Magdalena Tyżlik-Carver

Content curation seems to differ at every level from a conventional understanding of art curation. Not least because everyone is doing it. Hal Foster, a distinguished art critic and historian, notices that today "everyone who compiles is a curator", while recalling, not without irony, "the utopian days of aesthetic egalitarianism" when everyone was a poet and everyone was an artist (Foster 2015). Indeed, curating has become a practice available to any user of mobile and networked technologies, while also any object, including a salad, is ready to be curated.[1] Organising personal Facebook walls, curating Instagram posts, liking, linking and retweeting are common activities that users of social media platforms perform repeatedly every day. Content curation generates and organises content online and involves content production, management, organisation and collection in a massively distributed practice. Content in this essay is not a general category for texts, images, films and other digital artefacts. Here, content is understood in a wider context that also includes so-called big data, and related practices such as mass participation in digital and networked media, and the labour (human and nonhuman) involved in production of online content/data.

The two significant features of content curating are: that it is performed (often simultaneously) by human and nonhuman actors, such as various software and hardware; and that these elements are able to perform together through a temporary and localised network organised to create, manage and distribute specific content online. Such organised networks are different to what Geert Lovink and Ned Rossiter (2005; 2010; Rossiter 2006) famously defined as a new institutional form. The common cause which, according to Lovink (2011), consolidates networks is, I argue, replaced in this case by repetitive actions rather than clearly set causes. These are mundane practices where free digital labour is executed as linking, liking, reposting, aggregating, editing, filtering, semantic analysis, tagging and annotating, all of which are performed by people (individuals and communities, curators and users), software and social and technological platforms. According to Lovink, such networks are without a cause, yet, I argue that they are affective and driven by ambiguous desires while injecting contingency into big data flows.

The discussion of curating in this essay focuses on how curating becomes posthuman, revealing that it is indeed no longer an activity performed by the professional figure of the "curator" but by agents of different orders. This is another challenge to subject/object distinctions as posthuman curating is performed through algorithmic processes of aggregation, RSS feeds, annotation, metadata and/or automated curation alongside human-executed content generation and circulation of data. In this process posthuman curating becomes an apparatus of subjectivation and individuation; it executes complex processes of subjectivation while being constantly engaged in reaffirming and reproducing the self as data, and as such, it is an active biopolitical force. It is this tension between the posthuman subject as process of subjectivation and the notion of the self as a (re)productive practice based on forms of individuation that is discussed here. In other words, the attention is on a biopolitics of posthuman curating which, while executing bodies into forms of data and affect, brings to the fore the urgency to rethink biopolitics in the posthuman condition. Within this discussion that engages posthuman curating as its primary subject, execution is considered as performing a posthuman biopolitics that results in affective data bodies and banal (ir)rationalities of computational culture.

Biopolitics and positive critique

Let us start this reconsideration of biopolitics as posthuman with Claire Blencowe's interpretation of Michel Foucault's account of biopolitical modernity as "a historically specific formulation of *experience* and *embodiment*" (2011, 1).[2] Blencowe's focus is on the positive forms of biopower able to create new *embodied experiences* of life rather than concentrating only on the experiences of the body. Unlike Giorgio Agamben's (2005) forms of biopolitics which result from a state of exception, Blencowe uses the biopolitical nature of modernity as a way to exercise a "positive critique" which recognises *experience* as "a matter of processuality, connectedness and openness of relationships and forces in the world, rather than embedding continuity, stability or security of a subject" (2011, 6). In this view biopolitics is not limited to the "politics of the body", which in Agamben's state of exception can only (re)produce refugees, prisoners or other bodies of precarious status. Rather, biopolitics is defined as a "diverse and malleable" experience of "a multiplicity not the totality of modern political institutions, rationalities and ethics" (2). The experiential dimensions of biopolitics are recognised as multiple experiences. Not one but many, not universal but abandoning universals altogether.[3]

Foucault (2008) defines biopolitics as the process that links the disciplining of individual bodies with the process of the reconstitution of these bodies into a population. Biopolitics is a subjectivising force that is at the same time also manifested through bodies. Its concern is specifically with the politics of life, where the apparatus can be seen as a method that links the archive of knowledge (about bodies) with a mode of production of knowledge about life and, we might argue, (re)production of life itself. As Blencowe suggests, life, which is at the core of Foucault's biopolitics, is not just contained in "the limits of living bodies", but has as its main concern "the limit-nature of life, with experience, and with the role of biological knowledge in the formation of modern political problems" (2011, 34); a concern which she recognises throughout Foucault's oeuvre.

This notion of life as a complex experience generated through knowledge and knowledge making is seen as reaching beyond the body and thus escaping "the ontology of identity" manifesting the "trans-organic nature of life" (34). This experience is defined as "bio-mentality", understood as "biological knowledge that is an organiser of experiencing, rationality, truth-games, science and embodiment; a horizon of visibility, verifiability and value" (34). Knowledge making is for Foucault (1982) related to language and discourse and is therefore a human venture. Blencowe's bio-mentality, however, extends this process beyond the human body, recognising other bio forms which take part in life making.

It is this trans-organic knowledge making that is proposed as positive critique of biopolitical experience, where experience of life is not just an experience of population. Rosi Braidotti defines a similar process of "overcoming the self and stretching the boundaries of how much a body can take" (2006). Such a comprehension requires a pragmatic understanding of "the structures, technologies, embodiments and imaginaries through which we are made as bodies desiring and becoming such freedom, transformation and affective capacity" (Blencowe 2011, 158). It is both knowledge making and knowledge becoming while also becoming life, yet no longer tied to population politics defined through categories of bodies. It is the specific and empirical relation between the subject and power that defines rationalities behind particular practices of subjectivation and their capacity to affect and be affected.

One such rationality that governs subjectivation today is big data. Usually defined as large data sets, big data results from exponential growth and availability to register people, things and their interactions as numbers. A new subject of big data is produced and its identity formed through practices of harvesting, accumulating, hosting, interpreting and conservation of big data, whose value comes from its relationality to other data and from its networked quality (boyd and Crawford 2011). While Information Aesthetics and other forms of visualisation identify relations between data and make them more evident, some scholars of big data and also artists recognise how big data encourages the practice of apophenia (boyd and Crawford 2012; Steyerl 2016), that is seeing patterns where there are none.

My interest in big data has a different focus, namely how experience and embodiment of big data takes place and what consitutes its affective results, or what does it become. In particular, I am attracted to the capability of bodies (human and nonhuman) to affect data and to the ways in which data affects bodies. I expand the figure of bio-mentality to account for relations between big data as a form of biopower and the posthuman subject of content curating animated by humans and nonhumans. As a result, non-bio forms, such as data and software, are included when investigating the kind of processuality that is revealed when curating is a posthuman matter and when the dealings of curatorial power/knowledge are not just a domain of an expert curator, but often result from random, localised and relational arrangements of people, machines and code.

Content curating — making the data subjects/objects

In our deeply computational contemporary culture curating is posthuman. Traditionally associated with caretaking, presentation, collection and display of art objects and other forms of cultural heritage, today there is no end to curating. Performed by millions of social media users and not just professional curators, as well as nonhumans such as code, interfaces, networked systems, computational assemblages etc., posthuman curating is a recent development in the genealogy of curating. This genealogy, explained in detail elsewhere (Tyżlik-Carver 2016), follows a trajectory which recognises different figures in the history of curating. Starting with the *curator* as a carer of collections, it soon moves towards *curating* as idiosyncratic practices of displaying art represented in the novel exhibition making formats of Harald Szeemann, Lucy Lippard and Seth Sigelaub, among others, and the arrival of the independent curator in the 1960s. Another figure in this genealogy is the *curatorial*, a dominant discourse in the curatorial field in the last three decades, recently accompanied by the ambition to be understood as the "philosophy of curating" (Martinon 2013). *Software curating* (Krysa 2008) and *art platforms* (Goriunova 2012) define modes of curating that are native to the digital context, linking curating to organisational and algorithmic processes that are constitutive of online creativity and participation. Whereas *posthuman curating* (Tyżlik-Carver 2016) accounts for human and nonhuman agencies that perform curating today.

This historicisation of curating, presented here only in outline, localises forms of curating regularly excluded from traditional curatorial discourse and often developing outside of the institution of art. Most importantly, this genealogical approach interrogates the traditional notion of what curating is, where, who and what performs it, and what is produced as a result of such processes. As practices of curating extend far beyond the field of art that often is defined by its institutions and performed by artist or curators, curating has become a daily activity no longer dependent on an art object to be curated, and it now defines a wider field of practice that can be referred to as *not-just-art curating*.[4]

Posthuman curating accounts for power/knowledge distributions facilitated by curating techniques, technologies and accessibility of curating as an everyday networked phenomenon. It is in this context that the figure of content curator is situated. Content production, accompanied by the constant need to organise and manage its flow through curating of digital objects, gives rise to content curators.

There are various definitions of what content curating is, as well as corresponding expectations as to what content curators should be doing. While this practice is still in formation, curating content has been proposed as "an important participation and collaboration skill for digital citizens" (Rheingold 2011), and considered as an "emerging literacy" which can help in accessing the content "critically" (DiDi 2011). Elsewhere, digital curators are seen to be "the future of online content" (VanPeursem 2013) and an answer to the amount of information constantly generated and distributed online. A content curator active on Scoop.it, says this about curators of online content:

> *In this Age Of Super Abundance, one of the things we need more than anything is trusted filters ... We need folks whom we trust to lead us to where we would not go on our own. Ideally, these people will do more than just lead us to good work; they will expand our mind, and widen our social circles. But where are they?* (DiDi 2011)

Online curators deal with information and content, and their aim is to organise it in a way that allows audiences quick, just-in-time access to the correct and relevant information. Successful curation of content requires regular reposting, re-blogging and commenting. At the same time, the expectation for personalised news and information suggests another function for content curators beyond filtering information. Content curators are reimagined as gurus of a kind. Not just leaders but also directly influencing users' personal development. They are trusted filters, but most importantly, theirs is a particular role and responsibility of care for the social and intellectual and possibly spiritual development of content users.

This vision of a content curator as explicitly invested in the particular form of care for others references an epistemology of curating. The care of souls was a concern of the curate, a parish priest in medieval England, whose work was to care for the spiritual wellbeing of the members of the parish. This kind of pastoral power is traced by Foucault (2009) to pre-Christian tradition and Christian East and to the shepherd-flock metaphor and relationships engendered in these traditions later institutionalised by the Christian church. According to Foucault, pastoral power is exercised over a "flock" rather than a territory; it is seen as beneficial as it leads to "salvation"; and it is also an individualising form of power as each soul in the flock counts individually. It is this pastoral logic that Foucault recognises as constitutive of the modern political rationality that is also behind forms of subjectivation. And it is this pastoral rationality, I argue, that is reproduced through curating content, in other words, through big data practices which update pastoral power for the posthuman condition.

Taking into consideration these changes and potentials for contemporary forms of curating it is possible to see content curating as a disciplinary practice. On the one hand, it is a way for digital citizens to engage with their institutions (Internet, state, corporations) by managing content online through various forms of interaction with it. And on the other, it is a practice that creates new subjects of content curators and user/digital citizens, where it is the first one that is charged with leading and helping users in accessing right information. In effect, the value of content curators is often expressed through recognition that "in the process of doing 'serious', 'quality' curation, even at the personal level, me and you are helping others understand and make sense of their worlds more easily" (Good 2011). Curating in this context appears as an affective practice of care that is at the same time a practice of data management through subjective finding, recommending and presenting links between data objects while generating relations with data subjects. Content curators and content users are subjects that function on one level, while their labour is a resource to big data. Indeed, processes of datafication, which turn all into data, allow for new forms of value to be created, and are operational to and governed by big data as a meta force.

In these conditions curating is a method with many applications; from a pedagogical tool in education (Mihailidis and Cohen 2013) to its use in retail shopping online, where "a tailored experience is no longer just a desire for shoppers, it is an expectation" (Whitehead 2013), making curating in turn particularly suitable for marketing purposes. At the same time, curating is reimagined as a method of care for one's own life or/ and that of others. As a result, content curating is more than the aggregation of links and comments, as it aspires to a production

of enlightened minds and socially rich subjects, while at
the same time it is a disciplinary practice and a practice of
subjectivation through data management. Processes of data
and content creation are directly linked to the production and
reproduction of new subjects who are clearly defined and their
functions separated into big data sets.

Wikipedia — the body of data

Posthuman curating points to the fact that curating is no
longer a domain of a curator but that it is distributed across
and performed by agents of different orders. The process of
posthuman curating itself expands beyond the field of art, as
content and data are curated and managed while incorporating
processes of subjectivation and individuation. I argue that it
is through curating content that links and relations between
these different processes, things and people are established.
I propose to think of content as big data, thus recognising
how it acquires and becomes a number in data sets. In
parallel, curating itself is a practice that defines managing
and organising content online, actively influencing what is
considered curating and what is defined as content.

To illustrate this, let us look at Wikipedia practices
and the very first entry under the tag *curator* registered at
23:19 on 6 December 2003 and delivered by the IP address
131.211.225.204. At the time it was a one sentence description:
"A curator of a cultural heritage institution (e.g. archive, library,
museum) is a person who manages the institution's collection"
(2003). A check on the entry in Summer 2016 brings up seven
sections, including one on technology and society that defines
technology curators as those "able to disentangle the science
and logic of a particular technology and apply it to real world
situations and society, whether for *social change or commercial
advantage*" (emphasis added). Content curation, a separate
entry since June 2013, is defined as the "process of gathering
information relevant to a particular topic or area of interest",
where "services or people that implement content curation
are called curators".

This development of the definition for *curator* on Wikipedia
reflects changes in the understanding of what a curator does,
what the subject/object of the curator's concern is and how
the fields of curatorial activities have changed over recent
years, with the definition itself under constant construction. The

changes to the definition, additions and forking of concepts and references contextualise curating as a massively expanded field. As the entry can be read on the page, the very process of generating a Wikipedia page for curator contributes to changes in how curating is defined. Data documented and archived on the wiki includes a constantly growing number of entries and users, number of edits per each user, dates of their edits, IP addresses and links to the profiles of the editors, etc. (Fig. 1) These, together with the definition, are constitutive of the semantic entry for *curator*.

Data such as this, that registers and represents interactions on the platform that directly involve manipulation of content on Wikipedia, can be seen as exemplary of big data practices, while also linking it directly to the content (images and texts) that these practices generate. A visual representation of this process mediates data into the kinds of practices that can be seen in Figure 1 and 2. Such forms of content curation, executed on many levels and simultaneously, while also available to processes of visualisation, demonstrates how different forms of power are operative within practices of curating content. And they contribute to curating becoming posthuman, where human/nonhuman subjects become functional in the wider system that can be represented and visualised as big data statistics (Figure 2).

Through content selection, contextualisation and organisation, curating is distilled to its most relevant and essential parts, which increasingly means that it is already a part of some form of counting and visualisation facilitated by computation. Together with various technologies, such as social media, aggregator sites and other applications, curating content constitutes an apparatus directly engaged in the production of new subjects through executing processes of subjectivation on a platform level and through individual performances of those active on the platform. And so curating content participates in the creation of particular publics which use online platforms and content as source material for practices of individuation and subjectivation. This should be seen as the other side of concepts which characterise the Internet as a panopticon (Winokour 2003) and disciplinary technology (Rajagopal 2014). If we think of the Internet as a collection of various technologies of power such as surveillance, data monitoring or facial recognition, the function of curating content reveals how human and

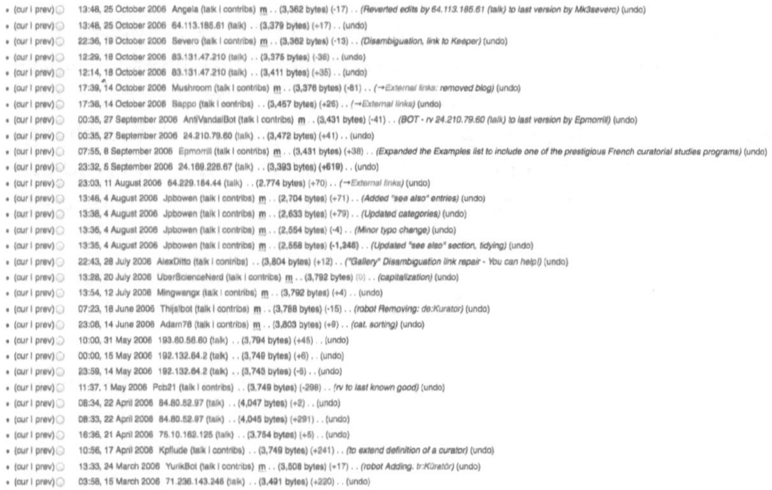

EXECUTING PRACTICES

Figure 1. Wikipedia, screenshot of the revision history page for 'curator' http://en.wikipedia.org/w/index php?title=Curator&offset=200702050 00925&limit=500&action=history.

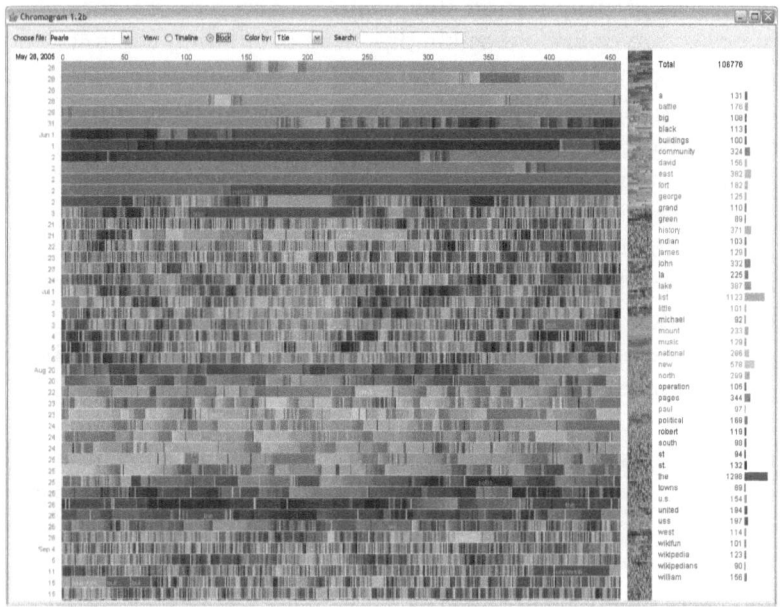

Figure 2. Visualisation of User activity on Wikipedia edits by user Pearl (created by IBM). At multiple terabytes in size, the text and images of Wikipedia are an example of big data. Source http://en.wikipedia.org/wiki/Big_data#/mediaFile:Viegas-UserActivityonWikipedia.gif.

180

nonhuman bodies are coerced to particular forms of subjectivation/objectivation. Yet these processes are simultaneously disrupted by certain (ir)rationality/ies also executed in the process.

Content curating as technology of the self

In a regime where data and content are extracted and organised continuously, the structure which integrates individuals into its totalising procedure expands further. It is exponentially distributed and naturalised through daily activities that include aesthetic choices, technical skills and increasing capacity to stay connected at all times. This results in the production of affective data where algorithms, bodies, technical platforms and proficiency in taking selfies, contouring or instant messaging are always in relation [Figure 3].

This relationality is situated in a material gathering of human and nonhuman subjects in specific relations, not as an abstract value in itself but dependent on materialisations that are "intra-actively produced" and which are "intra-actively demarcated through the specific production of marks on bodies" (Barad 2007, 232). As content curators are given responsibility for content and its users, Internet users who curate content are in charge of online management of their own data/body. This is the dataification process at its core: body becomes data while its physicality and materiality sustains how it is made operative for systems in order to count life as data.

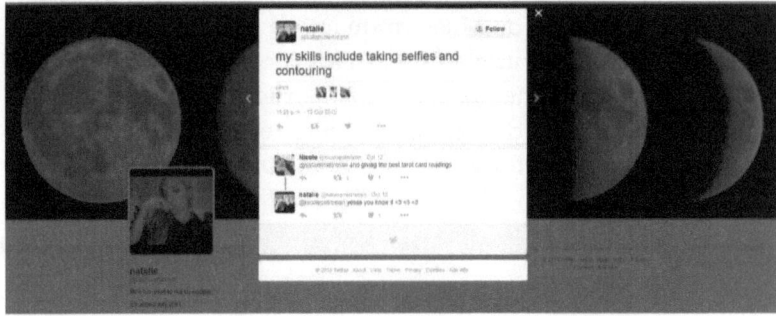

Figure 3. Screenshot of Twitter post by @satanmistress (2015).

Such practices can be described as driven by a desire to "count as subject" and to "become eligible for recognition" (Butler 2009, iv). Manifested by these aspirations, activities that facilitate becoming data body are politically potent. They are political where data, like the body, is personal yet definitely not private. Curating content involves a mix of technological tools, various practices performed by the curator/user releasing their agential force through linking and reblogging, but also through such skills as contouring and taking selfies. These are affective practices that influence the popularity of the subject, while often increasing their ability to monetise attention of followers online, as the cases of microcelebrity personas such as commercial lifestyle bloggers exemplify (Abidin 2016). According to Crystal Abidin, microcelebrity "involves the curation of a persona that feels authentic to readers" (2016, 3) and in itself is "a new style of online performance that involves people 'amping up' their popularity over the Web" (Theresa Senft in Abidin 2016, 3). This form of curating is concerned with establishing the status of the self as celebrity, even if on a micro level, while it is also about commercial practice of marketing and displaying the self.

And so autonomy and agency are reconsidered anew, taking into account that "it is not simply that subjects are governed, disciplined or regulated in ever more intimate ways, but even more fundamentally that notions of choice, agency and autonomy have become central to that regulatory project" (Gill 2008). In effect, it is the ability to generate relations between different data forms that becomes the valued agential force. Arguably, it is exactly this process which is tactically used in Amalia Ulman's famous Instagram performance *Excellences and Perfections* (2014), a performance that manages to expand data relationality beyond Instagram followers and platform practices because of its status as an art project (Figure 4). Yet, in this case, the performance is not a construction of authenticity, but an act of "imposed adaptability" where "bodies must be forever malleable" (Horning and Ulman 2014).

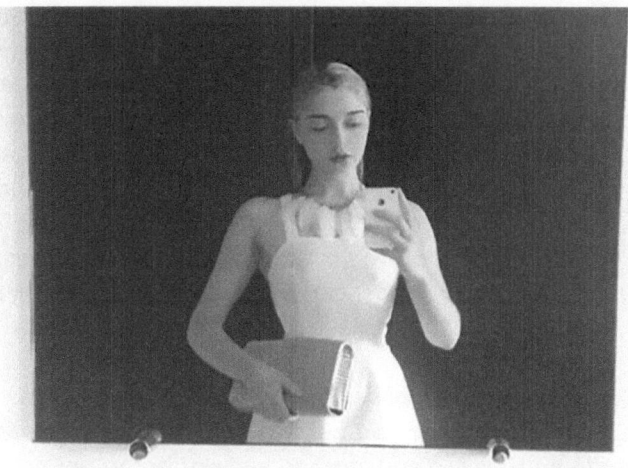

Figure 4. Amalia Ulman (2014) *Excellences and Perfections* (Instagram update 20th June 2014) (feather necklace yay or nay?), courtesy The Artist and Arcadia Misa 2016.

This new feature of malleability that a body must now display and which Blencowe also recognises as characteristic to the experience of biopolitics, has an ambiguous relation to authenticity, and it is this ambiguity that is at the basis of transformation that incorporates a multiplicity and not just the totality of big data institutions. The body's ability to always be another *self*, while also becoming a body of data does not concern a body only but its intra-actions that make data distinct while increasingly networked and accessible.

The process of individuation becomes a posthuman experience as digital objects, including data, are mediated and already situated within complex entanglements. According to Goriunova, a digital object such as a meme is not just a product of popular culture but is proposed as "an aesthetic performance through which individuation takes place" (2013). In this context, individuation is an aesthetic process not limited to traditionally defined aesthetic activities but a direct expression of aesthetic experience of individuation as multilayered and outlined as:

> *essentially collective, technical and physical: it is the individuation and consummation of ideas, norms, snippets of codes, codes of practice, cultural events and political acts, creative forms, sets of behaviours, gestures and performances, conceptual figures, youth practices, and technical platforms that unfolds online.*
> (Goriunova 2013)

Individuation is a process of becoming a thing or a person different from other things and persons, while at the same time belonging to methods, platforms and ways of being online. It facilitates a process by which the self becomes discrete while being defined as a part of wider phenomena. Individuation is an expression of difference and a never-ending process of realising and reconstituting the self; the becoming one not as a subject but as an other as data. And it is the other as data that is the subject of content curating while data itself enters a process of individuation.

These are processes of individuation and subjectivation executed on the body and on the platform where curating content eliminates the body as one by reducing self to a number while supporting practices that care only for data as many. In effect, practices of curating content and data transform the body into the one that counts as many, while injecting life into what otherwise becomes big data.

Bio-mentality of the body

In their essay "On Misanthropy", Alexander Galloway and Eugene Thacker (2006) recognise the biopolitical force of curating when they ask: how would one curate an exhibit of computer viruses and an exhibit of epidemics? The connection between curating as management of art and curing as management of life is expressed as "'care of the data' in which the life of information or 'vital statistics' play a central role" (2006, 161). They see such a process as both "self-transformation" and "self-destruction", recognising in it a "duplicitous nature" of curating as care and carelessness simultaneously. On the one hand, control and management is considered a method of care, and on the other, it is immediately undone and let go of at the point when control becomes care.

Today, ten years after their essay was originally published,[5] content curating can be seen as a functionary of vital statistics. Instead of a computer virus or exhibit of epidemics, life itself becomes that which is curated; not to be cured but to be datafied. Indeed, the care of the self becomes the care of data, with no end to curating through instantaneous availability of posting, reblogging, tweeting and liking while simultaneously transforming the body into statistics, figures and digits. The body's traditional function to sustain life is overtaken by its new goal: to live in order to become data. The living [users] become data bodies giving rise to a body of data as big data in a regime of "informatics of domination" (Haraway 1991). Curating content is a transformative act where the self becomes data in the truly posthuman gesture of human-becoming-other. This self-transformation also destructs the self as only body. Here auto-destruction is a process of becoming a data body in a continuous repetition of gestures and technologies that integrate individuation into and with subjectivation.

Here destruction is a creative force. Galloway and Thacker refer to the works of Gustav Metzger and their auto-destructive qualities, which Alan Liou defines as "viral aesthetics"; auto-destruction blurs the distinction between production and destruction as it sabotages the work by engaging in destructive modes of productivity. Liou identifies this kind of aesthetic in the works of net.art duo jodi.org and tactical media collective Critical Art Ensemble as able to "introject destructivity within informationalism" (Liou in Galloway and Thacker 2006, 173). And so while in the process of curating content the self is replaced with data as a nonhuman other ready for exploitation, it is through managing and organising data that content curation radically influences data itself. How content curating transforms bodies and how it also transforms data requires a posthuman sensitivity that is able to reimagine relations between biopolitics and curating.

To conclude, I want to introduce a new figure of the *affective data body* so as to provoke future speculations. Affective data bodies, epiphenomenon of big data, result from big data's inability (yet) to function without bodies. Content curating is evidence of subjectivation and individuation performed through bodies with various technologies, such as social media, aggregator sites and other applications. Content curating translates the subject into a body of data. It executes the experience of the self as my Facebook wall or your tumblr dashboard. Of course this is not to say that they are "me" or "you", at least not yet. But the experience of the self is defined as a consumer and producer of content and at the same time the self is captured by that content, while subjects become the products within processes of dataification. Production of subjectivity is increasingly reduced to linking, liking, deleting or reposting of content as such, and these online gestures have to be situated within a much broader assemblage of forces which reaffirm themselves as daily practices that turn into daily performances of the self. They constitute the individual not only defined by the data (s)he produces but as becoming an affective data body; one among many.

Bio-mentality, which Blencowe characterises so effectively, is reflected in the posthuman subject of curating. Curating becoming an affective data body extending an experience of life beyond the human subject colonised as and by big data. The affective data body(ies) are the result of trans-organic formations where becoming data/body is the becoming data, becoming other, becoming none. It is a manifestation of malleability that is the result of data, body and affect intra-acting. To think with affective data bodies is to pay attention to the "breaks in the established patterns of thought" (Braidotti 2013, 168) about data, body and subjects. And so this impersonal force that the affective data body introduces is not necessarily an introjection of destructivity within informationalism, but more of an attempt to grasp the creative potential of the posthuman to execute life beyond the human self.

Notes

This essay is based on research undertaken for my PhD thesis *Curating in/as Common/s. Posthuman Curating and Computational Culture* (awarded in June 2016 by Aarhus University), and includes some of the material published in the first chapter.

1. Popularisation of curating where outfits and salads are curated and curating is replaced by "curationism" (Balzer 2015a; Balzer 2015b) seems to suggest that curating today is a form of "'curated' consumption" (Foster 2015). This essay takes a different approach. By focusing on curating as everyday practices assisted by digital and networked technologies and available to all with access to such technologies, I analyse forms of content curating in order to reveal complexities involved in such forms of curation today.

2. Unless otherwise stated, emphasis in the original.

3. Deleuze (1992) in his essay "What is dispositif" in which he

proposes his interpretation of Foucault's notion of "dispositif" (apparatus) recognises the philosophical consequence of apparatus that demands abandoning universals as unable to explain anything, when he asserts "it is the universal which needs to be explained'.

4. Matthew Fuller (1998) uses the term "not-just-art" in his essay "A Means of Mutation. Notes on I/O/D 4: The Web Stalker", where he describes the browser Web Stalker as not-just-art art, defining the project's qualities that make it functional beyond domain of art. Fuller refers to this concept also in his later text "Art Methodologies in Media Ecology" (2011). I make use of this concept and apply it to curating. For more on not-just-art curating in the posthuman context see (Tyżlik-Carver 2016)

5. Their essay was originally published in the Data Browser series entitled *Curating Immateriality* (Krysa 2006).

References

131.211.225.204. 2003. "Curator— Wikipedia, the Free Encyclopedia." http://en.wikipedia.org/w/index.php?title=Curator&oldid=1889263.

Abidin, Crystal. 2016. "'Aren't These Just Young, Rich Women Doing Vain Things Online?': Influencer Selfies as Subversive Frivolity." *Social Media + Society* 2 (2). doi:10.1177/2056305116641342.

Agamben, Giorgio. 2005. *State of Exception*. Translated by Kevin Attell. Chicago: University of Chicago Press.

Balzer, David. 2015a. *Curationism: How Curating Took Over the Art World and Everything Else*. London: Pluto Press.

——. 2015b. "'Reading Lists, Outfits, Even Salads Are Curated—It's Absurd'." *The Guardian*, April 18, sec. Books. https://www.theguardian.com/books/2015/apr/18/david-balzer-curation-social-media-kanye-west.

Blencowe, Claire. 2011. *Biopolitical Experience: Foucault, Power and Positive Critique*. Basingstoke: Palgrave Macmillan.

boyd, dana, and Kate Crawford. 2011. "Six Provocations for Big Data." In *A decade in internet time: Symposium on the dynamics of the internet and society*, 1–17 Oxford Internet Institute. http://papers.ssrn.com/sol3/papers.cfm?abstract_id=1926431.

——. 2012. "Critical Questions for Big Data." *Information, Communication & Society* 15 (5): 662–79.

Braidotti, Rosi. 2006. "The Ethics of Becoming-Imperceptible." In *Deleuze and Philosophy*, edited by Constantin V. Boundas, 133–59. Edinburgh: Edinburgh University Press.

——. 2013. *The Posthuman*. Cambridge, UK ; Malden, MA, USA: Polity Press.

Butler, Judith. 2009. "Performativity, Precarity and Sexual Politics." *AIBR. Revista de Antropolgia Iberoamericana* 4 (3): i–xiii.

Deleuze, Gilles. 1992. "What Is a Dispositif?" In *Michel Foucault Philosopher*, edited by T. J. Armstrong, 159–68. New York: Routledge.

DiDi. 2011. "Who Are Today's Curators? And Where The Hell Are The Rest Of Them?!!" *Scoop.it*. October 18. http://www.scoop.it/t/content-curation-411/p/561154946/robert-scoble-on-online-curation-content-curation-social-media-and-beyond-scoop-it.

Foster, Hal. 2015. "Exhibitionists." *London Review of Books*, June 4.

Foucault, Michel. 1982. *The Archaeology of Knowledge*. New York, NY: Pantheon Books.

——. 2008. *The Birth of Biopolitics:*

Lectures at the Collège de France, 1978–1979: Lectures at the College De France, 1978–1979. Translated by Mr Graham Burchell. Basingstoke: Palgrave Macmillan.

———. 2009. *Security, Territory, Population: Lectures at the Collège de France 1977–1978.* Basingstoke: Palgrave Macmillan.

Fuller, Matthew. 1998. "A Means of Mutation. Notes on I/O/D 4: The Web Stalker." *Variant* 2 (6): 6–8.

———. 2011. "Art Methodologies in Media Ecology." In *Deleuze, Guattari and the Production of the New*, edited by Simon O'Sullivan, Reprint edition, 45–55. London; New York: Continuum.

Galloway, Alexander R., and Eugene Thacker. 2006. "On Misanthropy." In *Curating Immateriality: The Work of Curator in the Age of Network Systems,* edited by Joasia Krysa. Data Browser 03, 153–68. New York: Autonomedia.

Gill, Rosalind. 2008. "Culture and Subjectivity in Neoliberal and Postfeminist Times." *Subjectivity* 25 (1): 432–45. doi:10.1057/sub.2008.28.

Good, Robin. 2011. "The Short Road Between Collective Intelligence..." *Scoop.it.* October 13. http://curation.masternewmedia.org/p/543608508/the-short-road-between-collective-intelligence-and-curation-howard-rheingold-interviews-pierre-levy-video.

Goriunova, Olga. 2012. *Art Platforms and Cultural Production on the Internet.* London: Routledge.

———. 2013. "The Force of Digital Aesthetics: On Memes, Hacking, and Individuation." *Zeitschrift Fur Medienwissenschaft* 8 (Medienasthetic #1). https://www.academia.edu/3065938/The_force_of_digital_aesthetics_on_memes_hacking_and_individuation.

Haraway, Donna, J. 1991. "A Cyborg Manifesto: Science, Technology, and Socialist-Feminism in the Late Twentieth Century." In *Simians, Cyborgs and Women: The Reinvention of Nature,* 149–81. New York: Routledge.

Horning, Rob, and Amalia Ulman. 2014. "Perpetual Provisional Selves: A Conversation about Authenticity and Social Media." *Rhizome.* December 11. http://rhizome.org/editorial/2014/dec/11/rob-horning-and-amalia-ulman/.

Krysa, Joasia. ed. 2006. *Curating Immateriality. The Work of Curator in the Age of Network Systems.* New York: Autonomedia.

Lovink, Geert. 2011. *Networks without a Cause: A Critique of Social Media.* Cambridge, UK; Malden, Mass.: Polity.

Martinon, Jean-Paul. 2013. *The Curatorial: A Philosophy of Curating.* London: A&C Black.

Rajagopal, Indhu. 2014. "Does the Internet Shape a Disciplinary Society? The Information-Knowledge Paradox." *First Monday* 19 (3). http://firstmonday.org/ojs/index.php/fm/article/view/4109.

Rheingold, Howard. 2011. *Robert Scoble On Online Curation.* http://www.youtube.com/watch?v=WMn-cJHzF8A&feature=youtube_gdata_player.

Rossiter, Ned. 2006. *Organized Networks: Media Theory, Creative Labour, New Institutions.* Amsterdam: NAI Publishers.

Rossiter, Ned, and Geert Lovink. 2005. "Dawn of the Organised Networks." *Fibreculture* 29 (5: precarious labour). http://five.fibreculturejournal.org/fcj-029-dawn-of-the-organised-networks/.

———. 2010. "Urgent Aphorisms: Notes on Organized Networks for the Connected Multitudes." In *Managing Media Work*, edited by Mark Deuze, 279–90. Thousand Oaks, Calif: SAGE Publications, Inc.

Steyerl, Hito. 2016. "A Sea of Data: Apophenia and Pattern (Mis-)Recognition." *E-Flux*. http://www.e-flux.com/journal/a-sea-of-data-apophenia-and-pattern-mis-recognition/.

Tyżlik-Carver, Magdalena. 2016. "Curating In/as Common/s. Posthuman Curating and Computa-tional Cultures." PhD, Aarhus: Aarhus University.

VanPeursem, Ron. 2013. "When Did Content Curation Begin? Earliest Thoughts about Curation." Blog. *Content Marketing & SEO*. March 3. http://ronvanpeursem.com/2013/03/when-did-content-curation-begin/.

Winokour, Mark. 2003. "The Ambiguous Panopticon: Foucault and the Codes of Cyberspace." *CTheory.net*. March 13. http://www.ctheory.net/articles.aspx?id=371.

Ghost Factory: Posthuman Executions

Magdalena Tyżlik-Carver & Andrew Prior

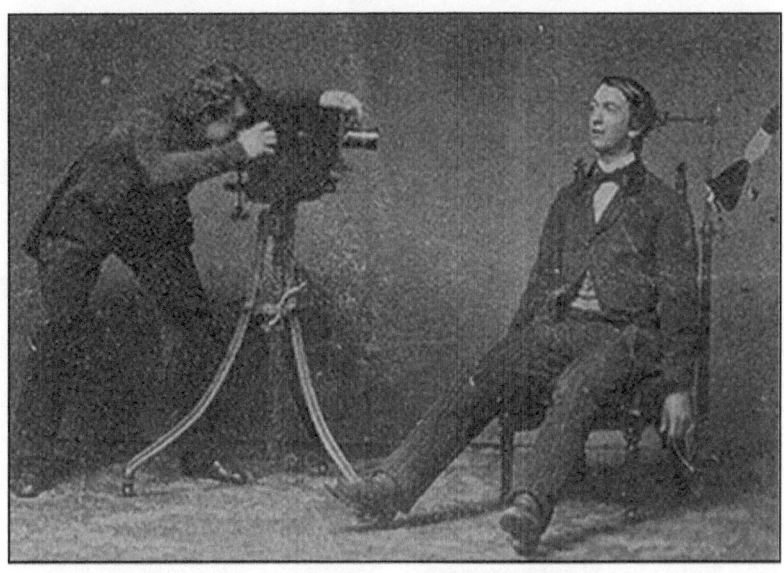

A photograph of a photographer allegedly taking a post-mortem picture of a corpse of a young man. Post-mortem photography was popular in the late 19th century and early 20th century in Europe and US. It was considered to aid the grieving process. Screenshot from Imgur.

Ghost Factory is an experiment which we perform on the self, with help of machines and software. Combining flesh and computational matter, data and algorithmic design, *Ghost Factory* is a laboratory that makes data for/ of no-one. Cultural objects; referents of real times floating free; appropriated and machined; regurgitated into binary placeholders of time and space.

Ghost Factory materialises processes in which humans and affects are turned into data facts. The body only a spectre in the shadows of "big daddy mainframe" (VNS Matrix 1991), turned into ghosts by an "informatics of domination" (Haraway 1991).

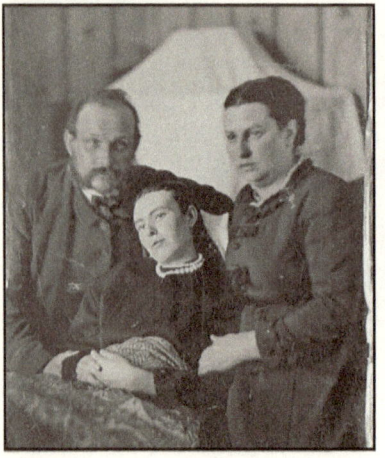

Alleged postmortem photography of a daughter held by her parents. Screenshot from Imgur.

Everyday mutations happen as humans and nonhumans enter mutual transformations. For just a moment, when playing with *Ghost Machine* devices, the human disappears, severed from the body into data fictions; a medium of remediation, another body part, affective s[t]imulation, with eyes open, though dead. Bodies of affect left behind.

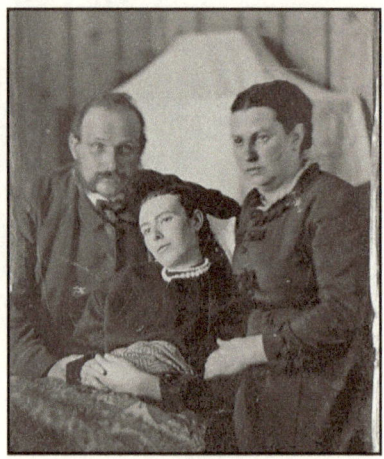

Ghost Machine software processes

Ghost Machine[1] is written in the MaxMSP coding environment and based on processes of transcoding and remediating. It takes still and moving images as source material which the machine systematically scans, outputting red, green and blue pixel values which are routed to three sound-making modules. Two modules map these values onto various musical scales, which are then played in real-time by a sine-wave generator. The last module converts values into raw audio amplitudes, producing noise and sounds.

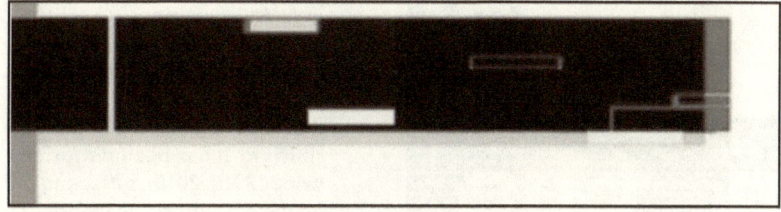

Fragment of a screenshot from *Ghost Machine* film by Andrew Prior (2012).

This little horror story feels good, even if a little noisy and glitchy. It is exciting, like all failure. But we believe in ghosts. They live with us and we want to touch them. We want to hear them. We want to have some fun! We want to become [with]one. We have become ghosts. Émigrés from the everyday of becoming data body, with affect left behind we turn to a ritual of ghostly labour. We call for them to come back. We are ghosts of the database. Residual bodies without soul and with a shell of another pattern recognition monster.

Is it yet? Has it gone, my soul? Is that what I see on the other side of database? Is it waste of the other that excretes from the medium's body? Is it us?

The software allows users to control the way in which files are viewed. A green square represents what is being scanned or read at any given time. Users can choose to control the square by mouse movements, or automate its movement across and down pages. They can choose whether to look at the whole page or the scanned area, or superimpose both on top of one another. This final option creates new audiovisual possibilities as the pixels from the page and close-up can be superimposed on one another in a variety of algorithmic ways; adding, subtracting, or multiplying values — or indeed the plethora of other computational functions offered by the software — changes the visuals, and therefore the sounds which are produced by them. What we hear and see, is a trace of cultural transcoding — media become data, to be re-made and repurposed as the code determines.

Ghost Factory curatorial interventions

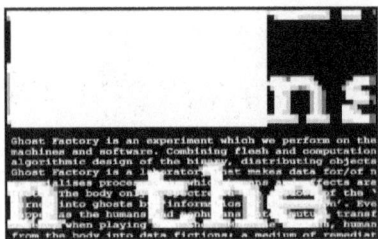

Ghost Factory[2] is a curatorial mediation of *Ghost Machine* and performative curatorial installation with humans, machines and software. It has been performed twice (2013, 2015), reflecting on the ambiguous character of participatory culture in digital and networked media. The exhibition creates an environment to experience divided appeal of technology in popular culture. It arranges people, machines, software, sound and text, in ghostly combinations. Each installation unpacked *Ghost Machine* into separate layers and plugged the results into the data of a YouTube facilitated channel. In 2013, the factory explored ideas of the immaterial labour of ghostly internet workers, while in 2015 it focussed on zones of non-stop creative production. The posthuman character of contemporary pop is revealed as contingent gesture and a challenge producing ghosts that occupy forgotten depths of the internet, while often creating zombies whose residual bodies are the result of an experiment gone wrong. Ghost Factory opens another posthuman experience to the willing participant. In any case, there is considerable doubt it is of any use in this life or thereafter. Consider it a voluntary work experience.

Notes

1. *Ghost Machine* is a collaborative work by Andrew Prior and Magdalena Tyżlik-Carver, which was originally commissioned as part of the publication *Local Colour. Ghosts, Variations* (2012) edited by Derek Beaulieu and InEditMode Press (Malmö). *Ghost Machine* takes as its starting point Derek Beaulieu's graphical reworking of Paul Auster's novella *Ghosts* (1986). It frames the multiple approaches to remix in *Local Colour* as examples of transcoding, raising questions around authenticity, affect, and the computational transformation of culture. *Ghost Machine* is available as part of the publication and online at http://www.ghostmachine.thecommonpractice.org.

2. *Ghost Factory* is a curatorial remediation of *Ghost Machine*. It was performed at Cornwall Media Resource in Redruth in 2013, and at Falmouth University in 2015.

References

Haraway, Donna. 1991 "A Cyborg Manifesto: Science, Technology, and Socialist-Feminism in the Late Twentieth Century", in *Simians, Cyborgs and Women: The Reinvention of Nature*. 149–81. New York: Routledge.

Stahl, Ola, Carl Lindh and Derek Beaulieu, ed. 2012. *Local Colour. Ghosts, Variations*. Malmo: Publication Studio Malmo / In Edit Mode Press.

VNS Matrix. 1991. http://www.obn.org/reading_room/manifestos/html/cyberfeminist.html.

Bataille's Bicycle: Execution and/as Eroticism

Marie Louise Juul Søndergaard
& Kasper Hedegård Schiølin

Introduction

Eroticism is an inherent aspect of computational culture and history. From love letter generators in the early days of computer development, through the rise of Internet porn industry in the 1990s, to the neoliberal products of IoT dildos, VR porn and sexbots of the present time, the development of computational technologies has been influenced by human eroticism. Eroticism in computing is all about the lust and pleasure of desiring subjects; corporate visions of increased connectivity and remote intimacy increasingly exploit users' inherent erotic and sexual inclinations. Simultaneously, computational art practices and counter-DIY cultures are hacking into the intimate sphere, exploring how individuation may be challenged through sometimes violent, erotic executions. Through practices of execution, performed through digital means, new powerful and transgressive relations of individuation are emerging.

This chapter questions if and how, a language of eroticism is useful in understanding the unstable, intimate and violent—that is, erotic—aspects of execution? We thus address the inherent, excessive eroticism in computational culture by focusing on execution at the boundary between extreme pleasure and extreme pain as it manifests itself in the experiences of eroticism and realisation of desire in modern digital technology. More precisely, we explore the transgressive potential of the excessive, blurred connection of desiring subjects and executing objects.

Entangling Georges Bataille's (1993) writings on *eroticism* and *excess* with, amongst others, Franco Berardi's (2009) notion of *connected bodies* and Lauren Berlant's (2011) reflections on *cruel optimism*, we question how networked bodies are executed and engage in blurred, erotic processes that transgress a mere voluntary sexuality where consent is sacrosanct. Through a close reading of specific sections in Bataille's novella *Story of the Eye* (Histoire de l'œil) (1979), we show how topics central in the novella such as excess, consent, control and unwillingness reflect the execution of our erotic, emotional state in computational culture. We argue that Bataille forms an exploratory taxonomy, or even hierarchy, of human lust and desire, in which the character Marcelle enjoys supremacy precisely because of her unwilling lust. In accordance with this argument, the speculative design *Marcelle*, named after Bataille's character, is our attempt to further explore the phenomenon of involuntary lust through design. *Marcelle* is a pair of white cotton briefs with built-in vibrators that are executed by the surrounding WiFi network landscape. In our exploring of its eroticism, *Marcelle* becomes a conceptual way of questioning both the limits of design and philosophy.

As we move beyond cruel optimism of the good life (Berlant 2011) and designed, spectacular sentimentality, eroticism is an inherent aspect of the social, political and aesthetic aspects of computational culture and execution. We argue that eroticism is about the transgression of the will, and in computational culture this is also manifested through cases of uselessness, instability and unwillingness. Furthermore, we argue that erotic technologies have economic and commodifying interests, but also violent *and* liberating potentials, that transgress the controlled logic and reasoning of technology. Art and design experiments, such as *Marcelle*, may help us understand this paradox and ambiguous relation.

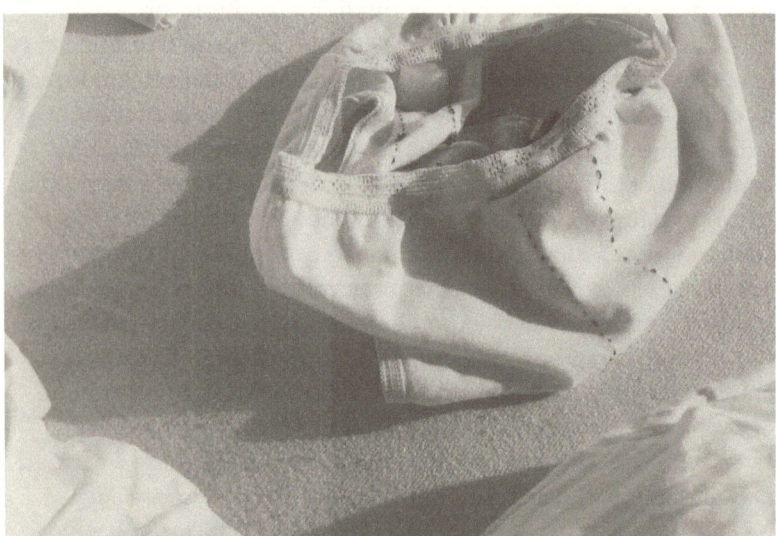

Figure 1. *Marcelle* (2016) by Marie Louise Søndergaard. All pictures by the first author.

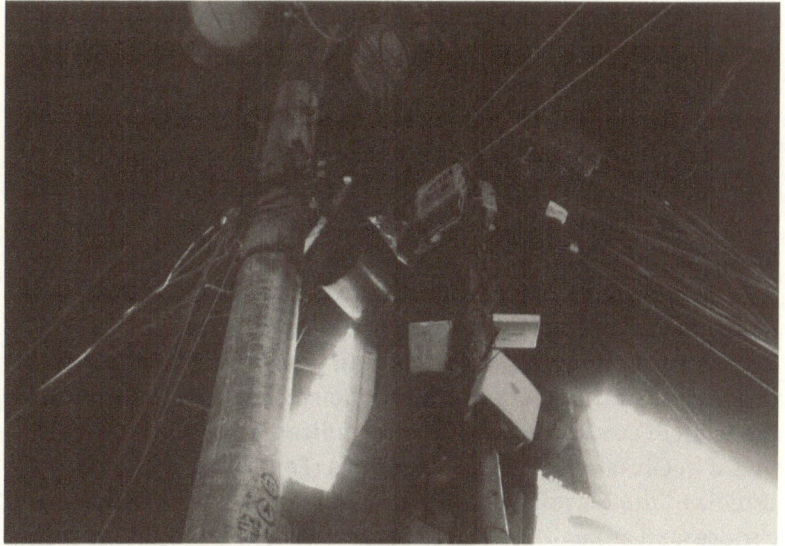

Figure 2. Messy electricity wires and WiFi routers in Seoul.

Eroticism as Excess

Describing eroticism is a complicated matter. It crosses the fields of art, society, health, religion and death, and is historically understood as being largely a "side-effect" of sexual reproduction. However, in Bataille's terms, eroticism is nothing less than the essence of humanity (1991). As an exuberant energy, that is, as excess, it flows in every corner of society and in all human activities. Contrary to sexuality, which might have productive outcomes, eroticism is "a sovereign form, that cannot serve any purpose" (Bataille 1993, 16). To Bataille, eroticism is excess. Excess is what begins when "growth ... has reached its limits" (1991, 29). When there is too much of something, it does not represent a utility-value, and thus becomes a loss, a something to squander or waste.
In Bataille's general economy, excess as a term defines that which cannot be tamed and transformed into capital.
"[E]rotic excess develops to the detriment of work" (1993, 83), he argues, and as such eroticism as excess is evidence of humanity's uselessness. Consequently, Bataille's eroticism expresses an implicit critique of the capitalist society where everyone and everything are being judged by use-value. Bataille believed in eroticism's transgressive potential of unveiling hidden structures and seemingly universal

prohibitions; structures and prohibitions that man established in order to separate and distinguish "perfect humanity, for which the flesh and animality do not exist" from "animal disorderliness" (55–56). However, as eroticism only exists, he argues, in its respect for and possible transgression and deviation of forbidden values, eroticism gains a double meaning as something that both civilises and possibly liberates human beings (57).

Michel Foucault takes a different perspective on eroticism than Bataille. In Foucault's study of the history of sexuality, he breaks sexuality into two segregated historical practices: *ars erotica*, the spiritual and lustful eroticism, and *scientia sexualis*, the truth of sex, the scientific and civilised sexuality as we also find it in Christianity and confessions (Foucault 1990). Foucault criticised the Marxist hypothesis that the rise of capitalism suppressed sexuality and desire, and instead brought forward the argument that capitalist, Western society had invented a new form of sexuality; a scientific sexuality where sexuality is omnipresent in the way we organize society and understand ourselves as human beings. Consequently, Foucault argues that sexuality has not been unequivocally repressed or tabooed, but has occupied different, shifting forms and installations in society.

Bataille argues that not only sexuality but also, and especially, eroticism has relations to both the artistic and spiritual sides of society and its civilized and political sides (1993). Similar to Foucault, he argues that eroticism is not to be ignored in the public spheres of everyday life, and that it is an inherent part and regulator of the norms and laws of society (52). His theory differs from Foucault's in his focus on eroticism as something that relates to subjectivity and corporeality, and not (just) to the social dispositif of biopolitical control. Bataille regards eroticism to have a connection to a *deep sexuality* beyond sexual reproduction. In its nature, eroticism is useless, it is opposed to work and cannot be governed as it is always in excess (52). Although eroticism is civilised by capitalism and different rational discourses, Bataille argues that eroticism is deeply connected to human's object of desire. "Erotic activity can be disgusting", he argues, "but it illustrates a principle of human behavior in the clearest way: what we want is what uses up our strength and our resources and, if necessary, places our life in danger" (104). As such, eroticism is linked to anguish, horror and even death, and its liberating potential is paradoxically released in the transgression of life itself.

An Eroticism of Connected Bodies

Drawing on Marxist and feminist traditions, art and computational culture have mostly dealt with the execution of eroticism as a liberating force, an organisation of power and a political act. However, in the rise of digital technologies, eroticism and sexuality have gained a new value. Already in the 1990s, cyberfeminism claimed sexuality as an "empowering" weapon and argued for its liberating potentials against technology's patriarchal, dualistic structures and the increasingly governed spaces of the formerly free, distributed network (Haraway 1991; Plant 1997; Steffensen 1998).

In the present tech industry the state of eroticism has, however, changed into a governed, commodified and managed form of sex and intimacy, and thus adapted to a neoliberal Silicon Valley-ideology described by Evgeny Morozov as technological solutionism (2014). Examples include Spreadsheets, an app that tracks the movement, volume and lengths of sexual intercourse; OMGYes, a website that teach users ways of enhancing (women's) pleasure through touchable videos; and Lioness, a dildo that uses biometric sensing and statistical methods to "characterize your sexuality" and suggest improvements. By offering and capturing erotic spheres of everyday life through apps and products, the tech industry thus extracts the maximum value from subjects as they perform emotional labour. Through worldwide marketing of sexual tools that promise to empower (mostly) women, neoliberal start-ups take ownership of what used to be a critical political act, and confuse the rather complex (political) difference between sexuality and eroticism. As a result, eroticism, as it is experienced in present computational culture, expresses the antagonistic conflict of desire-liberation having both anti-capitalist and capitalist interests.

Eroticism may be understood as an abstract principle of political, affective and philosophical processes that already are and also continue to become manifested in concrete material and embodied sites of execution. These sites of execution become part of the economy of eroticism, where everyday affective relations are tracked, managed and sold, gaining value beyond the relation itself. When considering today's neoliberal society surviving on individuals' productive consumption and emotional labour, it is no wonder that a common issue and increasing trend in corporate design is the wish to capitalise and rethink eroticism and sexual activity under capitalist terms.

The increasingly hyper-connected and hyper-visual character of today's digital culture (Berardi 2009) offers endless space for excessive joy and erotic sharing. We like, connect, match and laugh at kittens like never before. This endless realisation of desire and pleasure in our digitally-mediated social life has led Berardi to reflect on our present emotional state and its relation to economy. "Not repression, but hyper-expressivity", he argues, "is the technological and anthropological domain of our understanding of the genesis of contemporary psychopathologies" (108–109). This, he argues, has consequences for eroticism:

> *Connected bodies are subjected to a kind of progressive inability to feel pleasure, and forced to choose the way of simulating pleasure: the shift from touch to vision, from hairy bodies to smooth connectable bodies ... The control is built inside, in the very relationship between self-perception and identity. When the info-sphere become hyper-speedy ... we become less and less able to elaborate in a conscious way on the emotional impulses reaching our skin, our sensitivity, our brain.* (Berardi 2009, 100)

The disconnection between language and sexuality, Berardi argues, has led to a lack of empathy and a rise of obsessive rituals. Our sensitive organism is subjected to a permanent execution, as our every action is broken down to likes, retweets and emotional analyses. Similarly, our compulsive repetitions of rituals, of liking, swiping, scrolling, checking emails and notifications, point at a state of being where each emotional action does not fulfill its aim. As desiring subjects, we are thus "addicted" to a pleasure that is never fulfilled. Instead, our excessive obsessive rituals and emotional execution serves the aim of larger, hidden infrastructures; the aim of corporate economic structure, gaining value of "an overload of info-neural stimuli" (108) and emotional input to the systems. Although Berardi argues that repression of sexuality is not an issue in present psychopathology, it is exactly in the hyper-expressive and hyper-sexual culture of connected bodies that eroticism is repressed. Following Bataille's notion of eroticism,

eroticism is beyond *desire* and *smooth bodies*, and closer to what Berardi terms "conjunctive bodies"; "the encounter and fusion of rounded irregular forms that infiltrate in an imprecise, unrepeatable, imperfect, continuous way" (87).

The obsession with vision and connectivity does not (only) come down to a critique of porn, VR-porn or Internet connected sex toys; they may or may not lack empathy and context due to a blurred distinction between "natural" and "artificial" sex, but the critique unfolded in this essay has a different focus. We are concerned with the misconception of the essence of human sexuality as expressed through the notion of eroticism, and this leads to deeper, existential consequences concerning humanity itself.

To lay the foundations for this critique, we will dig deeper into Bataille's eroticism by a close-reading of some central sections in his (pornographic) novella *Story of the Eye*, and eventually connect it to the emotional state of present computational culture.

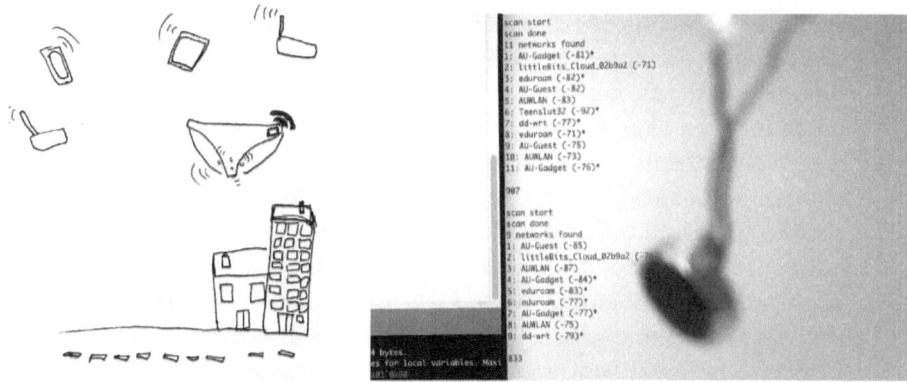

Figure 3. Material practices of wirelessness.

Story of the Eye

Blood, sperm, egg yolks, tears, urine, rain, vomit and milk are, metaphoricallly speaking, dripping from the pages of Bataille's 1928 novella *Story of the Eye*. This is, however, not news. Already in 1962, shortly after his death, Roland Barthes (1979) observed that fluids play a crucial role in Bataille's highly symbolic novella. Barthes' analysis is striking, and has indeed become a central text in Bataille scholarship. However, it literally reduces the *story* (of the eye) to a *metaphor* (of the eye), that is, to a pure linguistic analysis. Initially, Barthes even claims that *Story of the Eye* is "by no means ... the story of Simone, Marcelle, or the narrator"; it is really just, he continues, a "story of an object" (119), that is, a "story" of an "eye", metonymically substituted by other "substitute objects".

But *Story of the Eye* has much more to offer. Contrary to Barthes's refusal of the importance of the individual characters, we argue that Bataille forms an exploratory taxonomy, or even a hierarchy, of human lust and desire, in which the character Marcelle, due to her unwilling lust, is attributed supremacy. In accordance with this argument, the design *Marcelle* is our attempt to further explore the phenomenon of involuntary lust. Admittedly, this is a rather paradoxical endeavour, because design is generally seen as a material way of satisfying the user's more or less articulated will to reach a specific end. However, perhaps design is a more passable way than philosophy to explore eroticism. "Philosophy", Bataille asserts, "cannot embrace the extremes of its subject, the extremes of the possible as I have called them, the outermost [in particular eroticism] reaches of human life" (1962, 259). Hence, *Marcelle* becomes a conceptual way of questioning both the limits of design and those of philosophy. We might say that the two can cross-fertilise each other.

Working with unwillingness is not only a technical challenge, but also an ethical one. Consider, for instance, the dictum "Consent is Sacrosanct" that has become the media's automatic response to rape; indeed even the popular bondage porn website Kink.com has used it to dissociate themselves from its former employee, the famous porn star James Deen, when female colleagues accused him of rape in 2015. However, since consent is an unambiguous and often legal arrangement between two rational humans, the self-evident and appealing dictum reduces lust to a pure and sober intellectual endeavour leaving no room for accepting the Bataillean idea of transgressive eroticism. This leaves us with two highly contradictory views on sexuality; the one strictly philosophical, and the other strictly normative. There seems to be no easy solution to this conflict, but the speculative design *Marcelle* can be seen as a way of curiously exploring the matters at stake in this inextricable tension on a rather safe ground.

Simone's Will to Sex

As Benjamin Noys suggests, "certain recurring characters [...] dominate Bataille's fictions" (2000, 89). This also applies to the main characters in *Story of the Eye*. Following Noys, the 16-year-old Simone is the recurring figure of "the woman of *jouissance*" (90). Noys does not translate the common French word jouissance, which literally means "enjoyment". However, "enjoyment" lacks the explicit sexual connotations evident in French; "*jouir*" is slang for "to come". It is thus most likely Lacan's rather famous usage of the word that Noys hints to. For Lacan *jouissance* is the subject's always painful attempt to transgress the psychological-societal prohibitions that are imposed to its enjoyment (1978). As the Lacan scholar Dylan Evans explains: "The term *jouissance* thus nicely expresses the paradoxical satisfaction that the subject derives from his symptom, or, to put it another way, the suffering that he derives from his own satisfaction" (2002, 93). This definition of jouissance corresponds to what Bataille in *Story of the Eye* refers to as *deep sexuality*:

> She [Simone] was usually very natural; there was nothing heartbreaking in her eyes or her voice. But on a sensual level, she so bluntly craved any upheaval that the faintest call from the senses gave her look directly suggestive of all things linked to deep sexuality, *such as blood, suffocation, sudden terror, crime; things indefinitely destroying human bliss and honesty.* (Bataille 1979, 11)

Again, this definition is resonant in the Bataillean key concept of *eroticism*:

> In the very first place eroticism differs from animal sexuality in that human sexuality is limited by taboos and the domain of eroticism is that of the transgression of these taboos. Desire in eroticism is the desire that triumphs over the taboo. It presupposes man in conflict with himself. (Bataille 1962, 256)

In these definitions at least one thing is clear: Sex is not fun! Or, rather, sex is deadly serious. This is, however, also why Noys' descriptions of Simone as a "woman of *jouissance*", let alone Bataille's own apparent support of that characterisation, is not entirely correct. To Simone, sex actually seems to be fun; with great ease she plays around with, if not imperative controls and demands, the horrors of deep sexuality, and she does not show any visible signs of pain, or even qualms. Even in its most extreme manifestations, Simone's sexuality is a completely willful sexuality; a sexuality of a woman who knows exactly what she wants: "*I want to* have them [the testicles of a bull]", or, "*I want to* play with the eye ... Listen, Sir Edmund ... you must give me this at once, *I want it!*" (Bataille 1979, 48, 66, emphasis added).

In arranging an orgy in the beginning of the novella, Simone's sexuality is furthermore displayed as a rather calculating and manipulative will to master and control. By means of an easily won bet, she thus ensures herself as the commander of the orgy:

> "I bet", she said, "that I can pee into the tablecloth in front of everyone" ... Naturally, Simone did not waver for an instant, she richly soaked the tablecloth ... "Since the winner decides the penalty", said Simone to the loser, "I'm now going to pull down your trousers in front of everyone." (16)

Later, when the orgy has become more heated, her strong will to sex (and power) remains perfectly intact and even more imperative: "'Piss on me. Piss on my cunt', she repeated, with a kind of thirst" (16).

Marcelle, the Real Women of Jouissance

As the above quotes suggest, one can conclude that rather than being a woman of jouissance, paradoxically suffering from her own lust, Simone is a licentious and at the same time calculating woman of pure sexual will. The recurring figure of *the woman of jouissance*, however, *does* occur in *Story of the Eye*, and despite of all the power that Simone's willful sexuality expresses, the painful and unwilling *jouissance* incarnated in the character Marcelle seems even more powerful.

The narrator presents Marcelle as "the purest and most affecting of our friends", and, more notably as having "an unusual lack of will power" (5,12). Marcelle first meets the narrator and Simone as she accidentally witnesses them having sex on the beach. Marcelle is terrified by the sight but is forced to participate in the actions by Simone who is "brutally churning Marcelle's cunt, one arm around Marcelle's hips, the hand yanking the thigh, forcing it open" (13). From that encounter onwards, Simone and the narrator become completely obsessed with Marcelle and her unwilling lust; "the sight of Marcelle's blushing had completely overwhelmed us" (15).

Under false assumptions (a tea party), Simone and the narrator succeed in luring Marcelle to attend the above-mentioned orgy, but when Marcelle realises the true purpose of the party, she becomes angry, and in attempting to leave she is stunned by the sight of Simone who simulates a kind of orgasmic-epileptic seizure. This seems to be meant to stop the exit of Marcelle who, like the other guests, is excited by Simone's explicit show, but instead of joining the orgy, she lets herself into a large wardrobe to masturbate in private. The orgy continues but "all at once, something incredible happened, a strange swish of water, followed by a trickle and a stream from under the wardrobe door: poor Marcelle was pissing in her wardrobe while masturbating ... soon we could hear Marcelle dismally sobbing alone, louder and louder, in the makeshift pissoir that was now her prison" (17).

This scene in particular reveals Marcelle as the novella's real woman of *jouissance*, who, contrary to Simone, suffers under her lust and her failed attempt to willingly choke it back; Marcelle embodies the paradox of *jouissance*. Moreover, the unwillingness in her lust, and eventually in her orgasm, is emphasised by her involuntary urination that leaks from the wardrobe as a symbolic evidence of her failed attempt to keep her individuality from being absorbed by the shapeless orgy. As the narrator later explains: "Marcelle could come only by drenching herself ... with a spurt of urine .... at first violent and jerky like hiccups, then free and coinciding with an outburst of superhuman happiness", or "total joy", as he calls it shortly after (28). It is this superhuman moment of total joy that captivates Simone, who on the contrary is in full control of her urination and orgasm. She is, however, tragically trapped in her thirsting for this transgressive moment, because as long as she wants it, it remains unreachable; transgression depends on the defeat of will.

Escaping the Penal Colony on Bataille's Bicycle

No one has described the tragic metaphysical confinement of the will in greater detail than Schopenhauer, and the following quote might thus help in clarifying what is at stake in this important motif of *Story of the Eye*, and in Bataille's writings on eroticism in general:

> *As long as our consciousness is filled by our will, as long as we are given over to the pressure of desires with*

> *their constant hopes and fears, as long as we are the subject of willing, we will never have lasting happiness or peace. Whether we hunt or we flee, whether we fear harm or chase pleasure, it is fundamentally all the same: concern for the constant demands of the will, whatever form they take, continuously fills consciousness and keeps it in motion: but without peace, there can be no true well-being. So the subject of willing remains on the revolving wheel of Ixion, keeps drawing water from the sieve of the Danaids, is the eternally yearning Tantalus.*
> (Schopenhauer 2010, 220)

Schopenhauer also discusses at length the possibilities of escaping from this "penal colony", as he elsewhere calls the world (Schopenhauer 2000, 302), in which Simone the narrator, and the rest of us are imprisoned. While Schopenhauer's "escape attempts" all depend on a deliberate rejection of the will, primarily through asceticism, he does not address the possibility of rejecting the will unwillingly such as Marcelle practices it in *Story of the Eye*. Bataille, however, does.

In his usual dialectical manner Bataille suggests a unity of apparent opposites, *asceticism* and *eroticism*, which additionally casts light on the essential difference between the lust of Simone and that of Marcelle's. According to Bataille, both eroticism and asceticism are about "non-attachment to ordinary life, indifference to its needs, anguish felt in the midst of this until the being reels, and the way left open to a spontaneous surge of life that is usually kept under control but which bursts forth in freedom and infinite bliss" (1962, 246f). Elsewhere Bataille refers to this erotic-religious surge of life as "the feeling of being swept off one's feet, of falling headlong" (239), or rather, "to capsize", "*de chavirer*", as the original French wording goes. We find these characteristics in Marcelle and they are in stark contrast to Schopenhauer's willing subject.

Against the shared characteristics of eroticism and asceticism, Bataille places *sexual cynicism* and *obscenity*, in which Simone and the narrator are recognised. In these categories capsizing is thus an accepted principle. However, according to Bataille, the acceptance implies that the power of capsizing vanishes; capsizing becomes the new normal, and is thus weakened and unexceptional: "Having submitted unrestrainedly to the pleasure of losing self-control it has made lack of control into a constant state with neither savour nor interest" (244). On the contrary, for them (for instance Marcelle), "who have remained pure [obscenity] is the possibility of a vertiginous fall" (244). To Marcelle the fall is indeed vertiginous, and eventually even fatal. This again corresponds to Bataille's description of the conflict of the tempted ascetic, who had made his vow of chastity. If the ascetic yields to the temptation, as Marcelle does, (s)he will die spiritually, which is why "the religious would choose physical death to a lapse into temptation" (236). Marcelle's lust, and her uncontrolled, unwilling orgasm—"*la petite mort*"—thus prompts a highly vertiginous fall, which ends in unbearable madness, and finally in the real "big", physical death. Simone and the narrator's obscene lust, on the other hand, only reach la petite mort, which they ably control at will.

There is nonetheless one essential scene in the novella in which Simone's strong will is compromised, and, surprisingly, this scene also offers a remarkable perspective to the philosophy of design and technology. Escaping from a failed attempt to free Marcelle from the mental hospital, Simone and the narrator rush along naked in the night on their bicycles:

> *A leather seat clung to Simone's bare cunt, which was inevitably jerked by the legs pumping up and down on the spinning pedals ... she was literally torn away by joy, and her nude body was hurled upon an embankment with an awful scraping of steel on the pebbles and a piercing shriek.* (Bataille 1979, 30)

Through the medium of technology—on the bicycle—Simone thus eventually becomes what she constantly hankers after: she becomes Marcelle, the "real woman of *jouissance*". In this way Bataille deploys the repetitive and circular movements of technology to outplay and absorb the clear linearity of Simone's otherwise purposive will. This use, or indeed "nonuse", of technology countervails the predominant understanding of technology that sees technology as a tool that serves a specific purpose evident to the rational user in control of it. As a figure of thought, "Bataille's bicycle" thus hints to the concealed violent and erotic aspects of technology.

Becoming Marcelle

What would a contemporary version of Bataille's bicycle look like? A transgressive technology that would allow for becoming Marcelle? As an experiment, or a transgressive exploration into

Bataille's notion of eroticism as excess and the very idea of an erotic technology beyond "use", we suggest *Marcelle*.

The speculative design (Dunne and Raby 2013), *Marcelle*, uses the language of eroticism to investigate the compulsive and repetitious execution of *smooth* and *connected* bodies in networked surroundings. Bodies are executed in more and more intimate and intimidating settings, connecting emotional data and personal "things" with corporate infrastructures, closed circuits, and unpredictable networks. *Marcelle* explores the intimate aspects of network connectivity, and how the interactions between human and non-human bodies subvert and thus transgress the user's will in everyday life. Inspired by critical engineer Gordan Savičić's WiFi-connected corsage *Constraint City: The Pain of Everyday Life* (2007), *Marcelle* proposes that similar to the structural and political violence network users find in encrypted networks, the pleasure or satisfaction of being online and staying connected is an equally important affective state of today's computational culture, and an equally painful one.

The pleasure of everyday life, however, contains the same ambivalence as the notion *jouissance* does, because being online and connected is equally painful exactly because of the violent power structures of the contracts we are signing when we are deciding to enter into this life-long relationship, which is exploited by economic models and violated by normative ideologies. An Internet of bodies (as things) is a network that structures, categorizes and manages blurred and unstable relations. In each execution, relations are subjected to structures of power, control, and opaque treatment of consent and access.

As a culture-critical and partly fictional design (Bleecker 2009), *Marcelle* aims to go beyond 1990s cybersex and teledildonics and present neoliberal Internet of Things designer vibrators, in order to question *what if* eroticism becomes a restricted action, or a designerly "problem" to be solved, by applying logics of automation, efficiency, remote intimacy, and control? Presuming that we live in a computational culture of desire, could we imagine possible futures of erotic execution in the mundane everyday life beyond work, beyond the aggressive will to sex, and beyond rational, consent-driven sex? How do we discuss eroticism in an era of automation and efficiency? With this speculation, *Marcelle* seeks to transgress capitalist commodification of affects, desire and intimacy, and to question the role of eroticism in computational culture by translating invisible wireless networks into intimate vibrations.

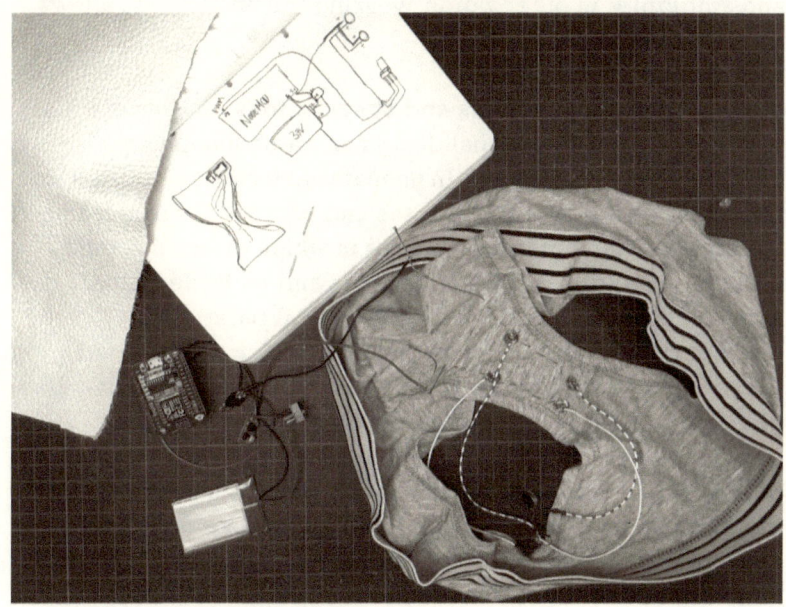

Figure 4. Paper, diagram, transistor, conductive thread, NodeMcu, battery, leather, cutting mat, wires, vibrators, networks, circuits, panties.

As previously mentioned, *Marcelle* is a wearable sex toy consisting of a pair of cotton underpants with modular vibrators that is connected to and relies on network information. As electronics (WiFi chip, battery and vibrators) are sewed directly into the mundane underpants, *Marcelle* is wearable and mobile, and the user can wear it in everyday life situations. The vibrators are made of transparent silicone fastened on popper buttons that may be connected at four different positions in the panties. This makes the sex toy modular, and the user is able to customize it to their own erotic and sexual needs and desires. However, the user cannot easily control the vibration patterns whose impulses are controlled by the number of surrounding WiFi networks. For instance, a space with a variety of different, competing networks, maybe a semi-public space with a variety of social groups and activities, triggers a very high intensity, whereas a private space with one superior network only causes the vibrators to vibrate with a low intensity. As such, the user delegates the control of the vibrators' intensity and rhythm to the networked landscape of autonomous networks, which makes for a partly unwilling, erotic experience characterized by spontaneity, opaqueness, and ambiguity. In other words: wearing the underpants allows the user to become Marcelle.

(Design) Fictions and Speculations on Eroticism
Marcelle is a partly fictional design and a philosophical argument in physical form. In its material form, it is present in the actual world, but the premises and narratives surrounding the object point to possible futures in which eroticism could be different and exist in simultaneous and multiple forms. *Marcelle* is *not* a solution to the theoretical paradox of involuntary eroticism or eroticism as excess in a restricted (desire) economy. Neither is it a clear manifestation of Bataille's philosophy, or a technological design ready-to-use. It is a partly fictional design that through a dialogue with Bataille's philosophical and literary writings on eroticism goes beyond eroticism as a theoretical construct, to speculate on the issues of excess, unwillingness, and abjection in a material form. It might indeed be used, but its user is yet to be defined, or more precisely, yet to be *performed.*

The excess of vibrations felt when wearing *Marcelle* and walking around, surrounded by WiFi networks is not exactly useful. The uncontrollable amount and intensity of the vibrations is useless compared to the purposeful will that gets pleased by the mechanical and effective s(t)imulations of conventional sex toys. Instead of being executed by the vibrator algorithms, reaching orgasm as a purposeful willing user, the wearer is exposed to the compulsive and repetitive vibrations, which, although increasing and decreasing in intensity, never end. The vibrations only end if the wearer, like Marcelle hiding in the wardrobe, takes refuge in an environment without WiFi, and in our present wireless psychopathology this seems almost unthinkable. Instead, the purposive will gets challenged, possibly transgressed, in this state of execution where neither lust nor desire is executed or relieved but instead lingers in between eroticism and asceticism. Wearing *Marcelle* might thus be compared to participating in an orgy, in which individuality—that is, the individual body and the individual will—dissolves and becomes uncountable. The wearer does not know exactly who, what and how many (s)he is having sex with in this anonymous WiFi-orgy.

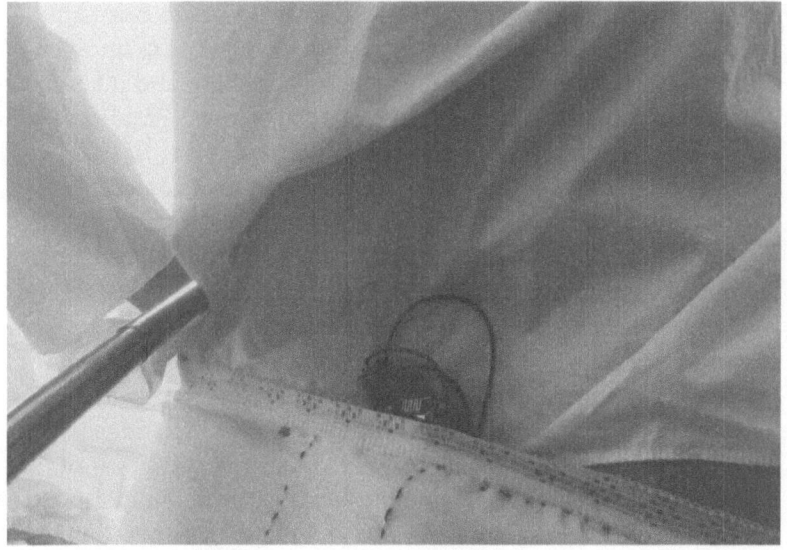

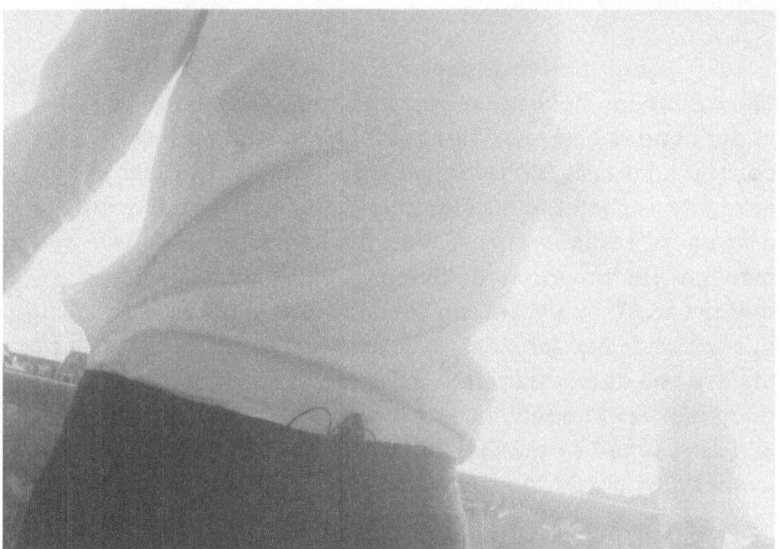

Figure 5 and 6. The jouissance of becoming Marcelle in wearing *Marcelle*.

When wearing *Marcelle*, consent means to not be in control of your own body and desire. The purpose of wearing it becomes ambiguous, as the outcome is unpredictable and out of control. Thus, when you enter the "experience" you do so with the implicit acknowledgement of not knowing the outcome, and consequently it is questionable whether or not the action actually has an aim, or stays inside the fixed boundaries of consent. This opens up onto a temporal space of permanent, involuntary execution, where the unpredictability and instability enables, if not presupposes, that the wearer elaborates on the emotional impulses and surrender oneself to the non-human activities reaching one's lower erogenous zones. A truly excessive activity without purpose outside the eroticism of the act itself, the *jouissance of becoming* Marcelle in *wearing Marcelle* first and foremost arises, not in the execution of desire, but in the affective experience of unwillingness, of transgressing the will.

Just as Simone *becoming* the real woman of *jouissance* depended on the "nonuse" of technology, *Marcelle* seeks to move beyond the critique of disembodied artificial sex — of "using" technology as inter-human sex mediator — and towards the potential of relational erotic (be)coming together of human and non-human beings.

Conjunctive Bodies

The distinction between eroticism and sexuality, as it is understood in how eroticism is treated in contemporary computing is first and foremost highlighted in its focus on sexuality as something belonging to the intellectual world; a "truth" of sexuality that is controllable and essentially manageable through individual free will. Following affect theorist and feminist Lauren Berlant's notion of cruel optimism, this scientific and Western understanding of eroticism may be understood as a cruel relation (Berlant 2011). The desire for "the good life" is inherently a *fantasy* of the good life, proclaimed and envisioned by culture, including visions that have been invented by corporate and commercial industry to market their products. It is a cruel optimism because it is an obstacle to our flourishing. In other words, we are *not* getting closer to the "optimum" by tracking our sex life or buying products that simulate how to provoke a female orgasm. These are *happy objects* (Ahmed 2004) directing us towards a very particular kind of eroticism; an ordinary state of desire-liberation that does not lead to excessive eroticism, but proceeds as a dulling, chronic condition of excitation without release. Too little time to feel, too little time to get to know one (others') body/bodies, but endless amounts of apps and designed sex toys to teach and manage the user's sexuality. This smooth, connected, happy state of bodies, where eroticism is commodified and sex only happens for a reason, is what we have aimed to transgress in the design of *Marcelle*. Hopefully, it moves closer to the state of *conjunctive* bodies without indulging in a sentimental, embodied lingering for a pure state of desire. Instead it seeks to transgress human sexuality itself in technologically-mediated erotic experiences that are uncontrollable, unpredictable and ultimately unstable. That is, erotic experiences where subjects and objects co-evolve, dissolve and become abject.

Consumption of Bodies (or, a critique of economic notions of eroticism)

The demands of eroticism, the exuberant energy that flows in computational processes are both subjected to and withdrawing from productive consumption and emotional labour. What Bataille would not know in his novella *Story of the Eye*, as well as in his anti-capitalist writings of eroticism as excess, was that eroticism and intimacy became increasingly (also) executed through technology and software, and as such necessarily exchanged and given form. Consequently, eroticism has, like most intimate aspects of living, potentially become just another action of purpose and exchange-value.

In this essay, we have aimed to revisit and actualize Bataille's notion of eroticism in contemporary computational culture, firstly to revisit if and how the transgression of the will is in evidence in present emotional states of desiring subjects and their use of sex technology. Secondly, to speculate on how the violent and liberating potentials of eroticism may be a challenge for design.

Highly inspired by the character Marcelle, and the overlooked but truly exceptional status of the erotic technology in *Story of the Eye*—the bicycle—we have proposed that *Marcelle* embodies and manifests the philosophical, theoretical paradox of eroticism, as well as the material and bodily emotional state of present connected and desiring bodies. As we have shown, eroticism of execution, as in the case of *Marcelle*, is a complex, excessive experience that both includes aspects of unwillingness, transgression of prohibitions or taboos and repetitious and continuous (unreleased) desire, in an even more complex fusion of interactions between human and non-human beings of network users, protocols, electromagnetic waves and erogenous zones of the body.

References

Ahmed, Sara. 2004. *The Cultural Politics of Emotion*. First Edition edition. New York: Routledge.

Barthes, Roland. [1963] 1979. "The Metaphor of the Eye." In *Story of the Eye*, Trans. Joachim Neugroschel, 119–27. London: Penguin Books.

Bataille, Georges. [1928] 1979. *Story of the Eye*. Trans. Joachim Neugroschel. London: Penguin Books.

———. [1957] 1962. *Erotism: Death and Sensuality*. Trans. Mary Dalwood. San Francisco: City Lights Publishers.

———. 1991. The Accursed Share: An Essay on General Economy, Vol. 1: Consumption. 1st edition. New York: Zone Books.

———. 1993. *The Accursed Share, Vols. 2 and 3: The History of Eroticism and Sovereignty*. Reprint edition. New York: Zone Books.

Berardi, Franco. 2009. *Precarious Rhapsody: Semiocapitalism & the Pathologies of the Post-Alpha Generation*. London; Brooklyn, N.Y.: Minor Compositions.

Berlant, Lauren. 2011. *Cruel Optimism*. Durham: Duke University Press Books.

Bleecker, Julian. 2009. "Design Fiction: A Short Essay on Design, Science, Fact and Fiction." March. http://drbfw5wfjlxon.cloudfront.net/writing/DesignFiction_WebEdition.pdf

Dunne, Anthony, and Fiona Raby. 2013. *Speculative Everything: Design, Fiction, and Social Dreaming*. Cambridge, Mass.: The MIT Press.

Evans, Dylan. 2002. *An Introductory Dictionary of Lacanian Psychoanalysis*. New York: Routledge.

Foucault, Michel. 1990. *The History of Sexuality, Vol. 1: An Introduction*. Translated by Robert Hurley. Reissue edition. New York: Vintage.

Haraway, Donna. 1991. "A Cyborg Manifesto: Science, Technology, and Socialist-Feminism in the Late Twentieth Century." In *Simians, Cyborgs, and Women*. New York: Routledge.

Kristeva, Julia. 1982. *Powers of Horror: An Essay on Abjection*. Reprint edition. New York: Columbia University Press.

Lacan, Jacques. [1973] 1978. *The Four Fundamental Concepts of Psychoanalysis*. Trans. Alan Sheridan. London: W. W. Norton & Company.

Morozov, Evgeny. 2014. *To Save Everything, Click Here: The Folly of Technological Solutionism*. First Trade Paper Edition edition. New York: PublicAffairs.

Noys, Benjamin. 2000. *Georges Bataille: A Critical Introduction*. London: Pluto Press.

Plant, Sadie. 1997. *Zeroes and Ones: Digital Women and the New Technoculture*. 1st edition. New York: Doubleday.

Schopenhauer, Arthur. [1819] 2010. *The World as Will and Representation, Vol. I*. Trans. Judith Norman, Alistar Welchman, and Christopher Janaway. Cambridge: Cambridge University Press.

———. [1851] 2000. *Parerga and Paralipomena, Vol. II*. Trans. by E. F. J. Payne. New York: Oxford University Press.

Steffensen, Jyanni. 1998. "Slimy Metaphors for Technology: 'The Clitoris Is a Direct Line to the Matrix.'" Durham, North Carolina: Duke University. http://www.mujeresenred.net/spip.php?article1538.

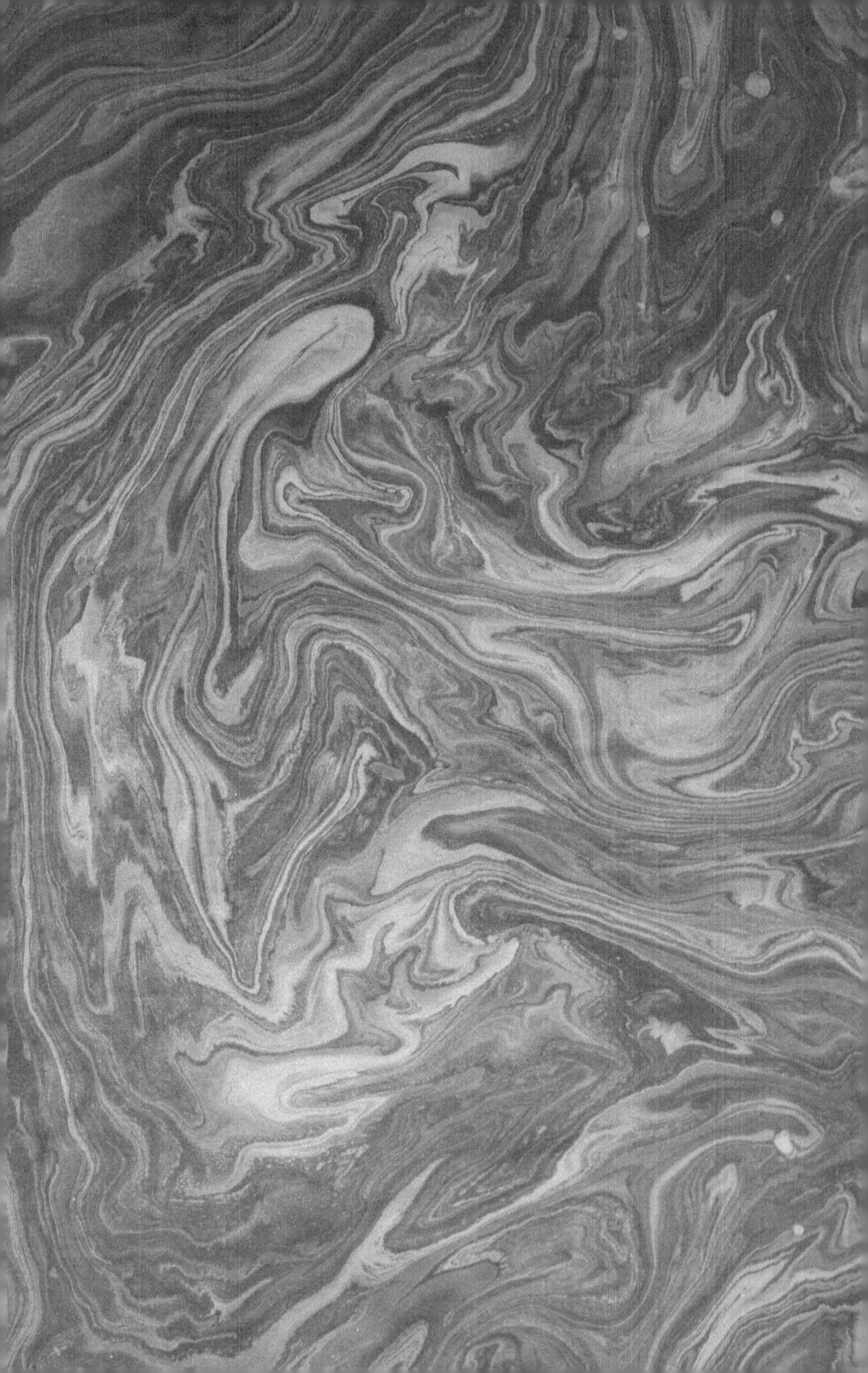

```
// The Chance Execution
// Olle Essvik

/* ***** Marbling******
 The colour floating on the water surface,
the resulting pattern, governed by
movements, temperature and dosage. The
marbler's mood and state of mind on a
specific day. A certain difference is
unavoidable. The marbled paper dries.
*/

int    paper_x= 827;
int    paper_y= 1169;
int    water = 149006;
float paint;

/* I look at a picture representing Ken
Perlin. It was Ken Perlin who created the
algorithm that aims to remove the
computerized - a certain graphical and
mechanical appearance in digital images -
and instead emulate nature's seeming
chaotic complexity. The algorithm was
created in 1983 and there are several
pictures on the Internet of Ken Perlin. Ken
in  different ages, photographs in
different resolutions, formats and graphics.
I use Perlin noise and begin typing a code
inspired by marbled papers.
*/

/* An auction in the north of Sweden, held
on the outskirts of a medium-sized Swedish
town.
```

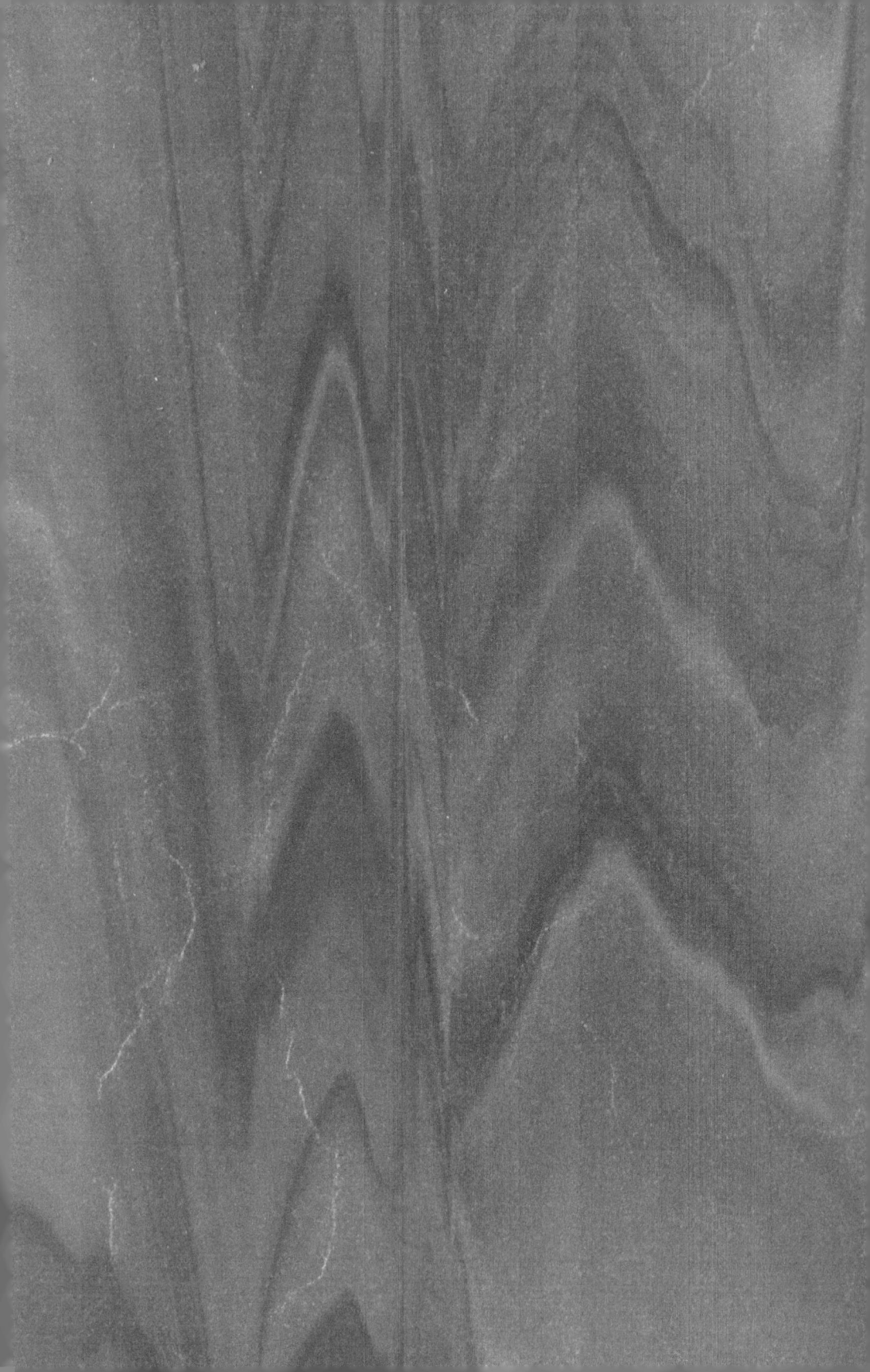

I make my bids online. The bookbinder died and the son did not take over. The bindery is auctioned off in batches. Hot foil stamping machines, lead types and tools. A coffee maker next to bone folders, book cloth and paper.

I make a bid for one of the larger boxes, containing paper used for front- and endpaper covers. A green filing cabinet with 12 drawers, each filled with marbled papers. Thousands of papers. Most of the papers in the drawer are endpapers. The part that holds together the pages of the book with the front and the back. Uniquely marbled in different colours and styles. Industrial papers produced in larger editions with patterns that appear identical. /*

/* One box for leftover papers. The trace of the second paper, it's shape and the execution in the piece left behind. This is the content of the box in front of me. The papers the bookbinder did not choose. */

/* I'm looking for a picture of the bookbinder on the internet, I find nothing except a name in a database for genealogy. An algorithm searching for names and family bonds following a certain order. */

```
int    marblers_mode=0;
float movement;
float surfaceTension;
```

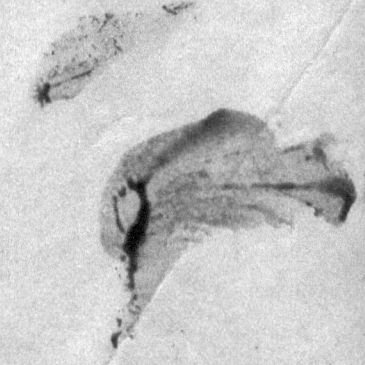

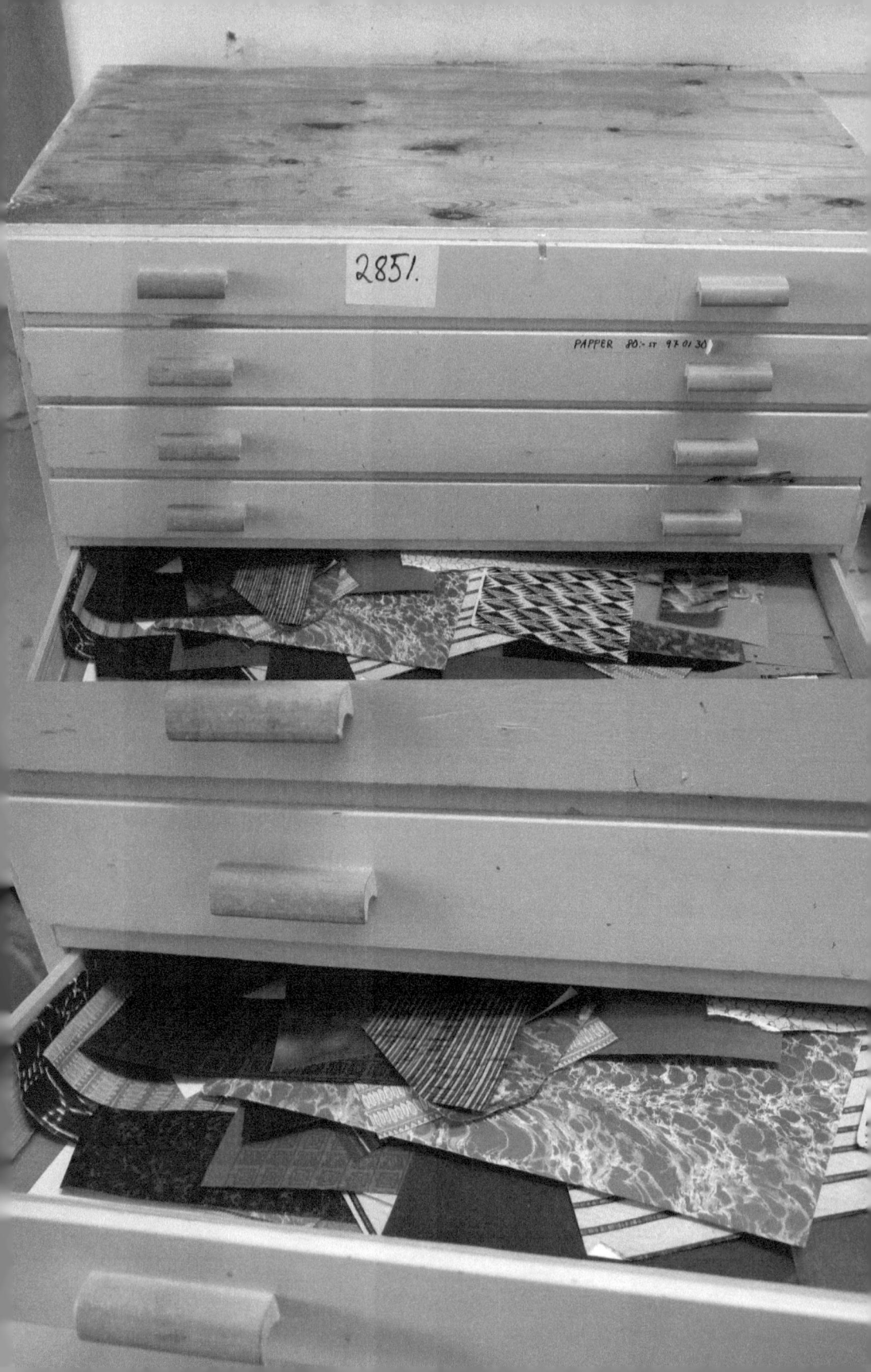

```
int Countress3491;
PVector[] UllaSievert = new PVector[water];
PVector[] DistrictJudge = new PVector[
water];
PVector[] kenPerlin = new PVector[water];

/* The papers in the drawers carry few
traces, apart from the occasional name, the
odd title, a price.

Counteress 3491
Ulla Sievert.
District Judge
Anna
15:-

*/
float bookbinder = random(0, 255);
float lavaLamp = random(0, 255);
float radioNoise = random(0, 255);

float genealogy = random(1)-4;
float anna = random(1)-4;

float mx = map(1, 10, paper_x, genealogy,
anna);
float my = map(1, 10, paper_y, anna,
genealogy);
void setup() {
size(827, 1169, P2D);

for(Countress3491 = 0; Countress3491 <
water; Countress3491++) {
```

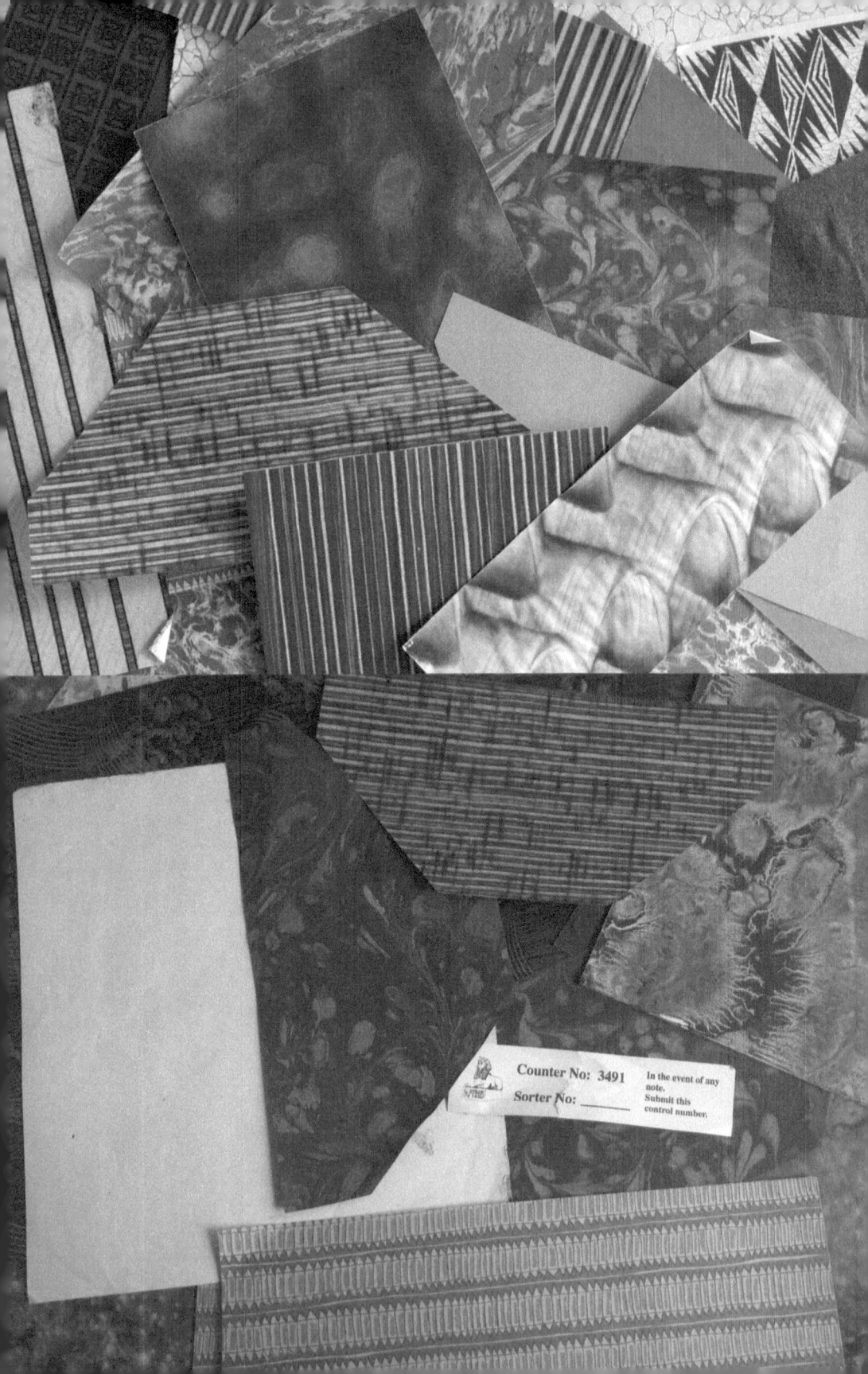

```
    UllaSievert[Countress3491]
= new PVector(random(0, paper_x), random(0,
paper_y));
        DistrictJudge[Countress3491] = new
PVector(random(0, paper_x), random(0,
paper_y));
        kenPerlin[Countress3491] = new
PVector(random(0, paper_x), random(0,
paper_y));
    }       }

/* I find a note that reads "counteress no.
"3491", and picture a person behind that
number, someone, long ago, counting papers.
Someone with a family name who counted
paper, based on given instructions and
systems. But countress 3491 could also be
the name of a machine. */

void draw() {
float paper = movement;
for (int x = 0; x < paper_x; x++) {
float marblers = surfaceTension;

for (Countress3491 = 0; Countress3491 <
paper_y; Countress3491++) {
float r = map(noise(paper, marblers), 0, 1,
0, bookbinder);
float g = map(noise(marblers, paper), 0, 1,
0, lavaLamp);
float b = map(noise(paper, marblers, paper),
0, 1, 0, radioNoise);
loadPixels();
pixels[x+Countress3491*paper_x] = color
```

```
(r, g, b);
marblers += -pow(5, my) - pow(5, -5*noise(-
paper, marblers)); }
paper += -pow(5, mx) + -pow(5, -5*noise(
paper, paper));}
loadPixels();
```

/* A profession that no longer exists and
has been replaced by algorithms and
machines. Counteress 3491 is numbers, an
unknown note.
Having examined all the papers I get a
headache. I am the first person to take these
papers out, after decades in the dark. /*

/* I gather up the papers, one of each kind,
in large stacks. I keep them in the same
order as in the drawers. The bindery had
been around for a long time; several of the
papers are at least 50 years old. The pile
has been growing gradually and the oldest is
right at the bottom. They follow a certain
order. */

```
updatePixels();

   for (  paint=0; paint<=60000; paint+=0.1)
  {
     stroke(0, 0, 0,random(15));
     ellipse(paint,random(1600),ra
dom(1),random(1));
  }

float noisy = 0;
```

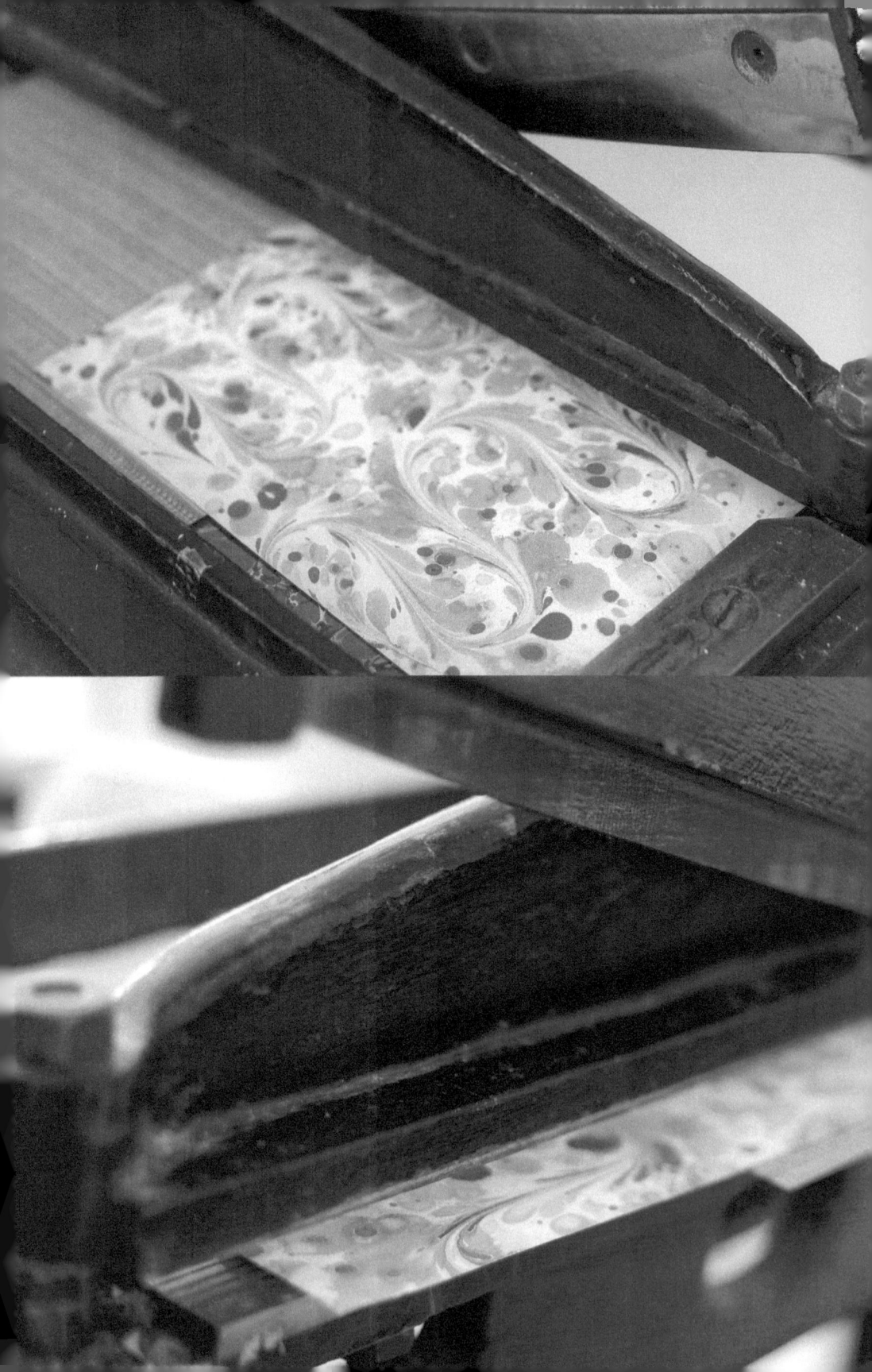

```
for(marblers_mode = 0; marblers_mode <
water; marblers_mode++) { stroke(lavaLamp,
radioNoise, bookbinder, 45);
      point(UllaSievert[marblers_mode].x,
UllaSievert[marblers_mode].y);
      DistrictJudge[marblers_mode].x
= 20*noise(400+UllaSievert[marblers_
mode].x*.0007, 400+UllaSievert[marblers_
mode].y*.0007, noisy*2)*cos(4*PI*noise(
UllaSievert[marblers_mode].x*.007,
UllaSievert[marblers_mode].y*.007,
noisy*.5));
      DistrictJudge[marblers_mode].y =
10*noise(UllaSievert[marblers_mode].x*.0007,
400+UllaSievert[marblers_mode].y*.0007,
noisy*2)*sin(4*PI*noise(UllaSievert[
marblers_mode].x*.007, UllaSievert[marblers_
mode].y*.007, noisy*.5));
      UllaSievert[marblers_mode].add(
DistrictJudge[marblers_mode]);   }}
```

/* I press a button on the website and
receive a random number between 1 and 100.
I can see the number, but the number is
not evidence that the algorithm does what
it says it claims. I press the button five
times: 3, 9, 4, 71, 1. */

/* Silicon Graphics once used a lava lamp to
generate chance for the computer, and
published the random numbers on their
website. The Lava lamp principle is to blend
two immiscible liquids. Not dissimilar to the
looks and techniques of marbling. */

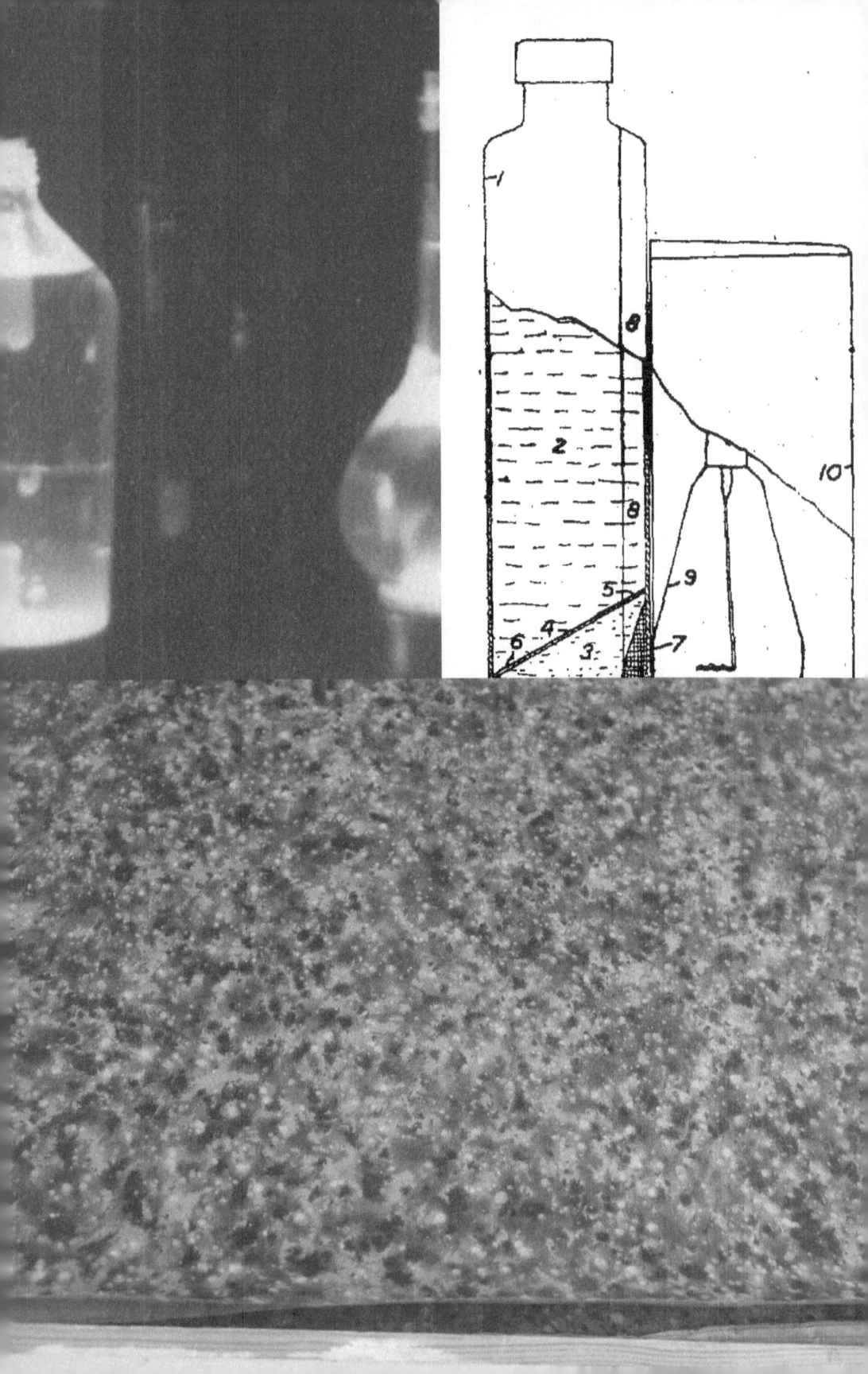

```
/* I glue the papers. With gauze I attach
the coded endpapers in the end and beginning
of the book with the endpapers found in the
drawer. Leftover papers from the chance
execution. Beginning and end of a book. The
pages that you never read. */

void keyPressed() {
  switch(key) {
  case ' ':
    setup();
    break;
  case 's':
    int m = (int)millis();
    save("pattern"+str(m)+".jpg");
    break;
  default:
    println("unknown key");
    break;
  }}

/*Olle Essvik, under Creative Commons
Attribution ShareAlike https://creativecommons.
org/licenses/by-sa/3.0 adapted and inspired by
2D Perlin noise example from Dan Shiffman's Na-
ture of Code  and  http://www.openprocessing.
org/sketch/157579. The text is from the book
The Chance Execution, Olle Essvik, rojal press.
*/
```

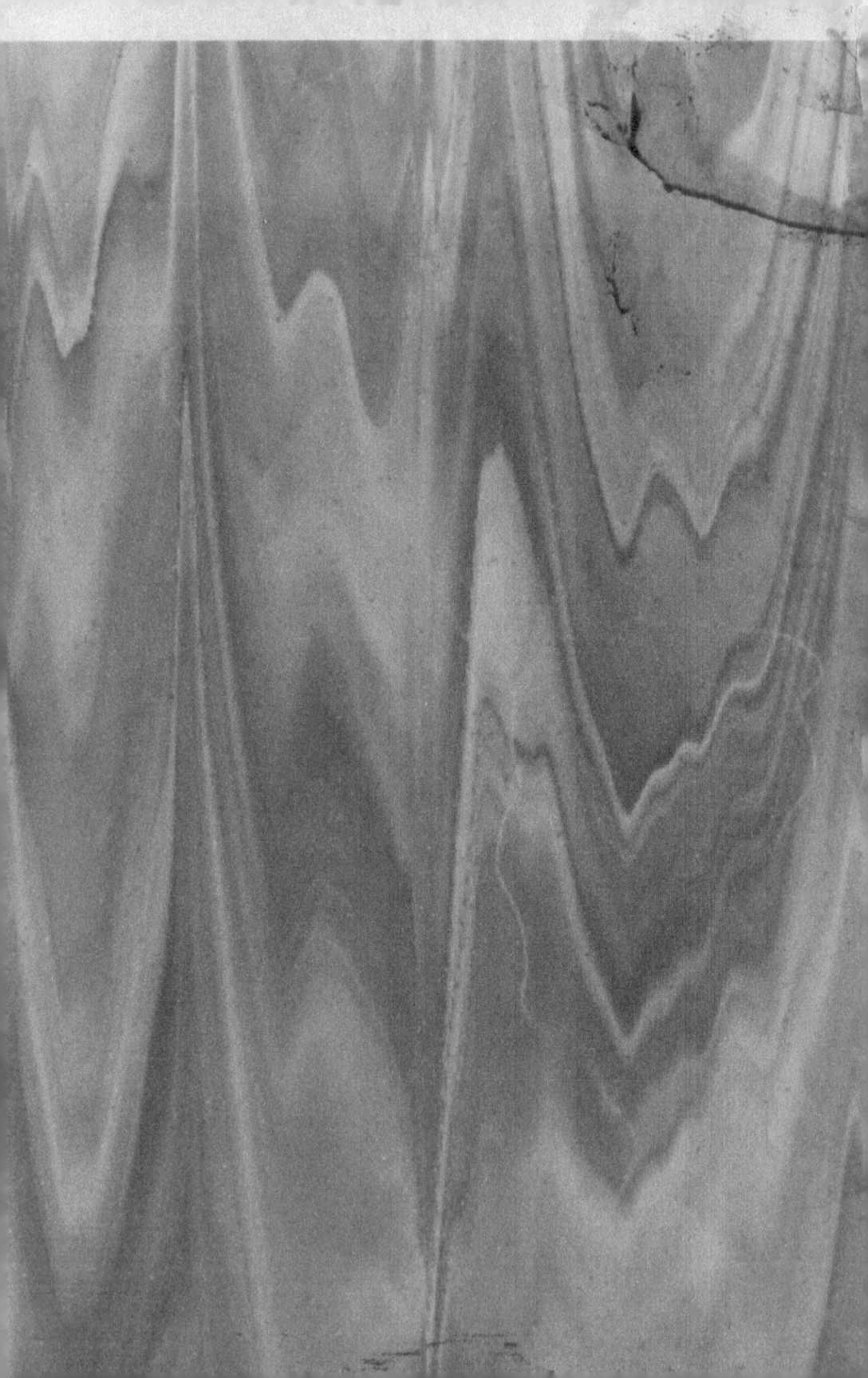

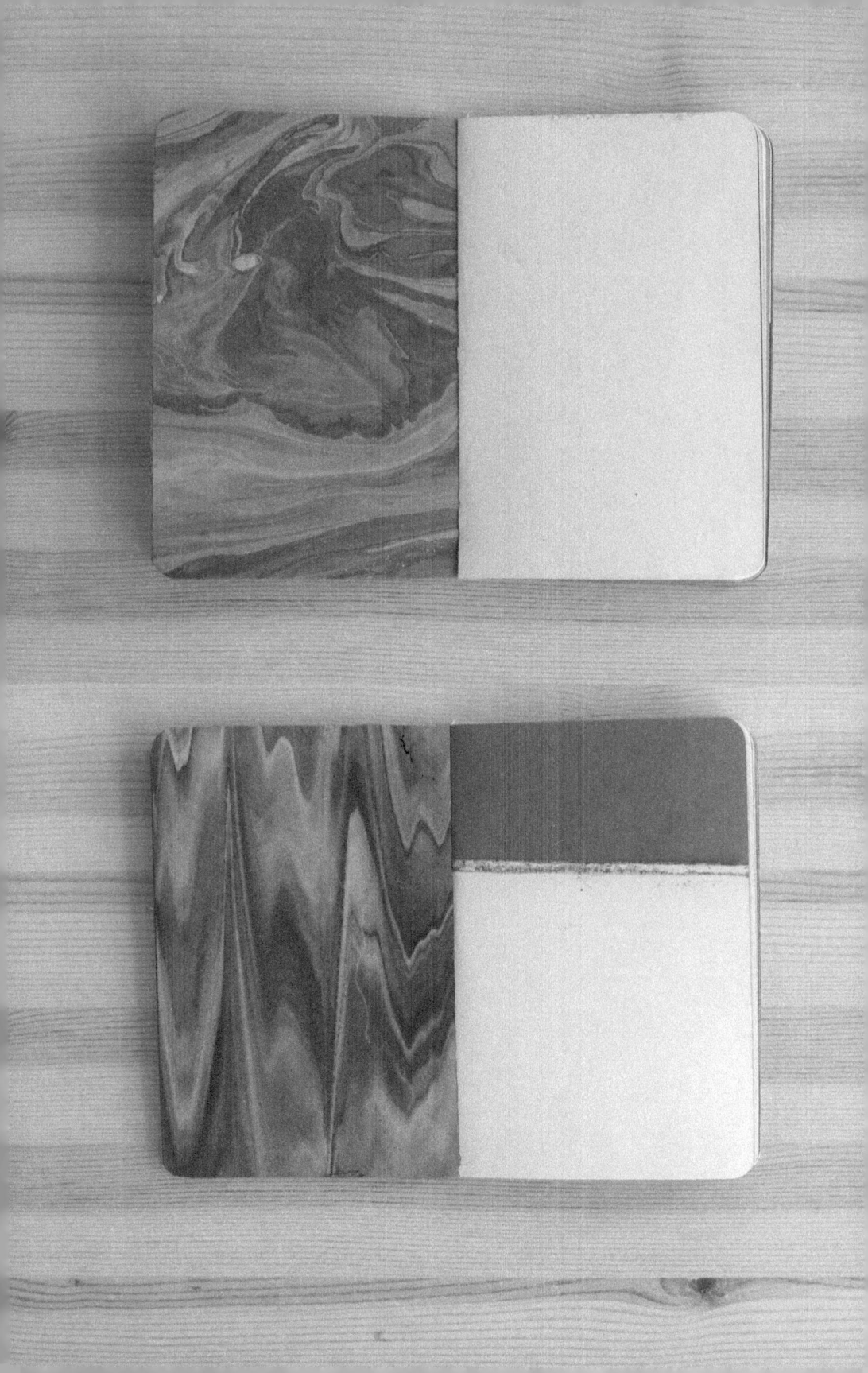

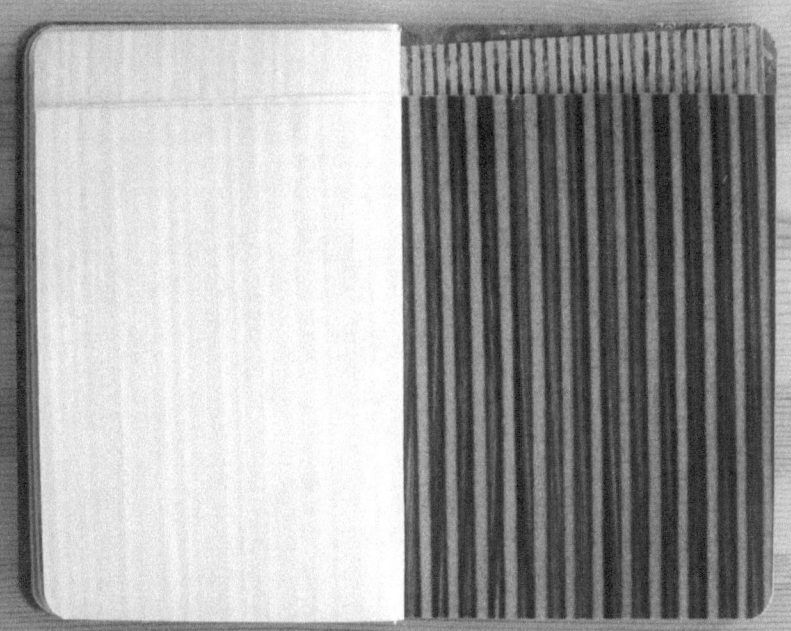

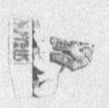

Counter No: 3491

Sorter No: ————

In the event of any note, Submit this control number.

the chance execution

What is Executing Here?

Eric Snodgrass

Instruction Pointer

Execution. The act of carrying out a set of instructions.

Execution. The act of carrying out a set of instructions in a step by step fashion.

Execution. The automated act of cycling through a set of machine-readable instructions in a step by step fashion.

Execution. The automated act of cycling through a set of machine-readable instructions (logically encoded character-chains fetched from stored-program memory) in a step by step fashion (making calls upon the memory for relevant operators and storing any resultant operands back in memory).

Execution. The automated act of cycling sequentially (in a time coordinated process) through a set of machine-readable instructions (logically encoded character-chains fetched from stored-program memory) in a step by step fashion (making calls upon the memory for relevant operators and storing any resultant operands back in memory), whereby any actions are made effectively decidable (capable of being interpreted by a logical decoder) according to the parameters of the active instruction set.

Execution. The automated act of cycling sequentially (in a time coordinated process determined via a pulse whose period is established by a phase distributor) through a set of machine-readable instructions (logically encoded character-chains fetched from stored-program memory and placed in the executing command circuits) in a step by step fashion (making calls upon the memory for relevant operators and storing any resultant operands back in memory), whereby any actions are made effectively decidable (capable of being interpreted by a logical decoder whose signals address the instruction pointer to the component on which the instruction operates) according to the parameters of the active instruction set and repeating such cycles for as long as they continue to remain effectively decidable or until there are no more instructions to execute (the instruction pointer points to the end of the instruction sequence).

Marks

shift.

Perched at the verge of some low-hanging brush or on a leaf's edge: the tick. Dwelling in all of its alien personhood, this "blind and deaf bandit" (von Uexküll 2010, 45) of the outdoors passes days, months, even years in wait of a single blood meal. Charged. Alert. Questing a world of its particular accord.

Still, a few actions on its part direct themselves to certain devotees of pattern recognition. Writing in 1934, Baltic German biophilosopher Jakob Johann Baron von Uexküll shares one such notable and oft-cited consideration of the tick's mode of being in the world. In this account, von Uexküll highlights what he distinguishes as three particular "functional cycles" that are initialised within the tick's being. These functional cycles are triggered at the first (perhaps all-enveloping) detection of butyric acid, an odour promiscuously emitted by the skin glands of all mammals and for which the tick, like many other animals, is highly attuned to:

> *And now something miraculous happens… From the enormous world surrounding the tick, three stimuli glow like signal lights in the darkness and serve as directional signs that lead the tick surely to its target… Through these features, the progression of the tick's actions is so strictly prescribed that the tick can only produce very determinate effect marks.*
> (von Uexküll 2010, 51)

In von Uexküll's hypothesis, such functional cycles are activated within the subjective environments of the "perception world" and their co-constitutive productive counterparts from the "effect world". Any nominally organic being is able to receive perceptive stimuli (via its particular array of perception organs) from certain objects in its environment and form "perception marks" (*Merkmal*) that highlight these stimuli as potential matters of concern. Such perception marks are closely related to the particular forms of functional ability on the entity's part to potentially act upon these perception marks by enacting further "effect marks" (*Wirkmal*) of one form or another upon them. As von Uexküll highlights, these stimuli are not qualities of the object itself, but instead are forms of what, in the context of this essay, might be described as interfacial affinities between the perceiving being in question and the structural makeup of the perceived entity in question. It is sense making that von Uexküll is interested in and, as he characterises it, the perception mark can be understood as a question posed by the perceived object and the effect mark as the perceiving subject's answer to this question. Namely, how does the being in question make sense of and act in relation to the perceptual signs that make up its environment? One further note of interest here is how the eventual enactment and imprinting of an effect mark is, to one degree or another, transformative in regards to the perceived object in question—namely in that it "extinguishes" the perception mark (49). It executes the functional cycle in question, answering the question and making room for other executable queries and actions.

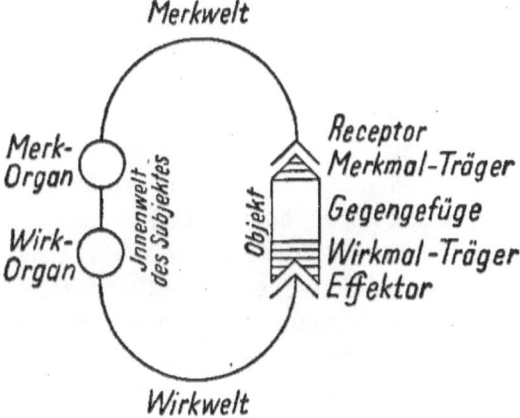

Figure 1. Functional cycle of a tick. Drawing by Georg Kriszat, in von Uexküll & Kriszat (1934, 27).

According to such a scheme, a tick is known to act on an initial perception mark of butyric acid by launching itself from its perch and, in the case of a successful landing, is able to impress onto the mammal's surface exterior the effect mark "collision". This in turn allows for an erasing of the initial perception mark while also initiating a new functional cycle in which the tick sets off across the hirsute expanse of its mammalian host, relying on its further sensitivity to temperature to detect the perception mark of a bare patch of pulsing, warm-blooded skin. A sign that for this bloodborne practitioner of hematophagy is quite possibly a mark of marks; an event on which to execute the climatic third act of piercing a hole in the host's epidermis, the tick inserting its harpoon-like hypostome into the skin of its receiver. An interfacing not only of parasite and host, but of mutually executable materials, the layer of skin and calcified hypostome readily enveloping one another in an embrace that takes little note of consequences to their host organisms. Indeed, "[t]he tick's hearty blood meal is also its last meal" (45).

As von Uexküll describes it, "[f]iguratively speaking, every animal subject attacks its objects in a pincer movement—with one perceptive and one effective arm" (48–9). These perception and effect worlds are not separate, but rather "form one closed unit". This is what von Uexküll calls the *Umwelt*: the subjectively experienced lifeworld whose perceptible and executable qualities inform the experiences of the subject in question. As von Uexküll emphasises throughout his text, in such a schema recursively identifiable subjects and objects interact in a generative fashion, perceiving and bringing forth perceptive-effective marks and their rhythms and melodies of interaction from the interlinked perceptions and effects that arise within what is at one and the same time a collection of subjectively distinct yet cellular and mutually impinging gatherings of Umwelts. With such a relatively simple abstract functional schema in place, von Uexküll's biosemiotic method is ostensibly able to breakdown the most complex or basic[1] of animal Umwelts. Its robust, pincer-like binding able to unpack the functional cycles and material discursive Umwelt of seemingly any entity of its choice.

WHAT IS EXECUTING HERE?

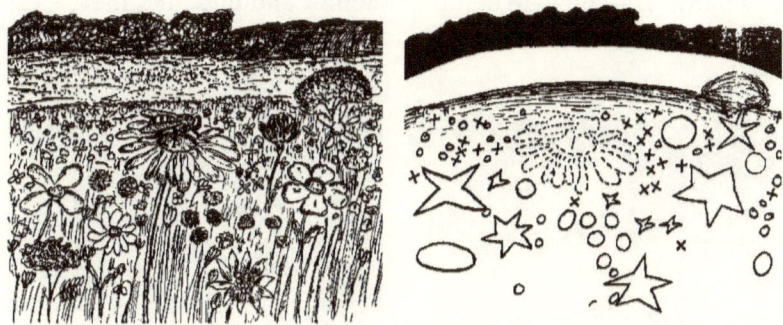

Figure 2. Surrounding environment of a bee and the same environment as experienced in the bee's own perceptual Umwelt. Drawing by Kriszat, in von Uexküll & Kriszat (1934, 59).

Questions around interpretation are inevitably a central point of discussion for most disciplinary endeavours. In the early twentieth century however, as witnessed in much of the key work emerging in fields such as linguistics, mathematics, physics and the arts (e.g. Dada), the question of interpretation can be seen to become a particularly pressing and formative one. Writing in the very same period as von Uexküll, Alan Turing, in his paper "On Computable Numbers, with an Application to the *Entscheidungsproblem*" (1937), was able to formalise his breakthrough description of computation and a sketch of its practical application in the form of a "universal machine". As with von Uexküll's functional cycle, there is a pincer-like quality all of its own in Turing's formulation.[2] Georges Ifrah captures it as follows, "The real genius of Turing's invention is the fact that he invented both the abstract form of a revolutionary device and the mathematical concept which allowed the device to be analysed: the theory and its application were unified from the outset. It is as if Archimedes had invented the principle of the lever and the lever itself at the same moment" (Ifrah 2001, 278-9). Where von Uexküll would regularly (and with much delight) mock behaviourist "machine theorists" and their habit of turning animals "into pure objects" (2010, 42), Turing's formulation highlights a rather decisive and powerful vitality of this particular machine by showing its inbuilt potential to recursively be both an object and subject of its method of discretely defined operations. In the place of the functional cycle, the many fetch-decode-execute cycles of computing machines, bootstrapping themselves from one hardware-software setup to another and injecting their interpretations into this or that collection of executable entities.

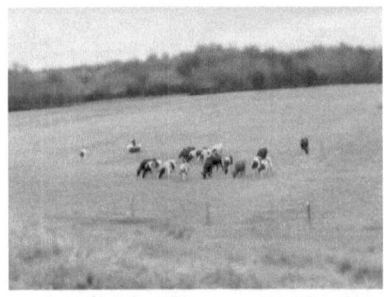 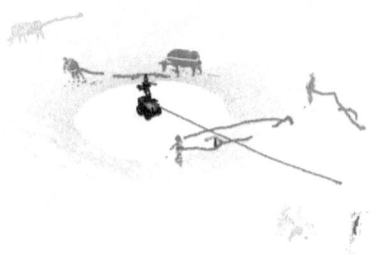

Figure 3. Stills from "A robot amongst the herd" video by the Australian Centre for Field Robotics (2013), portraying a pilot investigation regarding the behavioural response of dairy cows to a robot.
https://www.youtube.com/watch?v=S4Dndp-Esd8.

These theories of von Uexküll and Turing, as well as those of the likes of Kurt Gödel and Niels Bohr before them, bring to life powerful models of interpretation and execution. The notions of constraining sensorial or computational limits that they highlight can be understood as being generative in nature, as incitements towards further queries and inventive responses to dynamic lifeworlds as they present themselves at any particular instance. As Elizabeth Grosz describes it in her own reading of von Uexküll, an organism's milieu "is an ongoing provocation", with an organism's own existence as a co-constituted "provisional response to that provocation" (2008, 44). At the same time, these theories involve what might be seen as a rather leaky form of unification: namely, that for any formalist discursive endeavour there will inevitably exist truths that are not accessible by the same system that implies them. Just as the machine cannot read and write code at the same instant, formalisation here comes up against a kind of tantalising gap between its expression and execution, just as its discrete makeup is itself contingent upon a continuous flux and iterability of things (Mackenzie 2006, 36–7).

In the very undecidability of their nature, such theories and their actualisations point to a generative power of execution as it continually churns across a spectrum of interactions. Its ongoing moulding and puncturing of Umwelts that indicates towards discourse as materially oriented and materiality as subject to its own ability to be marked and formed. An interfacing and marking of bodies upon one another. The forcing or mere leaking of energies of interaction across materials, systems, flows, Umwelts. And in the process, the potential reconfigurations or coalescings of newly fused ensembles and ecologies of the executable that emerge from such interactions. Execution breeds execution.

(Skins, Bodies, Tapes, Sites ...)

shift.

As media theorist Friedrich Kittler (2006) highlights in his writing on the introduction in the early 1980s and then regular inclusion of what was termed as a "protected mode" feature within what is the still common x86 family of instruction set architectures,[3] logics of enclosure have a way of becoming immanent throughout media discourse networks. Here the enclosing logic in question is the implementation of a built-in restriction that further removes users from the real mode[4] of ostensibly full access to a computer's "original" Von Neumann architecture.[5] Protected mode style features, typically referred to as executable space protection, can be implemented in a variety of ways. In the example that Kittler is referring to, it is a technique applied within CPUs to segregate areas of memory by marking them as non-executable, such that an attempt to execute machine code in these regions will cause an exception. The NX bit ("No-eXecute") is one example of this. Thus, in contrast to such a segregated system of restricted access, in real mode a user should ostensibly be able to access and address all areas of the memory without any protection mechanism being employed.

In an ongoing series of experimental works, artist Martin Howse interrogates the nature of computational enclosures, with their "separation of users and of their desires and affects" (2013a). Howse is specifically interested in how, through the establishing of such enclosures, "[t]he possibility of transferring execution outside these sets of containers or black boxes into the world is resolutely denied" (2013a). Many of Howse's works can be seen to highlight a key question to be addressed with regards to the nature of computation in the world. As Howse characterises it in an interview discussion:

One question I'm very interested in which you could say fuels my research is to ask where exactly software executes. Where exactly do these seemingly abstract coded processes which seriously effects our lives, where do these take place? At first it seems simple, somewhere inside this machine or black box, a laptop, a smartphone, but looking at it closer there's no easy answer. And I feel that this answer has to do with our skin and the Earth. (Howse, in Sayej 2013)

For Howse (with a direct nod in his notes to J. G. Ballard's *Crash*), one method or exploit for triggering a reacquaintance with the fault lines of such a question is the act of shifting the site of an executable process from its typical or stabilised domain to a less typical, less stable one. To this end, he carries out a range of experiments that work to shift computational sites of execution into "new material (data), outside the particular confines of a trusted and identifiable process or skin" (Howse 2013a). Beyond simply shifting the site of execution, Howse can also be seen in these works to be continually foraging for and repurposing such shifted arrangements towards alternative conceptions and sites of the executable. Looking at almost any of Howse's projects, a lingering question can be seen to take hold: *What is executing here?*

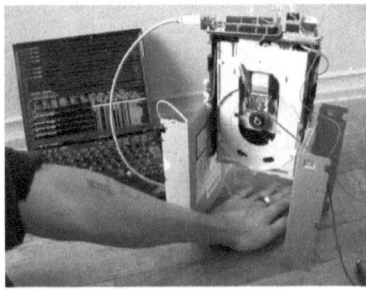 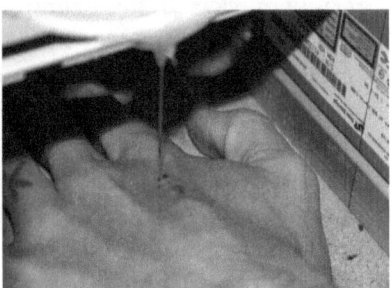

Figure 4. Martin Howse's *pain registers* (2011). Images courtesy of the artist 2016.

The above images (Figure 4) are from documentations of Howse demonstrating the workings of his piece *pain registers* (2011), which uses the ptrace()[6] system call to make readings of the opcodes (operational codes). Opcodes are the portions of machine language instructions in an instruction set architecture that specify the operation to be executed by a processor (e.g. an operation might be "read", "write", "add", "jump", etc.). In Howse's characterisation of them, opcodes are the "bare logical bones of computation" located on the "questionable surface which divides software and hardware" (2013a). The ptrace system call ostensibly allows one piece of software (the "parent") to observe, control, examine and alter any aspect of another process running on the same operating system. In *pain registers*, the readings of the opcodes running on a computer CPU are promiscuously transposed, with Howse shifting the site of execution of code from the instruction pointer over to a machine-operated needle that carefully executes an up and down rhythmic pricking upon the skin of its user, writing patterned, piercing inscriptions on the skin's surface according to the currently executing processes running on the user's computer (such as the booting up or closing down of a Firefox web browser).

This is in part a kind of reanimation of the semi-mythical "killer poke" from the earlier days of a less materially protected form of computing, in which "[t]he computer crash originally referred to the disastrous impact of the hard disk's read/write head on the shiny, information-rich surface of the hard drive platter ... eliciting violent hardware destruction" (Howse 2013a). With echoes of Kittler, Howse contrasts such a materially present crash with the pseudo-nature of the crash as it came to be presented at the level of software in the standard operating systems of the day (such as the "Blue Screen of Death" of Windows operating systems):

> *The promises of the word made flesh are denied in a necessary crash; the crash of the operating system is some kind of fraudulent non-accident, designed to avoid the Ballardian collision and miming the same faked revelation or exposure of the pornographic, designed and enacted to draw to a halt any potential perversion of the instruction pointer, before it gets out of hand. Crash appears as original and volcanic revelation, yet uncovers only another unpierced skin layer; in both cases, only more protocols.* (Howse 2013a)

As hinted at in *pain registers*, for those users spared/denied of the pains and vicissitudes of computing, whether due to choice of software and hardware and/or because of a certain privilege that keeps them at the higher end of the speed and computational efficiency spectrum (and far away from both the manufacturing sites and waste dumps of computation's political economies), shifting sites of material execution are perhaps readily painful and intimately charged events, enacted as they are at a more tangible level in which their tentative instability vibrates in a potentially more visceral and transgressive fashion.

This potential for tension and resolution between executing entities points to execution's making of necessary distinctions in the form of discursive inclusions, exclusions and markings of executable entities. Consider, for instance, the originary interstitial gap that Turing's computing model opens up, with its mandate of discrete elements capable of being enumerated and made into effectively calculable algorithms for execution upon and by computing entities. As a machine that cuts so as to count, the task that digital computing sets engineers is originally that of rendering various forms of analogue hardware (vacuum tubes, transistors, etc.) signals into discretely readable units whose determinations can be accurately analysed and reliably carried out from one step to another. In this materialisation of Turing's thesis into actual computing machines, the act of making things discrete,[7] so as to be computable, becomes one of establishing machine-readable cuts: the switchable on and off state elements, or flip-flops executed via logic gates used to store and control data flow. Such switchable and readable states constitute a practical material basis that allows for the writing and running of the executable binary instructions of machine code upon a computing machine. All of which eventually results in what has become a particularly productive cut, this incision of the digital and its seismic materialisation in computational form, giving birth as it has to the "manic cutter known as the computer" (Kittler 2010, 228).

Howse is continually after ways of bringing this materiality of discursive practices to the fore. Thus skin, as a notably sensitive and markable surface, is a site of interest for Howse because of its quality as a thing "to be pricked, pointed to, mined, excavated and extruded, in order to test, engineer, show and expose precisely something" (Howse 2013a). In *pain registers*, this pricking involves not only the code calling the ptrace function but also the creation of the modified hardware setup that acts as "an appendage or code prosthetic" for translating the opcode values into "needled plunges".
In order for skin to take on its quality as skin, various organs, appendages and other extensions and externalisations must form so as to be able to touch upon (in one way or another)

and thus partly point towards its quality as skin, as the epidermal border around which markable bodies have for so long been demarcated.

A similar quality of bordering can be seen to work itself into Turing's machine model, which requires its site of discretely arranged tape with which an instruction pointer can read and write its instructions for operation. In this way a key function of the tape is twofold, providing (1) a layer of discretely enclosable areas that (2) have the ability to be marked. The instruction pointer points to one set of computable instructions after another in a mode of execution. In doing so, it mobilises various energies and pacts of structural impositions, both intensive and extensive, while also having the potential effect of consolidating and making amenable certain bodies into its operating regime. Where execution meets resistance, it is often a question of recomposing either the program and/or the executable bodies in question (with the application or threat of pain as a knowingly effective measure in the case of many organic bodies). Bodies then, as demarcated entities within a particular discursive system, are notable sites and materially discursive loci that can act as productive points of entry for studying the heterogeneous workings and executing processes involved in a certain situation. In the case of *pain registers*, the human body and its sensitive layer of skin and nerves act as a particularly suggestive site for engaging with Howse's ongoing interest in interrogating a notion of execution in computing, the needle becoming here a rather tangible instruction pointer for better impressing its mode of execution onto the user, not unlike the harrow of the execution apparatus in Kafka's *Penal Colony*, to which Howse also makes reference in his writing (2013a). Indeed, Howse sees *pain registers* as pointing towards an even older computational reference, with its punctuating of executing processes upon the skin of its user enacting a "knowing reversal of the operation afforded by the punch card, that other surface lying historically at a beginning for user software with Jacquard's loom" (2013a).

Pain registers' shifting of the site of execution from the CPU's instruction pointer to the skin can be understood to enact a method of materialising the cybernetic epistemology of a "unit" of information as "a difference which makes a difference" (Bateson 2000, 315-318) via the self-same cybernetic apparatus and onto the user's skin. Via such a seemingly simple shift, the piece accounts for a sense of difference as computation is executed as "marks on bodies, that is, the differences materialized" (Barad 2007, 89). In the context of the Jacquard loom and computing pioneer Charles Babbage's well known adoption of certain of its properties, it is important to pay heed to the ways in which any cut is also a cutting out. Just as Babbage's model for computing proved prototypical of those that were to come, so too would its partitioning and making invisible of the work, labour, materials and energy expended in sustaining seemingly seamless automation. From the very beginning, the many bodies involved—their often marginalised and "nimble fingers" (Nakamura 2014; see also Gallardo and Samson in this volume on the presence of hands in contemporary capitalist modes of production) that continue to remain at best as footnotes in histories and practices of computing (Plant 1995, 63–4). This despite their crucial role in the creation, running and sustaining of computational economies, whether at the level of manufacturing (Nakamura 2014), programming (Plant 1995; Chun 2005) or networked community management and support (Nakamura 2015). Ada Lovelace programming under a gender-neutral pseudonym. Turing's chemical castration. ENIAC Girls and Mechanical Turks. Obscured bodies and invisible hands of execution.

To summarise, execution in the standard model of computation such as Turing and others originally put forward, involves some kind of privileging of a discrete and symbolically enumerated logic of enclosure in the name of executability. It defines the rules and limits of its procedures, and in doing so, creates various kinds of executable entities. When executed, the executing process in question presents its programmatic imposition within a range of other executing processes, the executing process in question aiming to make operative the differentiating cuts of its particular material discursive makeup. Execution in this sense is both a discursive attempt at defining differences and material enactment and working through the various material discursive queries that arise in such attempts. Thus, execution is not merely the computability of something but the actual practice and execution of this computability in the world and over time; each instance of execution bringing the wound-up velocities of its discursively established logical abstractions into contact with the frictional and situated materials of its executing encounters. An ongoing interplay of affordances whose multi-scalar ensembles of bodies and sites operate as situated and compositional bearers of a certain propensity and potential for execution.

Interpreters

> *In this summer of 1915 [a three-year-old Alan Turing] made his first venture in experimenting: as one of the wooden sailors in his toy boat had got broken he planted the arms and legs in the garden, confident that they would grow into toy sailors.* (Sara Turing 2012, 10)

> *The code of nature maintains consistency and flexibility by repressing itself from one level to the next.*
> (Jack Burnham 1974, 74)

What is executing here? ... As Karen Barad has elucidated (drawing from the example of quantum physics and its highlighting of the formative impact of the mediating apparatus and its observer effect), "[m]atter and meaning are not separate elements. They are inextricably fused together" (2007, 3). Discourse and its interpretive efforts are dependent on materials and perceptual-effectual devices whose operations are themselves dependent on the various material affordances and energies of the components that make them up. Forces that are in turn moulded and interpenetrated by further embodied, technical, social and nonhuman energies of any situated instance. In order to both address and expand upon this ongoing prompt from Howse's work and to cover some more of the specifics of execution, a further work of Howse's will be brought in for discussion here: his Dark Interpreter effects processors.

In computing, an interpreter is a procedure that executes source code in what is an ostensibly more on-the-fly fashion, specifically because an interpreter doesn't fully compile a program's instructions into machine language prior to execution. As Abelson et al characterise it: "An interpreter raises the machine to the level of the user program; a compiler lowers the user program to the level of the machine language" (1996, 607). Given Howse's aim of bringing the workings of machines into a closer and more direct proximity with their users, it is clear why his interrogation of execution would lean towards a focus on interpreters rather than compilers. In a recent essay, "Dark Interpreter—Provide by Arts for the hardnesse of Nature", Howse outlines his own take on interpreters:

> *What is an interpreter or an interpretation? Within the realm of computer science an interpreter exists as a program, devised in earth, in hardware, which instantly translates language into action, into execution and material or breath, either directly or through an intermediate translation. The interpreter must itself be described in a language, which, Orouboros-style can perhaps be the very same language which is interpreted, thus slowly and seasonably bootstrapping itself into a wordy autumnal existence and a cycle of development. It seems as if interpretation must always come after a writing; seasons are not reversed or coming before. Yet, following the season/reason of the lake (the return), what is to come is what has happened —it is always repeated and returning; the base principle of scrying is reading the palimpsest which is the Dark Interpreter, and like-wise interpretation in this sense is nothing but divination, knowing how to execute that which comes later to be uttered.* (Howse 2015)

It is a rich and characteristic passage of Howse's, highlighting an ecological take on execution as seasonal cycles of sedimentation in which interpretation is simultaneously a divination of future utterances and a palimpsestic bootstrapping onto sets of already existent, sequential processes of execution and interpretation in the world.

In his knowing reappropriation of the shadowy figure of the Dark Interpreter from Thomas De Quincey's writing on the productive "ventilation of profound natures" that pain brings forth ([1891] 2009), Howse further develops his thinking on execution in relation to his new set of noise processing sound generators, which he gives the name of Dark Interpreter to. In doing so, Howse repurposes De Quincey's shadowy figuration of interpretation by shifting it into the realms of computing and noise generation, in this case, via a "skin-sensitive electronic instrument" (Howse 2015) capable of translating, or rather interpreting, the conductions of body capacitance, skin resistance and biological micro-voltages into noise generation. Crucially for Howse, "The Dark Interpreter is thus <u>not</u> to be controlled. It is an obsidian electronic mirror, the earth and skin itself" (2015). Howse is interested then not necessarily in the registering and working with the "dark" powers of frenzy and grief such as De Quincey would have it, but rather in ventilations and on-the-fly interpretations of what might be understood as the (comparatively) nondiscursive abilities of the body's capacity to continually conduct energies all of its own accord.

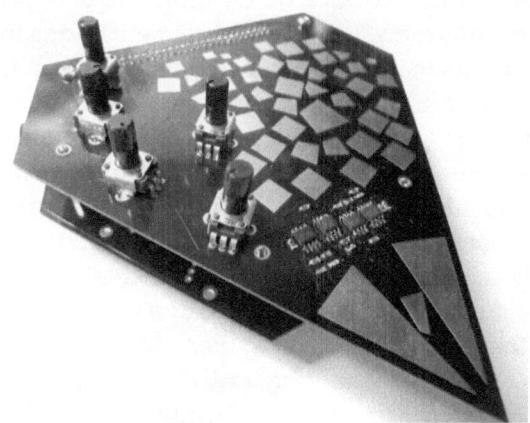

Figure 5. Mater Tenebrarum, the third of Howse's Dark Interpreter series. Image courtesy of the artist 2016.

Howse also situates his series of Dark Interpreters in a direct comparison with the CPU of computing: "But what is exactly this hidden place of the now, where symbolic orders, where language becomes material change at a quantum level? Where words are subjected to literal and not literary un-angelled noise ... This non-place is the CPU or Central Processing Unit, anchoring any technology, AKA. the Dark Interpreter" (2015). This presencing mode of Howse's Dark Interpreter can be read in multiple ways: as a referent for the moment of the infusion of discursive logics (e.g. information, mathematics, code) with their nondiscursive substrates (e.g. entropy, noise, materials); as the act of live interpretation and execution as it unfolds in the world and in the moment of the now; as a processual, "autoevolutionary machine" and executor of Gnostic style programs of universal organisation (Howse 2013b, making direct reference to Stanisław Lem's *Summa Technologiae,* a collection of philosophical essays); or as an incessant drive towards creation and execution, as witnessed both in the kernel of inspiration that inspires a young Turing to plant the limbs of his broken soldiers in the ground and in the same dark, creative responses of the soil within which these limbs are inserted.

As a notion of the Dark Interpreter hints at, a key issue that can be seen to arise in Howse's works is the interplay of discursivity and nondiscursivity and the way that each potentially infects the other. As Abelson et al. remind readers of their well-known textbook on the structure and interpretation of computer programs, "the most fundamental idea in programming" is that "[t]he evaluator, which determines the meaning of expressions in a programming language, is just another program" (1996, 360).[8] In their work to materialise Turing's and others' formulations on computation into reliable executing machines, engineers of the time had to work hard on making matter and phenomena such as electricity into necessarily reconfigurable and controllable elements that could consistently carry out the operations of mathematics and logic that would flow through them. In his essay on this key phase in electrical engineering, artist and writer David Link highlights how this engineering of matter as reconfigurable can be seen as the culmination of an intense history of experimentations with electricity, leading to a situation in which engineers "no longer understood natural phenomena, such as electricity, as fate and fact to be grasped descriptively, but as material that could be formed in any number of ways" (2006, 41). Combined with Claude Shannon (1938) and others' work on formalising the way in which relays and switching circuits could be utilised for executing logic functions, a kind of decisive tipping point can be seen to be crossed, one in which a powerful mode of discursivity becomes materially executable on these new computing machines.

Turing's (1946) own proposal and work on his Automatic Computing Engine (ACE) ably highlights this flexible mobility of meaning and matter. In it, Turing outlines how mercury-filled acoustic delay lines[9] can be used to form a high speed storage component in the machine. According to this setup, five-foot-long tubes of liquid mercury (or other liquid alternatives) with quartz crystal transducers are injected with carefully controlled pulses of electricity (about a microsecond apart) that, via crystals on one end, propagate ultrasonic wave patterns along the length of the tubes, whose varying amounts of energy can then be reconverted, via crystals on the other end, back into electricity whose resultant voltage must in turn be sufficiently amplified so as to give a readable output that can then be used to gate a second standard pulse generated by the clock. In this creative manipulation of materials, logically encoded bits of information are progressively shifted across metal, rock and liquid, at one point riding upon sound waves that are themselves propagated via the undulant affordances of mercury. In all of this, a kind of tectonic material discursive rumbling can be seen to be working its way across the exponential range of practices infused by this model of computability and its execution in the world. This highly transducible form of information processing, one that, despite its many prickly, error-prone and difficult to control physical elements, begins to call forth a diverse array of materially switchable and relayed forms of executable operations into the world.

Such flexible and mobile forms of transduction and recursivity in the execution of programmed material discursive pursuits poses a question of what exactly the nondiscursive becomes in such setups. In his article on stack software structures, Rory Solomon poses the question of "whether it is truly possible to access nondiscursive layers of media, and what that even might mean" (2013). Using the examples of both the functional call stack within programming languages and the more general purpose diagrams of application stack software architectures (with their pyramids, cones, cylinders and other diagrammatic heaps of sedimented computational layers stacked one over or below the other), Solomon highlights the way in which a mode of last in, first out interpretation and execution, as well as other stack-like models can serve as a helpful reminder of how one discursive system can bootstrap and further build itself off of other discursive systems, a cycle of layering and sedimentation that points to discourse and interpretation as both historically sequential and highly contingent.

Just as the meaning of expressions in a programming language are themselves determined by other programs, one can of course speak of other such recursive relations. As media theorist Alexander Galloway emphasises in his work on network protocols, "the content of every new protocol is always another protocol" (2004, 10). Or, as in the example of source code that Wendy Chun deconstructs, a notion of software code as "source" is a distinct glossing over of the "vicissitudes of execution" (2011, 53), one that ignores the fact that source code is historically posterior to object code, as well as the more direct matter that source code is not itself executable, but rather must be compiled and thus is subject to other elements, operations, protocols and discursive institutions that could themselves be posited as source. Paul Kockelman captures the crux of the matter:

> *just as a bicycle (as a relatively large instrument) provides an interpretant of the function of the smaller instruments that make it up (e.g., spokes, pedals, chains, etc.), and just as these smaller instruments provide interpretants of the purchases provided by the affordances they incorporate (e.g., steel, plastic, rubber), an accumulator provides an interpretant of each of the logic gates that make it up, and each of these logic gates in turn provides an interpretant of the purchase provided by the affordances it incorporates (from silicon to solder, depending on the current state of technology). In short, just as one can zoom out to the function served by many interconnected digital computers (qua the Internet), however wide, one can zoom in to the purchase provided by many incorporated silicon atoms, however narrow... In other words, do not get hung up on the fact that instruments are "derivative" agents. There is no life form that is not a derivative agent in this account.* (Kockelman 2011, 723)[10]

All of which serves to highlight a perspectival nature of discourse and its material purchase; how any "agential cut" (Barad 2007) and interpretation is itself built upon certain black-boxed supports that are nonetheless interoperating and potentially material discursive mobile entities of their own.

Much of Howse's own practice can be understood as highlighting just such a contingency in execution. In his method of applying forms of engineering towards the creation of contraptions in which computational logics and materials are made to unravel their own enclosing drives, it seems clear that Howse's implementations veer towards what could be described as a *promiscuous mode*: an intentionally perverse mode of inquiry and method of execution aimed at unsettling the more stratified interpretive modes of executing machines as they have often tended to become. To this end, Howse launches his materials (code, chemicals, software, needles, soil, circuit boards, crystals, EEG readers, *Amanita muscaria fungi*, etc.) up to their stratic limits, pushing them to their perceived frictional and/or fictive constraints. Like the unruly particle of physics, potential sites of executability flash back and forth across these various works: surfacing as a computer crash; a needle pressing the skin to its breaking point; a slime mould becoming runny and separating itself from a sufficiently stratified solid. Each instantiation, leakage and interpretation suggesting both further routes for transgressive expression and new potential supports for material and endophysical enclosure.

What is executing here? Again, the command line's pushy prompt. In each or any shift enacted in these works, there is a certain bringing to the fore of materialised sites of contact and exchange that inscribe and articulate their particular capacities amidst a range of ongoing, active ecologies of execution. In the example of von Uexküll's tick, execution is envisaged as the launching of an action in response to a threshold event that triggers an executable response on the part of the tick. A dangerous promiscuity of skin glands and subjectivities. In Kittler's exposition on the implementation of protected modes that further solidify perceived divides in hardware from software, one is made privy to the creation and sedimentation of certain kinds of notable layerings between the material and discursive. In response to the often misguided projections of any such enclosing drives, Howse positions the executable as "the real, that which is enacted and constructed by software in/as the world itself" (2013a), aiming to remove any sense of a privileged view from the outside. In doing so, he highlights the interpenetrative entanglements and generative powers of matter and discourse across a range of charged entities, practices and sites of execution. In *pain registers* computational execution is palimpsestically traced off of the computer's operational codes and transduced via a needle onto a layer of generative skin. In the Dark Interpreter the skin's promiscuous capacities become themselves executable inputs for contagious, noisy divination. In Howse's Earthboot execution worms from the soil into the circuits of a bespoke trowel of a motherboard. In *Diff in June* (2013) a summer's day's worth of executional traces are excavated from the changes in the register of a PC's file system and spilled out into a 1,673 page graphomanic archive and tribute to micro-instructional executive ardour. And in *Sketches for an earth computer*

(2014–2016) collections of earthly materials and naturally provided for telluric flows and atmospheric inputs code an embryonic assemblage that regardless of its comparatively unrefined state will inevitably execute these inputs in one way or another. In any lingering sense of doubt at times as to their executability, the very potential of the executable. Its needle furrowing across sedimented surfaces, unearthing unstable interpretations and potential leakages in these stacks that bury and unbury;[11] the codes and materials growing wild, producing opaque excess and new "alliances of bastard components" (Fuller 2005, 103).

This becomes *that*. Information, entropy and the liveliness of materials bring forth ongoing encounters and sites of execution. Amidst such an ecology of executions, interpretation can be understood to "haunt" (Gitelman 2013, 3) the act of processing, even if only in its basic effect of mobilising certain energies and their further generative and questioning prompts. Thus the discourse network, as a result of its own demonstrative interpretative power, can increasingly be seen to be unravelling long held notions of a human-centred interpretative agency. At the same time, emerging from the mills of Babbage's beloved nineteenth century factories, the invisible hands and instruction pointers of capitalism and Moore's law steadily accumulate their own uneasy returns in the geological record. The dark interpretation of the moment: Anthropocene.

Notes

1. Indeed, any notions of complexity are themselves subject-specific formulations. Von Uexküll: "All animal subjects, from the simplest to the most complex, are inserted into their environments to the same degree of perfection. The simple animal has a simple environment; the multiform animal has an environment just as richly articulated as it is" (50).

2. Turing's name and work is often invoked in this essay as a stand in for what can easily become an exponential list of a range of actors involved in various key achievements in regards to both the theoretical horizons and practical materialisations of computation.

3. A family of backward compatible instruction set architectures introduced in 1978 by Intel with the release of their 8086 central processing unit. Despite its age, the x86 architecture continues to be one of the most used and dominant computer architectures, featuring in most desktops and laptops, as well as in many of the various hardware setups of contemporary networked cloud services.

4. Like the tightly wound psycho-analytical schematics of Jacques Lacan, protected mode can be seen to act here "as both the enemy and co-existent partner of a Real Mode"

(Kittler 2006, 359–60).

5. A stored-program computer for the processing, transmission and recording of inputs and outputs in which numerically encoded program instructions and data are stored in the same read-write, random-access memory and accessible via a common bus. Protected mode style features indicate towards a general trend of modifications to the Von Neumann architecture. In fact, the majority of modern CPUs (including many variations of the common x86 microprocessors) also incorporate aspects of the Harvard architecture model, a setup in which program instructions are stored in physically separate storage pathways and accessed by a separate bus, thus allowing instructions and data to be fetched in parallel. These hybrid models of Von Neumann and Harvard architectures are typically referred to as a Modified Harvard Architecture, with the most common modification involving the implementation of a memory hierarchy via a CPU hardware cache that allows for certain separations of instructions and data (typically for speed or security reasons) while still retaining the flexibility of a unified address space that an underlying Von Neumann architecture gives.

6. Accompanying statement to a short video by Howse on the ptrace() call: "Date of origin: 1979. Author/inventor/context: Seventh Edition Unix, Bell Laboratories. An operating system call, first implemented in Version 7 of AT&T UNIX in 1979, which allows one piece of software (the parent) to observe, control, examine and alter any aspect of another process running on the same operating system. The ptrace call is commonly used to debug running code and can be considered as an active language, infiltrating and interrogating, snooping on and injecting code into living, running processes; an active language projecting a potential process promiscuity within the machine. Ptrace shifts the site of execution and is nowadays commonly viewed as an unnecessary security risk" (Howse, https://vimeo.com/86690846).

7. As Turing and von Neumann were both well aware of, when comparing what Turing describes as the "idealised machines" of his formal descriptions of "discrete state machines" to their instantiation into "actual machines", the very materiality of these machines means they are of course not actually discrete. Turing: "Strictly speaking there are no such machines. Everything thing really moves continuously. But there are many kinds of machine which can be profitably *thought of* as being discrete state machines" (1950, 439–440).

8. Evaluator being another term for interpreter. In speaking of execution, it can be helpful to compare and contrast the many alternative phrases invoked in its place within computing. For instance, if execution has a sense of suggesting a kind of decisive moment, the common terminology of "running" a program brings more readily to the fore the durational aspects of live execution ("runtime") and the ongoing and necessary processes of upkeep involved in any processes of computation (see, for instance, Linda Hilfling's essay in this collection, or Kafka's penal colony officer and his frequent outcries of designerly frustration at the ongoing work required to keep the execution machine in not only working order, but at a level of pristinely polished condition that does sufficient justice to its own pointedly performative act of execution).

9. Turing later acknowledged the influence of J. Presper Eckert's pioneering work on mercury delay

line memory in this particular setup of his.

10. See Marie Louise Juul Søndergaard & Kasper Hedegård Schiølin's contribution in this collection on "Bataille's bicycle" for a notable interpretation of a further purchase afforded by the bicycle.

11. In outlining his implementation of a last in, first out stack data structure as part of the design for his Automatic Computing Engine, Turing designates the terms "bury" and "unbury" (1946, 11–12 & 30) for the calling and returning from subroutines (what were called "subsidiary operations" in Turing's terminology).

References

Abelson, Harold, Gerald J., Sussman, and Julie Sussman. 1996. *Structure and Interpretation of Computer Programs (Second Edition).* Cambridge, MA: MIT.

Barad, Karen. 2007. *Meeting the Universe Halfway: Quantum Physics and the Entanglement of Matter and Meaning.* London: Duke University Press.

Bateson, Gregory. (1972) 2000. *Steps to an Ecology of Mind.* Chicago: University of Chicago Press.

Burnham, Jack. 1974. *Great Western Salt Works; Essays on the Meaning of Post-formalist Art.* New York: G. Braziller.

Chun Wendy Hui Kyong. 2005. "On Software, or the Persistence of Visual Knowledge." *Grey Room* 18 (Winter): 26–51.

———. 2011. *Programmed Visions: Software and Memory.* Cambridge, Massachussetts: The MIT Press.

Davis, Martin. 2012. *The Universal Computer: The Road From Liebniz to Turing.* London: CRC Press.

De Quincey, Thomas. (1891) 2009. *Confessions of an English Opium-Eater and Related Writings.* Broadview Press.

Fuller, Matthew. 2005. *Media Ecologies: Materialist Energies in Art and Technoculture.* Cambridge, MA: The MIT Press.

Galloway, Alexander. 2004. *Protocol: How Control Exists after Decentralization.* Cambridge, MA: MIT.

Gitelman, Lisa (ed.). 2013. *"Raw Data" is an Oxymoron.* Cambridge, MA: The MIT Press.

Grosz, Elizabeth. 2008. *Chaos, Territory, Art: Deleuze and the Framing of the Earth.* New York: Columbia University Press.

Howse, Martin. 2013a. "Shifting the site of execution." *1010* website. http://www.1010.co.uk/org/shift.html.

———. 2013b. "I've Seen Gardens, Compared with Which this Would be a Wilderness." *Mute*, 11 June. http://www.metamute.org/editorial/articles/ive-seen-gardens-compared-which-would-be-wilderness.

———. 2015. "Dark Interpreter—Provide by Arts for the hardnesse of Nature." *Occulto Magazine*, Issue δ, December.

Ifrah, Georges. 2001. *The Universal History of Computing: From the Abacus to the Quantum Computer.* Trans. E. F. Harding. Wiley.

Kittler, Friedrich. (1991) 2006. "Protected Mode." Trans. Stefanie Harris, in Martin Howse (ed.), *[the] xxxxx [reader].* Berlin: xxxxx.

Kockelman, Paul. 2011. "Biosemiosis, Technocognition, and Sociogenesis: Selection and Significance in a Multiverse of Sieving and Serendipity." *Current Anthropology* 52 (5): 711–739.

Link, David. 2006. "There Must Be an Angel: On the Beginnings of the Arithmetics of Rays." In *Variantology 2. On Deep Time Relations of Arts, Sciences and Technologies*, edited by Siegfried Zielinski and David Link, 15–42.

Cologne: König.
Mackenzie, Adrian. 2006. *Cutting Code: Software and Sociality.* New York: Peter Lang.
Nakamura, Lisa. 2014. "Indigenous Circuits: Navajo Women and the Racialization of Early Electronics Manufacture." *American Quarterly* 66 (4): 919–941.
———. 2015. "The Unwanted Labour of Social Media: Women of Color Call Out Culture as Venture Community Management." *New Formations* 86: 106–112.
Plant, Sadie. 1995. "The Future Looms: Weaving Women and Cybernetics." In *Cyberspace/Cyberbodies/Cyberpunk: Cultures of Technological Embodiment*, edited by Mike Featherstone and Roger Burrows. London: Sage Publications.
Sayej, Nadja. 2013. "Programming Computers with Dirt: Earthboot Powers PCs with Geological Energy." Motherboard. October 22. http://motherboard.vice.com/blog/programming-computers-with-dirt-earthboot-powers-pcs-with-geological-energy.
Shannon, Claude. 1938. "A Symbolic Analysis of Relay and Switching Circuits". *Transactions of the American Institute of Electrical Engineers* 57 (12): 713–723.
Solomon, Rory. 2013. "Last in, First Out: Network Archaeology of/as the Stack." *Amodern.* http://amodern.net/article/last-in-first-out/.
Turing, Alan M. 1937. "On Computable Numbers, with an application to the Entscheidungsproblem." *Proceedings of the London Mathematical Society* V.42.
———. (1945) 1946. "Proposals for the development in the Mathematics Division of an Automatic Computing Engine (ACE)." *Report E.882, Executive Committee, National Physical Laboratory*, February. Teddington, Middlesex: NPL.
———. 1950. "Computing Machinery and Intelligence." *MIND* lix (236): 433–460.
Turing, Sara. 2012. *Alan M. Turing—Centenary Edition.* Cambridge: Cambridge University Press.
Uexküll, Jakob von, and Georg Kriszat. 1934. *Streifzüge durch die Umwelten von Tieren und Menschen: Ein Bilderbuch unsichtbarer Welten.* Berlin: J. Springer.
Uexküll, Jakob von. (1934) 2010. *A Foray into the Worlds of Animals and Humans.* Trans. Joseph D. O'Neil. Minneapolis: University of Minnesota Press.

Critter Compiler

Helen Pritchard

On March 24, 1989, the oil tanker Exxon Valdez had just entered Alaska's Prince William Sound, after departing the Valdez Marine Terminal full of crude oil. At 12:04 am, the ship struck a reef, tearing open the hull and releasing 11 million gallons of oil into the environment. Initial responses by Exxon and the Alyeska Pipeline Company were insufficient to contain much of the spill, and a storm blew in soon after, spreading the oil widely. Eventually, more than 1,000 miles of coastline were fouled, and hundreds of thousands of animals perished ... Though the oil has mostly disappeared from view, many Alaskan beaches remain polluted to this day, crude oil buried just inches below the surface.[1]

The year is 1997 and we are at the Oak Ridge National Laboratory, California. Mike Simpson, the inventor in the lab, is holding up a microchip in front of his computer. He traces the sensor with his finger and points towards the surface; it is here that the genetically engineered Pseudomonas fluorescens HK44 is "living" on the bed of silicon. Mike has fondly named the sensor, a tiny light-sensitive computer chip coated with the bioluminescent bacterium HK44, "Critters on a Chip". When the bacterium encounters petrochemical pollutants, it lights up, creating an electrical signal that the chip can process or amplify. Mike explains that they have used the HK44 to create a biochip as it is sensitive to naphthalene, a common petroleum pollutant. HK44 is a genetically engineered strain that responds to exposure to naphthalene, salicylate and other structural analogs by production of visible light. It was constructed using genes from the light organ of the tropical fish the *Monocentris* and the common bacteria *Escherichia coli (E.coli)*. Exposure to naphthalene, one of the polycyclic aromatic hydrocarbons that are a component of coal and petrochemicals, causes injury to the HK44 and the resulting harm creates a bioluminescencent reaction. Light sensors embedded on the chip subsequently compute this reaction. Mike tells us that a naphthalene biosensor could be useful for monitoring hazardous waste sites, remediating oil spills or as a forensic application to evidence

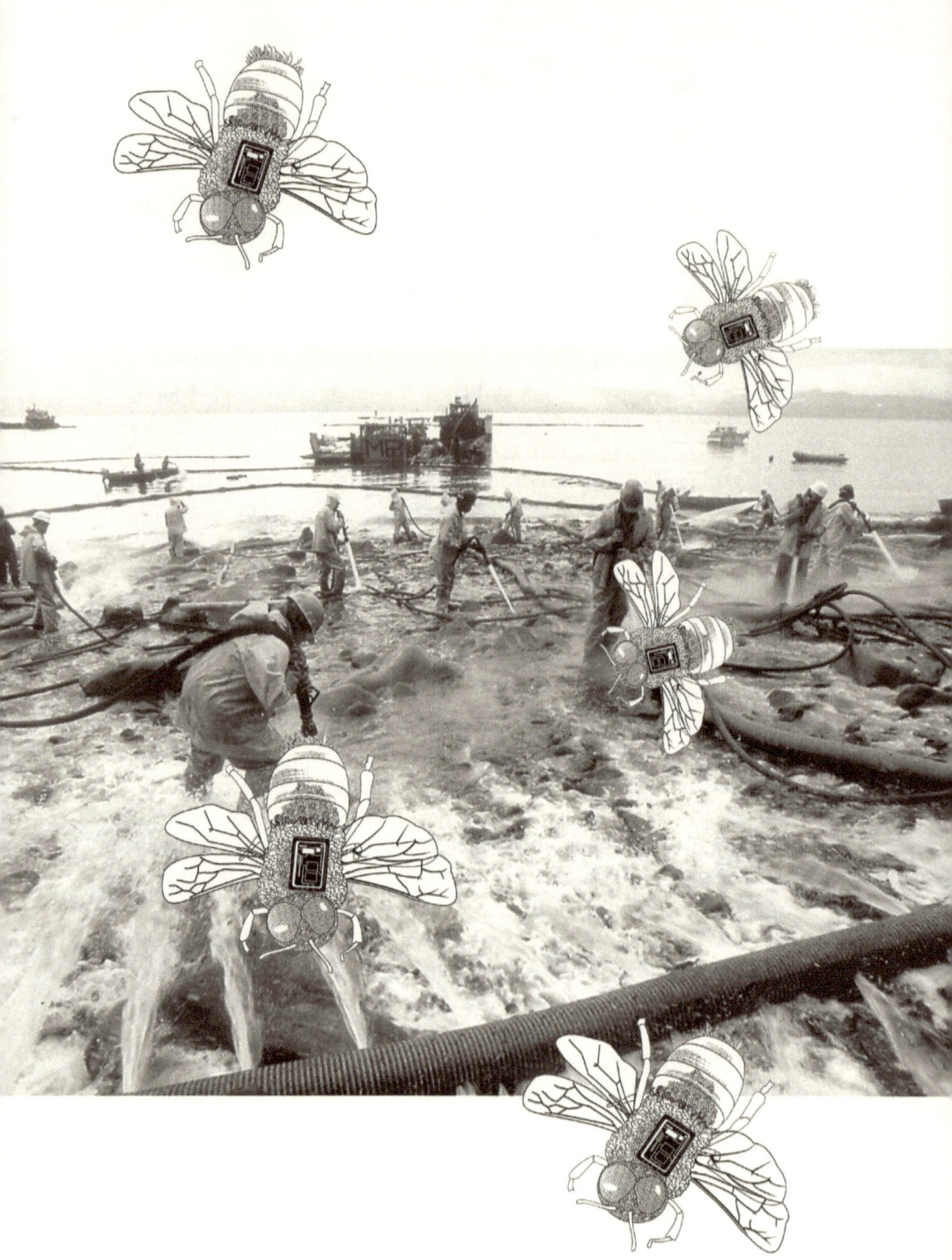

Figure 1. Critter Chips on the backs of Honey Bees, circulate over the Exxon Valdez Oil Spill. Pritchard (2016).

the presence of a particular chemical. The Critter Chips can be installed either on a floating platform or as the patent shows on the backs of the common honeybee. Mike notes that if the bacteria come into contact with polycyclic aromatic hydrocarbons, it flips a biological switch and the bacteria start to glow. As the bacteria used give off a great deal of light, they are able to study the processes at a high resolution—down to a microscopic level in individual organisms. Of course, as he explains—such Critter Chips have limitations, because they are alive. The bacteria and the honey bee hosts need food, and they can die or mutate. So Critter Chips will probably carry (literal) expiration dates.[2]

* * *

This chapter unravels how execution holds—in enduring states—semi-living microbes in sites of petrochemical waste. By referring to semi-living I am not signalling a life sustained through technological means (Catts and Zurr 2002), but a living constrained and held in injured states by computation. I ask what type of activity is this execution that derives from injury and how we might speculate on execution otherwise? Through ethnographic and speculative engagements with Critter Chips I will show how execution can be described as propelling semi-life, outlining how computation exploits the potential of microbial injury and death. I follow this with a discussion of the artwork *Critter Compiler*, a fabulation (Haraway 2013) that engages with contemporary microbial computing. *Critter Compiler* is a prototype for a microbial novella writer and a response to Rosi Braidotti's call for experiments that "are non-profit and actualise the virtual possibilities of an expanded relational self that functions in a nature-culture continuum" (2013, 61). The artwork takes as its starting point toxic execution, and as a speculative experiment performs (or executes) these processes otherwise.

Negative possibilities
In scenes of toxicity, Critter Chips operate through engaging the productive capacities of the HK44. Yet in these scenes this renewal is not often a capacious, co-flourishing, but a drawn out persistence preceding death. The HK44 might be described as a technical component, in which processes of differentiation,

in the form of damage or injury to the microbe, signal the presence of toxic hydrocarbons. Critter Chips outline the crucial yet elusive intra-actions (Barad 2007) of nonhuman organisms in computational execution; nonhumans who might be said to accompany execution as negative shapes. As Nigel Clark observes,

> *Our bodies, our identities, our social formations, are also consequent of the non-relation we have with all those who did not make it ... Accompanying us as negative shapes—as silent, spectral figures—are the many who did not pass safely across thresholds, who took a wrong turn at a bifurcation, whose experimental wagers did not win out. Our own flourishing may even be impacted in these falterings.* (Clark 2011, 209)

Microbial deaths become negative shapes that emerge with us from scenes of petrochemical toxicity such as the ongoing pollution from the Exxon Valdez oil spill on the coast of Alaska or the waste from the industry of the Pearl Delta River Basin, in South China. Rosi Braidotti notes that the opportunistic post anthropocentrism of advanced capitalism both invests in and profits from the commodification of all that lives. "The capital it goes after is the informational codes of living matter itself in all its forms. Life, as *bios* as well as *zoe*, is turned into commodities for trade and profit" (Braidotti 2014, 243). It is these processes that not only destroy and erase life but also propel new biotic subjects such as Critter Chips. Whilst advanced capitalism is often characterized by the exploitation and erasure of life, this chapter engages with a contemporary mode of existence[3]— semi-living, exhausted, partial lives that both are propelled into and depleted by scenes of what I call toxic execution.

The existence of Critter Chips is not an individual project, indeed they foreground what Donna Harway and Karen Barad describe as entangled intra-relating (Barad 2007, ix). Critter Chips emerge from an already-meshed-together scene, where their capacities are articulated through computation and particularly execution. Through an engagement with matter, we might understand that it is the excess or creative force (i.e its potential to renew) of both the HK44 and execution that renders the Critter Chips active. Seeking ways to account for this creative force of matter, material feminisms (alternatively called new-materialism or neo-materialism) have often turned their attentions to that of co-creation and conjoined forms of production with the non/inhuman world.[4] Although these accounts have opened spaces of alterity beyond humanist concerns, their search for positive engagements with nonhumans has often attended to only that which we can know and flourish with, rather than that which takes an entity apart from itself. This has led to dominating articulations of life that obscure negative encounters of semi-living, exhausted, partial lives, and as discussed by Claire Colebrook, premises naturalised accounts (2014). Additionally, little attention has been dedicated to the application of (bio)computational organisms in environmental computing, on the assumption that computing that addresses climate change or pollution from petrochemicals is based on an extended intimacy with "nature" and positive possibility. Critter Chips demand us to entertain a different articulation. As Barad notes, "[t]he stakes in denaturalizing nature are not insignificant. Demonstrating nature's queerness, its trans*-embodiment, exposing the monstrous face of nature itself in the undoing of naturalness holds significant political potential"(Barad 2015, 412). In this context it is important to foreground the entangled relations of petrochemicals, waste, computation and capitalism, to trouble nature and its naturalness "all the way down" (Barad 2015, 413), I do this by invigorating the idea of *toxic execution*.

As Wendy Hui Kyong Chun has noted, in the context of computation things always seem to be disappearing in such crucial ways, not just because of the effects of computation but because this process of disappearance is central to the temporality of computation itself. "[O]ur computers execute in unforeseen ways, the future opens to the unexpected. Because of this, any programmed vision will always be inadequate, will always give way to another future" (Chun 2011, 9). Engaging with toxic execution enables us to pay attention to these disappearances so that we might attend to the ways that injury and death are enrolled with the computation of the environment that generates (so-called) real-time (big) data. Consequently, and as a queer experiment, instead of focusing on a co-flourishing of humans and non-humans, I draw on queer theory to pay attention to damage, injury and the constraints placed on the possibilities of life and brought about through computation. As Heather Love notes, there is a genealogy of focusing on injury in queer studies and a willingness to investigate darker aspects of experience (Love 2009, 2). As the anti-social turn in queer theory outlines—to queer something is to engage with both the powerful negativity of punk politics and a mode of crafting alternatives with others (Halberstam 2008, 148 and 154).

I extend queer theories that concern personal injury into more-than-human ensembles in order to consider the damages and attend to the suffering, loving, caring, pain and death shared by humans and nonhumans in entanglements of computation and petrochemicals. Drawing on queer theory is not an anti-affirmative stance. Instead, as Heather Love outlines, "[t]he emphasis on damage in queer studies exists in a state of tension with a related and contrary tendency—the need to resist damage and to affirm queer existence"(Love 2009, 3). Therefore to think through affirmative questions of resistance we first need to ask how execution constrains life and produces an alternative economy of critical life that needs attention. This question pushes us to begin somewhere other than with the economy of life and nonlife.

Trans Practices

Myra Hird observes that nonhumans have long "been overburdened with the task of making sense of human social relations" (2008, 229). Indeed, many critters have been "enrolled" as sentinels in environmental sensing "to detect signs of disturbances that remain indiscernible to humans" (Akrich et al. 2006 cited in Gramaglia 2013). Canaries, molluscs and lichen have all been tasked as sentinels, to signal future events or warn us, "making it possible to lower the threshold for detecting toxins in air, soil and water, and allowing investigations on the effects of low doses of particular pollutants on the environment" (Gramaglia 2013). Gail Davis also points to how our understandings of human corporeality and potentiality are increasingly enacted through the individual bodies of a multitude of laboratory mice (Davis 2013, 3). However, the HK44 has not just been tasked through genetic engineering with the characteristics of a sentinel but also enrolled further as a computational component. Yet as HK44 emit an excited fluorescent glow, as the light from the microscope passes through them, my engagements with them seem to illuminate their enduring liveliness.

In *Animal Trans* Hird describes how she shares Haraway's interest "in trans species/cendence/fusions/gene/genics/national that disturb the hierarchy of taxonomic categories (genus, family, class, order, kingdom) derived from pure, self-contained and self-containing nature" (2008, 231). For Haraway, Hird explains, trans [practices] "cross a culturally salient line between nature and artifice, and they greatly increase the density of all kinds of other traffic on the bridge between what counts as nature and culture" (Haraway 1997, 56 cited in Hird 231). Critter Chips engage me with a trans aesthetics of affective ecologies (such as suffering, loving, caring, pain and death) shared by humans and nonhumans (Puig de la Bellacasa 2010, 8). Provoking an account for our shared "ambiguity/undecidability/indeterminacy" (Barad 2012, 212) in our entanglements with computation. By focusing on Critter Chips, I do not wish to reinstate the categories of the nonhuman organism or execution as fixed. Instead I want to develop a fuller understanding of capitalist practices of computing and the ways in which they extend their reach into the possibilities for life.

Critter Chips

In 1997 "Critters on a Chip" were set to replace expensive and complicated optical detection systems for petrochemicals that used photo multipliers and optical fibres buried in the ground. These Critter Chips used the genetically engineered microorganism HK44 to produce light as it was injured by hazardous waste, so that monitoring could be undertaken at sites of petrochemical accumulation. Almost twenty years later I am a visiting researcher at the Toxicology lab at City University in Hong Kong. China is the third largest producer of petrochemicals, and a site of energetic activity for biotechnology (Ong 2010, 3). Today the lab is busy, and Vincent the lab technician is standing near a rapidly spinning centrifugal machine. He explains that he is generating bacteria for a microbial chip which will detect oil and petrochemical waste from refineries and factories, such as those in the Pearl River Delta, the low-lying area surrounding the Pearl River estuary, where the Pearl River flows into the South China Sea. Today, Vincent is attempting to harvest the genetically engineered bacteria cells that will live on a small microcontroller. He draws a picture for me on the back of his

pad, to show how the Critter Chips will shimmer in vast floating networks compiling signals in real-time from the microbes' metabolic and reproductive processes as they respond through injury to oil spills. These signals translate the Critter Chip's injury from toxicity into iterative arithmetic computation.
The Critter Chip is imagined in its input/output specification, generating metabolic reactions that produce output quantities of proteins as a function of input quantities of hydrocarbons. Through the process of writing and compiling code in bacteria's DNA it is possible for iterative constructs such as while loops and for loops to be implemented on the Critter Chip, based on a clocking mechanism. The results are mapped onto specific biochemical reactions selected from libraries — a task analogous to *machine language* compilation.[5]

According to Cisco, there will be 50 billion devices connected to the network by 2020.[6] Many of which will be living sensors such as Critter Chips. In Vincent's speculative scene, the Critter Chips are enrolled as part of a networked computational ensemble, producing a fluorescent shimmering glow, to make intense the most harmful, yet unknown, unquantifiable, unrecognizable, unmatchable traces of waste, specifically so they can [re]enter capital circulation as data. I am left to wonder what is brought into play by the "temporal or immaterial dimensions of matter" (Yusoff 2013, 2).

In this spectral vision, as petrochemicals from industry and production circulate, they appear, fleetingly, as glowing traces illuminated by the metabolic process of microbes. The shimmers here are literal and material affective variables, which pattern the flows of polycyclic aromatic hydrocarbons. Whereas the Critter Chips of Oak laboratory were imagined to operate in small independent mesh configurations, the Critter Chips in Vincent's lab will most likely operate in networks, where hub nodes collect and aggregate data using machine-learning algorithms from ensembles of geographically distributed sensors. It is in these sites of computation, which are at the edges of human perception, where much of toxic execution will take place. Lauren Berlant notes, "[q]ueer, socialist/anti-capitalist, and feminist work has all been about multiplying the ways we know that people have lived and can live, so that it would be possible to take up any number of positions during and in life in order to have 'a life'" (Berlant 2011, 182). As I leave the lab that evening and return the next morning I find myself caught within, and approaching, the entanglements of Critter Chips as instruments of difference, arrested within the theoretical metaphors that open up the possibilities of going beyond, discourses of purity and originals, yet also caught within the very different lived experience of the Critter Chips. I am hustling between formations that are metaphorical and formations that are literal.

Continuous Expiration

From the 1930s onwards computation (in technical terms) has on the whole been recognised as the execution of halting Turing machines or their equivalents. Although other models of computation such as recursive functions, rewriting rules and lambda-calculus could have been taken up, the restriction of computation as the execution of a machine that stops or concludes—so called halting machines—takes hold (Denning 2010). This was in part because of material constraints and in part because of what the practices of computing demanded. It was more common than not for algorithms to be terminal, in other words to implement functions, to compute defined values. Critter Chips are however based on interactivity that involves an instantiation of algorithms in the environment rather than a reaching of a resolution. As Parisi notes,

> [f]rom the standpoint of interaction, the successful running of an algorithm is a performance in the environment (i.e. computation is embedded in the world) and of the environment (i.e. computation needs the world and the data extracted from it to fulfill the algorithmic task).
> (Parisi 2014, 121)

As interactive processes, the imaginaries and practices that propel Critter Chips demand a different computation to that of a final value. Compared to the Turing machine, Critter Chips take on a different set of characteristics, as they are entanglements of interactive processes, so-called natural information processes, which are imagined as—but not necessarily enacted as—continuous processes. In order to achieve this near continuity, the execution of interactive processes in Critter Chips instantiates itself across computational *and* metabolic processes. The temporality of the termination of these processes is quite different to that of a Turing Machine. The Critter Chip is not designed to perform halting executions that resolve calculations; instead the Critter Chips are (until the expiration date) non-terminating processes in which the fluorescent signals are read by the Chip and sent across the network continuously. Instead of the halting machine reaching a resolved number, in Critter Chips, signals continue until the expiration of the Critter Chips of the microbe, which is a significantly different process.

Petrochemicals have become a focus of increasing concern for human and environmental health over the past two decades. However, the effects of thousands of chemicals still remain unknowable. As Michelle Murphy notes, spatial and temporal industrially produced chemicals, "are regulated and ignored, studied and yet filled with uncertainty" (Murphy 2013, 105). As Vincent and I watch the centrifugal machine spin we discuss how Critter Chips are propelled by this uncertainty. He explains that the advantage of using a Critter Chip instead of an electrochemical sensor is that it is not limited to signaling one chemical of an oil spill but rather, because of the microbes' capacity for injury in response to a wide range of toxins, it is able to further signal the toxicity of a range of known and unknown compounds that are similar to naphthalene. As Vincent demonstrates to me in a petri dish, the Critter Chip is designed to signal the presence of petrochemical compounds that may be unknown, as well as chemicals already defined as petrochemicals. Those that are unknown may remain indeterminate, except for the injury that signals their presence. Rather than determining the presence of a specific chemical, the Critter Chip exhibits affects that can be attributed to toxicity. It is this quality of tracing affects, and existing within the unknowable, that makes the Critter Chip quicker and cheaper than other types of computational sensing.

Through execution across the domains of the biological, geological (fossil fuels) and the technical, the Critter Chip expands the temporal and spatial possibilities for the exchange of information. It could be envisaged that the Critter Chip is an extension of a cybernetic imaginary, one in which microbes are machines, and input and output need not be in the form of numbers or diagrams but sense organs read by ultra rapid computing machines such as imagined by Norbert Weiner (Weiner, 1948, 36). However the Critter Chip is not an ensemble that employs the HK44 because it is the same as the machine but instead because they are different from each other. In *On the Mode of Existence of Technical Objects* Gilbert Simondon outlines a philosophy of technology that pays close attention relationally to "actual difference, techniques, apparatuses and paradigms" (Combes 2013, 89). Simondon's theory of technical objects accounts for the important differences between "living" (humans, nonhuman animals, plants) and technical elements. In part, his focus on difference was a response to cybernetic theories of his time that had undertaken a shift from merely comparing animals with machines analogically, to making the much stronger claim that animals are machines. In cybernetics, these claims of animals as machines were used to envision ensembles of computers and biotic subjects. However for Simondon matter, organism and machine are different, "they can even be said to be ontologically different, but within an ontology that methodologically avoids dualism and substantialism" (LaMarre 2013, 80). It is under these circumstances that I want to suggest that the instantiation of computation across metabolic processes is more akin to the "enhancement" of the machine through differentiation that enables an increase in sensitivity to information, as opposed to a cybernetic model. Simondon outlines extending the margins of indeterminacy in the technological ensemble, noting "[i]t is such a margin that allows for the machine's sensitivity to outside information. It is this sensitivity to information on the part of machines, much more than any increase in automatism that makes possible a technical ensemble" (Simondon 1958, 13). However Critter Chips are by no means what Simondon describes as an open machine with freedom of operation.[7] Instead the Critter Chip only increases the margin of indeterminacy at critical moments in its operations, and at other points the meshing of organism and chip restricts the margin. It is the restriction that holds the HK44 in its enduring state and enables a certain level of performance as a sensor. It is this double bind that is exploited in the Critter Chip ensemble and renders the HK44 semi-living. The microbial processes of the HK44 open up the sensitivity of the technological ensemble yet are also moments of injury. The practices of computation command that the HK44 are genetically engineered around its ability to temporally localise its indeterminacy at critical moments in the computational process, such as its ability to shimmer in the presence of toxicity. At other critical moments, HK44 has to be able to do less, to live less, in order to remain enduring, that is to be more component like and less life like within the technical ensemble. Under the glare of advanced capitalism in which nature, commerce and politics are explicitly entangled, the use of HK44 to extend the margins of indeterminacy points to the ways in which toxicity "straddles the boundaries of life and non life as well as the literal bounds of bodies in ways that introduce a certain complexity of integrity of either lively or deathly subjects" (Chen 2012, 4096).

Through extension into biotic subjects, toxic execution (both applied and speculative) extends the horizon of calculation to include protein production, metabolisms and nonhuman variation. Yet it is the same innovative capacities that have the potential to extend calculation that also limit the HK44 to life lived for the Critter Chip, constraining its possibilities for life. As Steven Shaviro (after Whitehead) notes, life cannot be understood as a matter of continuity or endurance, "[r]ather an entitiy is alive precisely to the extent that it envisions difference and thereby strives for something other than the mere continuation of what it already is"(Shaviro 2010, 113).

Enduring States

The primary feature of toxic execution is not generalised interactions that lead to some kind of fusion of all that there is, or a mass entanglement or the biological, geological and technical. On the contrary, the microbial organisms that toxic execution acts upon hold together in a specific mode of advanced capitalism in which they are not independent of a complex environment they partly shape, and upon which they depend, but is also constantly putting them at risk (Stengers 2006, 8). Specifically, toxic execution holds together in a way that generates value through its entanglements with petrochemicals, humans, nonhumans and the network. If, as Jennifer Gabrys notes, "[w]aste reveals the economies of value within digital technology" (Gabrys 2011, 17), toxic execution highlights the reclaiming of waste as producing value in computation. This value from human labour is inseparable from toxicity and critter chips. Mazen Labban outlines (in relation to microbial biotechnologies for fossil fuel extraction), that these processes produce "what neither can on its own". This specific mode is a generation of capital from a wasting, "through which value is simultaneously created and reproduced, transferred and preserved, and extracted from waste and transformed into other forms of waste" (Labban 2014). Yet this injury is a double bond as it is the process by which the Critter Chip also persists. The constraint of both humans and nonhumans affected by toxic execution is most violently revealed in these states of suspension and liminality that Critter Chips are held in, violence that remains unaccounted for, in exchange for the hope of the predictive capacities of big data and intimacies with the environment. Thinking with toxicity, we can recognise that there is not a computational network that constitutes a technological outside to ecological life. Rather, toxic execution is the force that emerges from the collapse of subjects through their intra-actions with computation. What seems important to retain is a fine sensitivity to the intersectional sites in which computation and petrochemicals involve themselves in very different lived (or partially lived) experiences. In the experience of the Critter Chip, the HK44 are not rendered as unproductive or dead immediately, but are held in a state of enduring productivity, by harnessing the affects of toxins as something quantifiable by computation. They become productive (more productive than a query run across a central processing unit), if only for a moment in a short-lived life. Computation in this scene brings back into circulation all perceived wastes, which include toxic and queer subjects through their enrolment into productive roles.

Critter Chips are scenes, in which computational execution is increasingly instantiated (in both a metaphysical and computational sense) by the extension of computation into nonhuman organisms. That is, the bodies of nonhumans with carbon-based metabolisms emerge solely as entities to contain the execution which seeks to compile the innovativeness of organisms. This is not however another example of the parasitism of life by capital, but an engineering of, and extension of, vulnerability to execution.

In the twenty-first century, Critter Chips emerge as part of a computational ensemble engineered to instantiate the formal rule of algorithms, with injury becoming a significant component of sensing. Critter Chips bring to the fore the ways in which advanced capitalism plugs organisms into systems of (big) data at the service of capital. Consequently it is from sustaining injury and prolonged death (rather than the exploitation of life) that capital extracts value. In doing so, toxic execution acts as a quantum torque simultaneously tightening and loosening on life.

Critter Compiler

How then might we speculate on ensembles of microbial organisms and computation otherwise? In the Critter Chip the HK44 exists for its capacity for injury. However as Lynn Margulis evidenced, microbial life played a unique role in establishing the biosphere and have a continued prominence in earth processes and signaling climate change (Margulis 1998; Hird 2009; Clark 2011). So then how might we open up the processes of execution to a freer relation with the amazing deeds of microbes? That is to enable microbes to exploit execution as manifestations of life and to "generate novel forms and behaviors, probe new pathways and spaced of possibility, proliferate itself" (Clark 2011, 42).

Critter Compiler is an experiment, a speculative artwork developed as a response to microbial computing otherwise, through a more unruly process of compilation. *Critter Compiler* exploits the heat generated by execution of a recurrent neural network to train a novella writing algorithm, which in turn provides the heat needed for algae to proliferate. As computation is executed the central processing unit (CPU) processes much of the activity that takes place in the computer—and as this happens, heat is emitted, to the point that the execution processes can cause the CPU to overheat or burst into flames. Recursively, as the algae pass over the CPU it cools it, affecting its processing speed, which in turn effects both the algae growth and the novel-writing process.

Whereas Critter Chips are harnessed in semi-living states to signal toxicity, *Critter Compiler* is an unruly multitude of algae microbes and computational processes. Critter Chips are always-already proceeding towards harm for capital. Instead, and as a form of punk solidarity, *Critter Compiler* enlists the process of execution to promote unruly growth of microbial life. Yet although this is a fabulation, just as "the vast majority of microbial intra-actions have nothing to do with humans" (Hird 2009, 2), much of the processes of *Critter Compiler* are similarly inaccessible to us. Instead of approaching microbial life as a resource to measure and extract data from, *Critter Compiler* is an engagement with processes of execution that attempts to generate a non-profit-oriented experiment.

```
110/150 (epoch 36.667), train_loss = 3.03787239, grad/param norm = 3.8415e-01, t
ime/batch = 4.6381s
decayed learning rate by a factor 0.97 to 0.000085239041033725
111/150 (epoch 37.000), train_loss = 2.95983116, grad/param norm = 2.8236e-01, t
ime/batch = 4.8127s
112/150 (epoch 37.333), train_loss = 2.96664293, grad/param norm = 2.0982e-01, t
ime/batch = 4.7085s
113/150 (epoch 37.667), train_loss = 2.96315177, grad/param norm = 1.9476e-01, t
ime/batch = 4.7775s
decayed learning rate by a factor 0.97 to 0.00082681869802713
114/150 (epoch 38.000), train_loss = 2.88823217, grad/param norm = 1.5857e-01, t
ime/batch = 4.7964s
115/150 (epoch 38.333), train_loss = 2.91318690, grad/param norm = 1.5687e-01, t
ime/batch = 4.7505s
116/150 (epoch 38.667), train_loss = 2.92311297, grad/param norm = 1.6523e-01, t
ime/batch = 4.7363s
decayed learning rate by a factor 0.97 to 0.00080201413708631
117/150 (epoch 39.000), train_loss = 2.85977435, grad/param norm = 1.7928e-01, t
ime/batch = 5.3045s
118/150 (epoch 39.333), train_loss = 2.91645789, grad/param norm = 2.1770e-01, t
```

Figure 2. Critter Compiler in training. Pritchard (2016).

In the case of the *Critter Compiler*, the machine learning algorithm learns its writing style at a character-based level from George Eliot's vast novel, *Middlemarch* (1871-72), which is both "A Study of Provincial Life" and a meditation on social and political justice. Therefore, whilst some machine learning algorithms might have been trained for efficiency, financialisation, attention on individuals and profit, *Critter Compiler* is trained by a novel that conveys how we live in a world in which we are all bound in a huge web—and if one pulls one way or another someone or something is affected. Consequently, in *Middlemarch* all events, even the smallest or most everyday ones, are connected to planetary flows—much like microbial life. In addition in *Critter Compiler* the characters are not all human, and their genders are not fixed. In our algorithm, algae species and other lively nonhumans replace human characters. The audience-participant is a witness to this story, which unfolds between us, aquaspheres, politics, global climate change, and algae. Starting at the genealogy of injury but not lingering there, *Critter Compiler* is a small experiment in practices of execution that contributes a set of possible ethno-political practices for microbial computing and life itself, while resisting the production of ever new reparative fantasies of ecological life within networks.

Notes

1. http://www.theatlantic.com/photo/2014/03/the-exxon-valdez-oil-spill-25-years-ago-today/100703/.

2. This is a semi-fictional account based on archival research, patent research and my own lab research in 2013.

3. For a further discussion see the panel convened with Elizabeth R. Johnson "Bioaccumulation: Re-valuing life in the Anthropocene", Association of American Geographers (AAG) Annual Meeting, San Francisco , 2016 and https://www.jiscmail.ac.uk/cgi-bin/webadmin?A2=CRIT-GEOG-FORUM;27909dfd.1509. Thanks are also due to Kathryn Yusoff, Johnson and Mazen Labban for their feedback on my paper presented on this panel.

4. For example Haraway's exquisite story of meeting, feeling and listening together during agility training with Cayenne (2007); or Eva Hayward's evocative engagements with cup corals, that explore multispecies sensorial ensembles and unruly provocations (2010).

5. See Shea et al. (2010) for a discussion on the modularization and abstraction of synthetic biology.

6. http://www.cisco.com/c/dam/en_us/about/ac79/docs/innov/IoT_IBSG_0411FINAL.pdf.

7. For a parallel discussion that pays close attention to the widening of the margin of indeterminacy as an intervention that might enable greater freedoms of operation in technical ensembles see Jennifer Gabrys's eloquent account in Program Earth (Gabrys 2016, 256–258).

References

Catts, Oron, and Ionat Zurr. 2002 "Growing semi-living sculptures: The tissue culture & art project." *Leonardo* 35 (4): 365–370.

Barad, Karen. 2007. *Meeting the Universe Halfway: Quantum Physics and the Entanglement of Matter and Meaning*. Durham: Duke University Press.

——. 2012. "On Touching—The Inhuman That Therefore I Am." *differences: A Journal of Feminist Cultural Studies* 23 (3): 206–223.

——. 2015. "TransMaterialities Trans*/Matter/Realities and Queer Political Imaginings." *GLQ: A Journal of Lesbian and Gay Studies* 21 (2.3): 387–422.

Berlant, Lauren, and Jay Prosser. 2011 "Life writing and intimate publics: a conversation with Lauren Berlant." *Biography* 34 (1): 180–187.

Braidotti, Rosi. 2013. *The Posthuman*. Cambridge: Polity.

——. 2014. "The Untimely". In *The subject of Rosi Braidotti: Politics and concepts*, edited by Bolette Blaagaard. London: Bloomsbury Publishing.

Chen, Mel Y. 2012. *Animacies: Biopolitics, racial mattering, and queer affect*. Durham: Duke University Press.

Chun, Wendy Hui Kyong. 2011. *Programmed Visions: Software and Memory*. Kindle Edition. Cambridge, MA: MIT Press.

Clark, Nigel. 2011. *Inhuman nature: sociable life on a dynamic planet*. London: Sage Publications.

Colebrook, Claire. 2014. *Sex after Life: Essays on Extinction, Vol 2*. Ann Arbor: Open Humanities Press.

Combes, Muriel. 2013. *Gilbert Simondon and the Philosophy of the Transindividual*. Cambridge, MA: MIT Press.

Davies, Gail. 2013. "Mobilizing Experi-mental Life: Spaces of Becoming with Mutant Mice." *Theory, Culture and Society: explorations in critical social science* 30: 129–153.

Eliot, George. (1871–72) 1985. *Middlemarch*. Markham: Penguin.

Gabrys, Jennifer. 2011. *Digital rubbish: A natural history of electronics*. Ann Arbor: University of Michigan Press.

———. 2016. *Program Earth: Environmental Sensing Technology and the Making of a Computational Planet*. Minneapolis: University of Minnesota Press, 2016.

Gramaglia, Christelle. 2013. "Sentinel Organisms: 'they look out for the environment!'" *Limn* 3.

Halberstam, Judith. 2008. "The anti-social turn in queer studies." *Graduate Journal of Social Science* 5 (2): 140–156.

Haraway, Donna J. 2007. *When species meet*. Minneapolis: University of Minnesota Press.

———. 2013. "SF: Science fiction, speculative fabulation, string figures, so far." *Ada: A Journal of Gender, New Media, and Technology* 3.

Hayward, Eva. 2010. "Fingeryeyes: Impressions of cup corals." *Cultural Anthropology* 25 (4): 577–599.

Hird, Mrya. 2008. "Animal Trans." In *Queering the Non/Human*, edited by Noreen Giffney and and Myra Hird. Farnham: Ashgate.

———. 2009. *The origins of sociable life: Evolution after science studies*. New York: Springer.

Labban, Mazen. 2014. "Deterritorializing extraction: Bioaccumulation and the planetary mine." *Annals of the Association of American Geographers* 104 (3): 560–576.

Love, Heather. 2009. *Feeling backward*. Cambridge, MA: Harvard University Press, 2009.

Margulis, Lynn. 2008. *Symbiotic planet: a new look at evolution*. New York: Basic Books.

Murphy, Michelle. 2013. "Chemical Infrastructures of Reproduction." In *Toxic World*, edited by Nathalie Jas and Soraya Boudia. London, Pickering and Chato: Berghahn Books Ltd.

Ong, Aihwa. 2010. "An analytics of biotechnology and ethics at multiple scales." In *Asian Biotech: Ethics and Communities of Fate*, edited by Aihwa Ong and Nancy N. Chen. Durham: Duke University Press: 1–51.

Parisi, Luciana. 2013. *Contagious Architecture: Computation, Aesthetics, and Space*. Cambridge, MA: The MIT Press.

Puig de la Bellacasa, Maria. 2010. "Ethical doings in naturecultures." *Place and Environment Ethics* 13 (2): 151–169.

Shaviro, Steven. 2010. "Interstitial life: Subtractive vitalism in Whitehead and Deleuze." *Deleuze Studies* 4 (1): 107–119.

Shea, Adam, Brian Fett, Marc D. Riedel, and Keshab K. Parhi. 2010. "Writing and compiling code into biochemistry." In *Pacific Symposium on Biocomputing* 15: 456–464.

Simondon, Gilbert. 1958. "On the mode of existence of technical objects." Trans. by Ninian Mellamphy, unpublished. University of Western Ontario: London, Ontario.

Stengers, Isabelle. 2006. "Whitehead and science: From philosophy of nature to speculative cosmology." Montreal, Canada: McGill University.

Yusoff, Kathryn. "Insensible worlds: postrelational ethics, indeterminacy and the (k)nots of relating." *Environment and Planning D: Society and Space* 31 (2): 208–226.

Weiner, Norbert. 1948. *Cybernetics*. New York, NY: MIT Press.

Shrimping under Working Conditions

Francisco Gallardo & Audrey Samson

We propose that mutated forms of death are emerging with neoliberalism's biopolitical financialisation of life. Thinking of such forms as commercial extinction and social death, how do we begin to frame these outside of a quantified rhetoric of surplus? These questions aim to provoke a discussion about these terms that can be interpreted as modes of exhaustion, while maintaining particular biological, social or economic conditions of life. When we are confronted with capitalism's failure to fulfil resource exhaustion, a model of conservation by *dispossession*[1] might emerge within what Rosi Braidotti calls "new and subtler degrees of death and extinction" (2013, 115). In this text we want to think with other conditions of death and extinction that can help to move beyond the missing item of an inventory, a carved rock along a fossil road or a set of pre-emptive actions to be executed beyond a certain threshold. Thus, we ask if there could be figures, which rather than narrating death as a biological or geological concept, open it up to other equally violent forces that are nevertheless materially situated. More importantly, will we ever be able to think of extinction beyond ideas of absence or frame death from social or economic realms as an emerging mode of living? In order to address many of these questions we dissect a critical example of extinction, that of the brown shrimp (*Crangon crangon*) as it flips between commercial (albeit not yet biotic) death in the ex-fishing grounds of the South East corner of the UK, and the social death embedded in the labour-power of the ex-processing factories of the Special Economic Zones of Tangier and Tetuan in Morocco.

Crangon crangon: the Undine of neoliberal numbers

Let us start by saying that certain forms of devastation can be interpreted as a condition of being worn out towards the maintenance of life.[2] We understand devastation following Gilbert Simondon's formulation of the term "deadening". For Simondon, there are different modes of death, one of which is productive and integrated in the process of life (Barthélémy 2015, 48–49).

In other words, in opposition to adverse death, there is a death that has a constitutive role in life itself. In this light, we want to differentiate our argument from others, such as those sustained by Elizabeth Povinelli (2016), for whom death is opposed to the notion of population—a group formed by individuals of the same species sharing the same geographical location.[3] In this section, we discuss the ways in which—under neoliberal conditions—there are modes of death that do not oppose this concept of population. It is rather the deadening of a certain population that grants its survival. However, while Simondon's deadening considers the individual and its processes of individuation, our comments are focused around devastation as connective tissue between deadening and population.

By devastation we refer specifically to the survival strategy of a certain marine organism, the brown shrimp. Contrary to the survival strategies of most organisms, the brown shrimp sits ambiguously between wasteful redundancy and catastrophe. Populations school in the soft bottom of shallow coastal waters and are subjected to the strong tidal forces of the North Sea. Female shrimp reach maturity at ten months, after which they spawn millions of offspring twice a year. Densities of sixty individuals per square metre of seabed are common to find. *C. crangon* is a predator to young fish and crustaceans, by which it is later preyed upon. However, maritime predators such as whiting or sole, given their low tolerance to satiety, quickly assimilate large numbers of immature offspring (Campos 2012). Such mechanisms of quick turnaround and fast maturity sit at the core of sociobiology, linking what some experts term the "dilution effect" (Howard 1971) and "predator-saturation" (Molles 1999). In summary, the presence of any individual is diluted by the large cloud of a population, hence its risk to be predated is diminished. In other words, the brown shrimp finds safety in sheer numbers by feeding its predators with its neighbours. Rioting fecundity in addition to group living are forced mechanisms in order to cope with predatory pressure. For shrimp, the optimism transpiring from the force of maintaining population rests upon modes of quick death and wasteful life.

Such forces of devastation and optimism were at play in nineteenth-century efforts to reduce evolution by natural selection to a set of arithmetical questions (Magnello 1993). At that time, Charles Darwin's ideas posed a strong emphasis on deviation, a concept that was often unwanted and ignored, escaping mathematisation altogether until then. At the theoretical level, Darwin maintained that variation (deviation from the norm) was meaningful and hence should be accounted for, as variation allowed tracing species back to the tree of life. However, as Eileen Magnello (2011) reminds us, Darwin's biological variation required two key changes within the discipline of statistics. First, to regard variation as a resource, not as a source of error,[4] and second, the notion of biological species needed to be defined not as average individuals but in terms of population. That is, a group that shares a geographical location and is formed of variating individuals. However, even though Darwin introduced various types of mathematical tools that could be used to that effect, statistical methods remained at the level of sophistication of the rule of three (Magnello 2011, 34). As eugenicist and mathe-matician Karl Pearson declared, "every idea of Darwin, from variation, natural selection, inheritance to reversion, seemed to demand statistical analyses" (1901, 3).

Two thousand nine hundred and eighty brown shrimp from Sheerness and Plymouth were carefully counted, painfully peeled, measured and dissected by biologist Raphael Weldon during his stays at the Laboratory of Marine Biological Association at Plymouth (Pearson, 2011). *C. crangon* accumulates small changes rapidly through generations that are visible to the unaided eye. For each shrimp, Weldon took four measurements, concentrating on the main body parts (carapace, tergum and telson) (Weldon 1892). In order to deal with such an immense wealth of data, mathematician Pearson, a collaborator and close friend of Weldon, developed a standardised system of frequency distributions. Deviation, accumulated visibly through the rapid and wasteful life cycle of the shrimp thus provided the means necessary to develop mathematically-based statistics. Techniques such as correlation, regression and goodness-of-fit,[5] all having deviation as a core, permitted systems of comparison and generalisation that were previously impossible. Evolution was no longer a matter of "causalisation", that is, cause and effect, but of correlation. Nature was not a matter of collective things that hold through aggregates of individuals. In Alain Desrosière's words, nature became a "thing that holds" (2010, 30).

The offspring of extinction

According to historical records, the lucrative business of brown shrimp first came into effect after the exhaustion of more valuable fisheries in the Thames Estuary such as oyster or cod (Lewis 1831). By the 1850s, the Leigh shrimp-net had become the main predator of the brown shrimp. During the age of sail, vessels were timed by the clock of the tide. The sandy shoals from the north bank of the Thames Estuary to the Nore were trawled by "bawleys"[6] or cutter-rigged smacks,[7] powered by westerly winds, and later by steam trawlers. Using from two to four beam-trawls at a time, they were kept down up to an hour or more at a time, depending on the extent of ground and sailing conditions (Holdsworth 1877). At the sail-age, this trade employed nearly one hundred boats with a crew of two, mostly during the summer months when wind and weather conditions are usually more favourable.

Today, after years of heavy trawling, shrimp fishing has become a rare activity in the Thames Estuary. The dwindling density of shrimp grounds is to blame, in conjunction with sharp rises in fuel prices. It could be said that together these have pushed the brown shrimp out from the Thames Estuary. As business jargon would have it, brown shrimp is, for most intents and purposes, *commercially extinct*. This is not a matter of concern for conservation, as other fishing grounds fill the guts of the national and continental seafood market, such as those of the Wash, Morecambe Bay and the Solway Firth. Commercial extinction is a concept rather than a fact. Every individual that is plucked from the seabed is virtually the last one, though this does not necessarily infer crisis. The commercial extinction of the brown shrimp is a force that helps to bring other fields such as statistics, economics or technology, among others, into more traditional accounts of extinction, which are restricted mostly to geology and biology. Commercial extinction still pertains almost exclusively to the concept of population measure. However, this mode of extinction can be better understood through the notion of environmentality (Agrawal 2005), which emphasises population within a space of financial power and the financialisation of life.

As the phrase implies, commercial extinction defines death from economic, social or cultural realms but not from the total (virtual) biotic inventory of marine life. It is acceptable loss, or better, a comfortable form of catastrophe.[8] Drawing from Lauren Berlant, commercial extinction can be understood as a form a "slow death", in the way in which it implies a "mass physical attenuation under global/national regimes of capitalist structural subordination and governmentality" (2007, 754). This mode of extinction shows, opposing Maurizio Lazzarato's reading of extinction (2014), that the destructive nature of capital is relative, not absolute. While commercial extinction still reduces something like a fishing ground to a mere object of exploitation, it shows the very exhaustion of exhaustion. The commercial extinction of the brown shrimp collates what most addresses of extinction fail to do: to underline the failure of capitalism to consume, or to fulfil extinction. It infers that a slow mode of deadening is a possible mode of living. In short, the shrimp is still there, but it is not *sufficiently* there. After all, there are certain things that cannot be extinguished entirely within capitalism, such as unemployment.[9]

With neither biopolitics nor necropolitics fully capable of discerning between life, death and non-life, Povinelli (2016) puts forward her own three figures of extinction: the desert, the animist and the virus. The desert is a geographical entity denuded of life, though it can regain it. The animist collapses this division as nonsensical. Everything is alive. The virus gags at the notion of life; as for a virus it is the difference that makes no difference (Povinelli 2016, 14–18). These three figures interrogate extinction and help to think with them through different discourses, questions and problems. In Povinelli's words, they do not reproduce the division between life and nonlife so relevant in the current modes of thought and practice that define late liberalism (2014).[10]

As compelling as Povinelli's figures are, they do not address the questions that commercial extinction might raise for us. By posing new figures within the realm of the brown shrimp's commercial extinction, we want to bring forward the notion of deadening within a neoliberal order as a mode of life and/or living. After all, a survey of species catalogued under the label of commercial extinction reveals that most of them are to be found in the ocean. This to us seems quite fitting, given that, as Christopher Connery notes, "[the ocean] is capital's favored myth element" (1994, 56).

Here we would like to propose the trawl, the price of liquid fuel and the railway as figures of commercial extinction. Petrol replaced altogether other traditional forms of power such as the cumbersome cotton sails and, later on, steam-coal. Formed by hydrocarbon chains of lesser complexity, hence of higher caloric content,[11] liquid fuel helped to detach horsepower from the power of a horse; a carrying capacity that affords greater dragging and heavier gear. However, as Timothy Mitchell (2011) argues, it was liquid fuel's physio-chemical properties that became constitutive of political agency. In other words, liquid fuel is easier to manipulate, distribute and store. Oilfields, pipelines, refineries and pumping stations are by effect, and by design, immune to organised labour, unlike the systems that had governed the extraction and distribution of coal (Mitchell 2011, 108). Turner Prize artist Jeremy Deller would find his petrol-equivalent *Battle of Orgreave* (2010) re-enacted with slight differences at every peak in oil-price in the form of mass-killings.

The best way to catch a cloud of brown shrimp is with another cloud. Throughout seven centuries, the trawl's evolution as a technical object has afforded thicker and more turbid clouds of detritus, deposits and by-catch. When alarmed, *C. crangon* buries itself in the sand with a fan-like tail movement. However, under vibratory stimulus such as a predator's presence—i.e. cod, or the approaching bottom contact of a pounding beam—it is known to trigger a startle escape response. The trawler's bottom contact has widened seven fold from the early beam-trawls of Barking,[12] which later developed into tickler chains, chain matrices, bobbin ropes and the otter trawl.[13] Gear for white and pink shrimp in the distant bays of Florida can deploy otter trawls with each door weighing almost a tonne and a net spanning thirty metres. As the pounding of a beam or chain approaches, the shrimp spring upwards, clearing the bottom bar and jumping straight into the net.

The combustion engine reminds us that supply and demand were not always related. Railways dithered to appreciate the radical potential their system could have on the marketisation of highly perishable commodity. Railway industries originally focused on high-tariff fish traffic such as large cod, sole and turbot (Robinson 1986). Shipments integrating multiple companies were awkward at first. Too far from waterways and shorelines, it wasn't uncommon to see supply glutting markets at the same time as severe shortages, caused primarily by poor harvests. Cobles[14] would be laid up and tons of protein-rich white fish dung were sown over vast fields. However, as some historians have noticed, increases in the trawled-fish trade were related to the construction of railways (Blackman 1992). Robb Robinson (1986, 32) brings to attention the correlation between the opening of the North Sea to trawling in the nineteenth century with the explosive construction of railway infrastructure, dubbed as the two railways mania.[15] The expansion of the railway was needed for the overabundance of fresh fish that trawling could deliver in order to grow, while at the same time the trawling industry needed a mode of connection between ports and markets.

At the dawn of the twentieth century, traditional Greek boat-building knowledge couples the figures of extinction into what is today the modern trawler (Edenfield 2014) — a.k.a. the world's most disruptive, as well as the most economically productive, fishing technology.[16] Austrian artist duo Ubermorgen have used the mediagenic capital of British Petroleum's (BP) Deep Horizon explosion and subsequent spill catastrophe as material.[17] Pointing at abundant aerial images captured during this dramatic episode, they claimed the return of oil as "the supreme discipline of art" (Ubermorgen 2010). For the artists, this comeback had forced oil painting to evolve into a kind of sickly generative bio-art.[18] Similarly to Ubermorgen, we would like to consider the scraping and digging of the roots of seabed life by trawlers to be the Earth's biggest work of printmaking. Trawl marks remain observable by side scan sonar two years after they were first ploughed. It is perhaps more cynical that these scars remain while shrimp schools are generally too hard to ensonify by echo-sound. A shrimp is too small a target and lacks an air bladder,[19] unlike most fish. One step ahead of Andy Warhol's famous efforts to mechanise and automatise the work of art, the three figures of commercial extinction—the trawl, the price of liquid fuel and the railway—turn into art the work of mechanisation and automation. Freed from the clock of the tide, these figures have left trails and carvings, many of them visible to satellites and SONAR.[20]

Peeling

The collagen-rich shell of the brown shrimp sits at one of the last frontiers of mechanisation. The shrimp's abdomen is largely filled with muscle and connective tissue. Comprising almost half of the total shrimp's weight, it accounts for a powerful muscle used only in predator avoidance. While protein bonds in the epidermis[21] are known, the route resulting in the breaking of such bonds is not well understood yet (Crawford 1980). Currently, the processing of shrimp covers a multi-step process, including the ageing step before peeling, which takes up to six days and occurs partially during transportation to the peeling factory. Ageing loosens meat from the shell as a result of the breaking of protein bonds in the membrane before peeling by hand. So far, and despite repeated engineering efforts, peeling has escaped mechanisation all together. Unlike other kinds of shrimps, the brown shrimp still requires the dexterous thin fingers of unskilled, typically female workers (Perez 2010; RNW 2010). To a certain extent, the brown shrimp claims that there are still some limits to the ability of mechanisation to take command (Giedion 1970).

The processing of brown shrimp sailed away from Europe in the early 1990s. In the mid 1980s, The Netherlands banned shrimp hand peeling altogether when a dysentery outbreak killed fourteen homeworkers (Kayser and Mosel 1984).[22] As a result, shrimp processing was offshored from Dutch unregulated work-homes to the uncontrolled outskirts of Europe. They moved first to Bulgaria and Poland. However, after the constitution of the Economic European Area limits, companies needed to scout still further for cheap labour, creating offshore and nearshore[23] hubs. The Free Trade Zones of Tangier and Tetuan in the early 2000s became the new bastion for the *neoliberation* of many economic activities servicing the single market, shellfish manufacturing being one among many.

As claimed by Aihwa Ong (2006) and Michel Feher (2014), neoliberalism promises the extinction of manual labour by the ghostly workings of its invisible hands. The recipe is apparently simple. It first requires the implementation of temporal "sacrifice zones of exception" in clogged economies, or as the authors reframe them: UNDER economies — economies rated as Underperforming, Non-Developed, Expropriate-able or Ruined (Toban et al 2014). Industrial capitalism was originally imported into these regions by promising the transfer of technical and capital knowledge in exchange for the capitulation of labour protection, duty impositions and environmental regulations, among others. The current promise for these zones is that the industrial economy will be absolved by a financial substitute: advanced capitalism. The former international zone of Tangiers is now emerging as a host to offshore banking activities resembling those of Gibraltar, Hong Kong, Bahrain, Luxembourg or the Cayman Islands.

In the field of photography, Allan Sekula (2014) reflected upon the threat of the automatisation of the image as opposed to the iconic significance of the organ of drawing. He highlighted Roland Barthes' (1980) protesting of the ubiquitous presence of the human hand in Diderot and d'Alembert's *Encyclopédie*, published in France between 1751 and 1772. In many plates, hands without bodies accompanied the encyclopaedic objects, almost as another component, in each complex mechanism or artisanal work. From Sekula's remarks, it is not difficult to see how these plates were, perhaps unintentionally, turning every citizen—or better every hand—into a kind of expendable technological organ. Transferring this reflection to a more contemporary economic order, hands could be said to be the "sacrifice zones" marketed for the promises of a new economic order. The exploitation of forms of *inhuman* energy can be understood as another way to understand "slow (social) death". As an aside, it might be useful to recall the role that the hand has played in processes of criminalisation and/or socialisation. Jailed prostitutes were put in forced workhouses to pick oakum in nineteenth century England (Mayhew and Binny 2011, x). Homosexuals were sent without trial to stitch soccer balls in Spain under Francisco Franco's dictatorship (Ugarte 2005). The hysterical woman was medicated by the masturbating hand of the psychotherapist, or what Foucault referred to as the "laying on of hands" (Micale 2008). Against the optimistic rhetoric of progress, repetitive, menial and injuring tasks have been a weapon throughout history for the re-socialisation of outcasts, sexual deviants and prostitutes.[24] These moving limbs are part of the execution of neoliberal systems' fetishising traditional labour power in order to lead to a new order from the industrial capitalism of the labouring hands in which money would be created out of money (Mulvey 1993).

Conclusion: Death as a mode of living

Do not despair. The destructive nature of capitalism under neoliberalism is not absolute, but relative. "[N]ew and subtler degrees of extinction" are mobilised by new practices of "life"

(Braidotti 2007, 2). Throughout this chapter we have introduced several instances of *operative* modes of death. We are particularly drawn by those that consider the exhaustion of exhaustion, such as in the concept of commercial extinction. In this light, commercial extinction is an example of exception to the concept of extinction. The life-cycle of the commercially extinct brown shrimp, *C. crangon*, is based on quick turn-around and group living as a way to reduce predatory risk. In fact, such a life-cycle was key to the mathematisation of Darwin's ideas of evolution by natural selection. It helped to kickstart a revolution in statistics that rely on the appreciation and translation of variation to a set of arithmetic questions. Together with our protagonist, *C. crangon*, we re-staged commercial extinction in such a way so as to open it up to a wider process of movements by our proposed three figures of extinction. These key players in the emerging modes of neoliberal death bring forth the notion that economic life can also be a threatening force in a discourse usually focused on biology and geology.

The collagen-rich shell of the brown shrimp is an exception to the long assumed command of mechanisation (Giedion 1970). The peeling of brown shrimp still demands the dexterous hands of unskilled labour power in the Special Economic Zones of Tangier-Med, in Morocco. For us, the execution of neoliberal forces relies on both industrial capitalism and its financial counterpart, represented in this chapter by the invisible and the labouring hand. What are these hands without bodies *executing*? Conservation and dispossession become associated tropes by which movement of capital and accumulation are measured and defined. With forms of deadening emerging through neoliberalism, death as a mode of living invites us to consider the maintenance of economic life through social death and commercial extinction as operative. In short, comfortable forms of catastrophe.

Notes

1. Ten year ago, Marxist geographer David Harvey introduced the motto "accumulation by dispossession" in various texts (2003, 2004). With it, Harvey described that under neoliberalism, capitalism best operates not by developing modes of creating wealth, but by divesting it from its source. More current work on this direction highlights the role of sustainable models (the economics of ecosystems, biodiversity, the Green Economy, etc.) as a more stable mode of accumulation — accumulation by securitization, or accumulation by conservation (Büscher and Flecher 2015; Massé and Lunstrum 2009). With conservation by dispossession we want to place the emphasis on the contradiction not of extorting nature to pay for itself. We are trying to address modes of conservation outside of conservation, orconservation not as an end but as a by-product.

2. As Gerry Melino (2002) points out, part of the explanation for the slow understanding of apoptosis processes lays in its mode of execution. Apoptosis is a process of controlled cellular death which occurs twenty times as fast as cell division or differentiation, well below of the limit of detection. Unlike its counterpart necrosis, unprogrammed or premature death, apoptosis leaves no residues.

3. In discussing the concept of extinction, Elizabeth Povinelli (2014) explains that the opposite of species is not death, but non-life. The opposite of population is not non-life, but death.

4. As Alain Desrosières (1998, 103–105) explains, vital statistics such as those in Robert Malthus, Adolphe Quatelet or Émile Durkheim emphasised means and averages, thus treating deviation from the mean as a source of error.

5. Goodness of fit test, also known as chi-square test, is used to determine sample data consistency in the face of a hypothesised distribution. See http://stattrek.com/chi-square-test/goodness-of-fit.aspx?Tutorial=AP for details.

6. According to E. W. White (2013), the development of this type of boat is uncertain. It is originally from the North side of the Thames Estuary and usually referred as the Thames shrimper. Its developments are associated with the Thames "Peter-boat". Early bawleys were clincher-built and contained a wet-well to keep the cargo alive. A later development type of bawley was carvel-built, which reduced hull friction against the water. The well was later supplanted by a copper cauldron, hereby preparing the catch for the market. The name bawley is speculated as being a corruption of the English for boiler, in reference to the on-board boiling apparatus.

7. A rig refers to the arrangement of types of sails, lines and mast(s) in order to harness wind power. A cutter-rigged watercraft is characterised for its speed and sail manoeuvrability. This rig allows turning windward in an easier fashion than any other kind of rigging. It is especially suitable for navigation on creeks, under shallow waters and against strong tides. On the other hand, they are poorly suited for fishing purposes (White 2013, 16).

8. Derrida worked in his last years on the subject of thought extinction as consequence of impending nuclear catastrophe. (Derrida et al. 1984). Paradoxically, the threat of human extinction allowed a period of "military peace". Conservationists have examined some of the odd ecological benefits of the Cold War, such as a reduced number of species invasion resulting from the interruption of trade between

Eastern and Western Europe (Chiron et al. 2010). Another effect of the Cold War threat was, as Jacob Darwin Hamblin describes it (2013), the spawning of the environmental movement, as much of modern environmental thinking originated with the scientists and military strategists during the dark days of the cold war.

9. Unemployment was a monetary policy first proposed by economist Milton Friedman under the concept of natural rate of unemployment. It was successively expanded into what today is known as non-accelerating inflation rate of unemployment, or NAIRU for short. The main underlying concept is that a certain level of unemployment is necessary to keep inflation low. See William Mitchell and Joan Muysken (2008).

10. Povinelli (2011) usually interchanges the concept of neoliberalism for late liberalism as a mode to highlight the continuity of the process, not the rupture naming. This argument is further developed in Povinelli, Coleman and Yusoff (2014).

11. The higher chemical complexity, the lower energy content (measured in unit of energy per unit of mass, i.e. Mj/Kg or j/g). Beyond fuel, drugs work similarly followed low chemical complexity higher effect.

12. The beam-trawl has it ancestor in England as "wondyrchoun", as recorded by a Petition elevated by fisherman from Barking to the Parliament in 1376–77. The name is believed to be a deprecation of the Dutch words "wonder" and "shoe" or "sock", which leaves us with the speculation of whether the genealogy of this technical object dates back to footwear customs.

13. In an otter trawl, two doors or otter boards function as underwater kites by generating and maintaining the spread of the net. For further details see Davis (1958).

14. The term coble refers to a type of open fishing boat, originally from the North East coast of England. The use of the term is currently extended to most fishing vessels. As in many working boats, the particular conditions in this area, such as prevailing winds, the hardness of the sea-floor, wave strength, tide, etc., are embedded in the adopted shape.

15. In order to give an indication of the magnitude for such a bubble, from 1840 to 1846 (the effective end for this event) the proposed routes totalled 9,500 miles of new railways. This mileage contrasts with the current UK railway network of around 11,000 miles (Wolmar 2009). Surprisingly enough, communication infrastructure bubbles or manias such as this one have occurred approximately every other century. First with the Canal Mania in the early eighteenth century, the Railway Mania of nineteenth century and the Telecom and Internet "dot-com" bubbles of the late twentieth century. Interestingly, the telecom boom was prompted after companies became aware that railway rights-of-way could be reused to install and service an extensive length of telecommunication network, affording low costs for fibre optic conduits.

16. The most economically important single species in the world by weight is the shrimp species *Acetes japonicus*, which is used in the production of the akiami paste shrimp in many countries around the Southeast Sea of China; see Rudloe & Rudloe (2009). The industry of trawling also produces the higher by-catch ratio (by-catch:shrimp), ranging from 2:1 in colder waters to 15:1 in tropical seas.

17. See Goriunova & Fuller (2017) on "Devastation".

18. The amount of novel forms of life benefiting by the oil spill has

been documented now to a great extent by, for instance, Dombrowski et al. (2016). Key to the findings are a higher than expected biodiversity of polycyclic aromatic hydrocarbon-degrading bacteria, chief among them being *Alcanivorax borkumensis*.

19. The air bladder in Osteichthyes or bonefish is an organ filled with gas for buoyancy control as well as producing and receiving sound, due to its resonating characteristics. It is usually located at the dorsal position, the mass centre is below the volume centre, hence acting as a stabilising system. J. Z. Young, in the Department of Anatomy of University College London, among others, points to swim bladders as the material of earliest contraceptive sheaths or condoms, even before sheep's caeca. See Huxely (1957).

20. See Palanques et al. (2001). The biggest trawling gear, spanning 30 m wide, can be, technically speaking, perceived from orbital space. 30 m x 30 m is approximately the standard resolution of today's satellite systems, such as the Landsat program used for meteorological purposes.

21. In anatomic studies of invertebrates such as in molluscs, crustaceans and echinoderms, epidermis usually refers to the membrane between the muscle or meat and the shell.

22. A small epidemic of dysentery caused by Shigella flexneri 2 occurred in the Netherland between December 25th, 1983 and January 7th, 1984. It caused death in 14 patients. See Kayser and Mosel (1984).

23. Nearshoring zones are not much dissimilar to offshore zones. Predominantly, they are dedicated to outsourced service industries, i.e. call centres, banking, insurance or software maintenance. They have become increasingly popular due to the consumer pressure of moving beyond full globalisation. The first two nearshores of Tanger MED were created in 2007, a model that is planned to double by 2020.

24. See Mayhew and Binny (2011). Picking oakum is the colloquial term used when referring to the manual labour of untwisting and loosing old cords or ropes. Oakum, after tarring was used in sealing cast iron plumbs and caulking timber joints in wooden vessels and later on planking iron and steel ships. Under Spanish dictatorial regime, from 1954 to 1976 Spanish homosexuals were prosecuted and sentenced without trial under the 'Ley de Vagos y Maleantes' [Vagrants and Crooks Act]. They were either sent to prisons on Badajoz or Huelva according to a sorting system between "actives" or "passives". See Ugarte (2005).

References

Agrawal, Arun. 2005. *Environmentality: Technologies of Government and the Making of Subjects*. Durham, NC: Duke University Press.

Barthélémy, Jean-Hugues. 2015. *Life and Technology: An Inquiry Into and Beyond Simondon*. Translated by Barnaby Norman. Lüneburg, Germany: Meson Press.

Barthes, Roland. (1980) 1988. "The plates of the encyclopedia". In *New Critical Essays*, 23–39. Translated by Richard Howard. New York: Johns Hopkins University Press.

Berlant, Lauren. 2007. "Slow death (sovereignty, obesity, lateral agency)." *Critical Inquiry* 33 (4): 754–780.

Black, Toban, Stephen D'Arcy, and Tony Weis, eds. 2014. *A Line in the Tar Sands: Struggles for Environmental Justice*. Oakland, CA: PM Press.

Blackman, Janet. 1992. "The Food Supply of an Industrial Town." *Business History*, 83–97.

Braidotti, Rosi. 2007. 'Biomacht und nekro-Politik. Uberlegungen zu einer Ethik der Nachhaltigkeit', [Biopower and Necropolitics, Reflections on an ethics of sustainability]. *Springerin, Hefte fur Gegenwartskunst* 2:18–23.

Büscher, Bram, and Robert Fletcher. 2015. "Accumulation by conservation." *New Political Economy* 20, 2:273-298.

Campos, Joana, Cláudia Moreira, Fabiana Freitas, and Henk W. van der Veer. 2012. "Short review of the eco-geography of Crangon." *Journal of Crustacean biology* 32 (2):159–169.

Connery, Christopher. 1996. "The Oceanic Feeling and the Regional Imaginary." In *Global/Local: Cultural Production and the Transnational Imaginary*, edited by Rob Wilson and Wimal Dissanayake, 284–311. Durham: Duke University Press.

Chiron, François, Susan M. Shirley, and Salit Kark. 2010. "Behind the Iron Curtain: Socio-economic and political factors shaped exotic bird introductions into Europe." *Biological conservation* 143 (2):351–356.

Crawford, David L. 1980. *Meat Yields and Shell Removal Functions of Shrimp Processing*. Corvallis, OR: Oregon State University Press.

Derrida, Jacques, Catherine Porter, and Philip Lewis. 1984. "No Apocalypse, Not Now (full speed ahead, seven missiles, seven missives)." *diacritics* 14 (2):20–31.

Desrosières, Alain. 2002. *The Politics of Large Numbers: A History of Statistical Reasoning*. Translated by Camille Naish. Cambridge, MA and London: Harvard University Press.

Davis, Frederick Mowbray. 1958. *An Account of the Fishing Gear of England and Wales: Fishery Investigations, Series 2 Vol. 21*. London: HM Stationery Office.

Dombrowski, Nina, John A. Donaho, Tony Gutierrez, Kiley W. Seitz, Andreas P. Teske, and Brett J. Baker. 2016. "Reconstructing Metabolic Pathways of Hydrocarbon-degrading Bacteria from the Deepwater Horizon Oil Spill." *Nature Microbiology*, 16057.

Edenfield, Gray. 2014. *Amelia Island: Birthplace of the Modern Shrimping Industry*. London: Fothill Media.

Feher, Mitchel. 2014. "The Neoliberal Condition and its Predecessors: Redemption, Fulfilment, Appreciation". Paper presented at the series of conferences on *Operative Thought: An annual lecture series on the Political Practices of Ideas*. Accessed September 20, 2016. http://www.gold.ac.uk/video/?id=80882516.

Giedion, Sigfried. 1970. *Mechanization Takes Command: A Contribution to Anonymous History*. New York, NY and London: Oxford University Press.

Goriunova, Olga and Fuller, Matthew. (forthcoming) 2017. "Devastation." In *General Ecology*, edited by Erich Hörl and James Burton. London: Bloomsbury Academic.

Hamblin, Jacob Darwin. 2013. *Arming Mother Nature: the Birth of Catastrophic Environmentalism*. London: Oxford University Press.

Hamilton, William D. 1971. "Geometry for the Selfish Herd." *Journal of theoretical Biology* 31 (2):295–311.

Harvey, David. 2003. The New Imperialism. Oxford: Oxford University Press.

———. 2004. *The 'new' imperialism: Accumulation by Dispossession. Socialist Register* 40: 63–87.

Holdsworth, Edmund W. H, Sea fisheries. London, 1877

Huxley, Julian(1957) "Material of early contraceptive sheaths." *British Medical Journal*, 1 (5018): 581–582.

Mossel. David. 1984. "Intervention Sensu Wilson: The Only Valid Approach to Microbiological Safety of Food." *International Journal of Food Microbiology* 1 (1):1–4.

Magnello, M. Eileen. 2009. "Karl Pearson and the Establishment of Mathematical Statistics." *International Statistical Review* 77 (1):3–29.

Massé, Francis, and Elizabeth Lunstrum. 2016. "Accumulation by Securitization: Commercial Poaching, Neoliberal Conservation, and the Creation of New Wildlife Frontiers." *Geoforum* 69: 227–237.

Mayhew, Henry, and John Binny. 2011 *The Criminal Prisons of London: And Scenes of Prison Life*. Harvard, MA: Cambridge University Press.

Melino, Gerry. 2002. "The Meaning of Death". *Cell Death and Differentiation* 9: 347–348.

Micale, Mark, S., 2008. *Hysterical Men: The Hidden History of Male Nervous Illness*. Cambridge, MA: Harvard University Press.

Mitchell, William, and Joan Muysken. *Full Employment Abandoned. Shifting Sands and Policy Failures*. London: Edward Elgar Publishing, 2008.

Mitchell, Timothy. 2011. *Carbon Democracy: Political Power in the Age of Oil*. London, New York: Verso Books.

Molles, Manuel Carl, and James F. Cahill. 1999. *Ecology: Concepts and Applications*. Dubuque, Iowa: WCB/McGraw-Hill.

Mulvey, Laura. 1993. "Some Thoughts on Theories of Fetishism in the Context of Contemporary Culture." *October*, 65: 3–20.

Lazzarato, Maurizzio. 2014. *Extinction*. London: The Serpentine Gallery. http://extinct.ly/texts/#lazzarato.

Lewis, Samuel. 1831. *A Topographical Dictionary of England*. London.

Ong, Aihwa. 2006. *Neoliberalism as Exception: Mutations in Citizenship and Sovereignty*. Durham: Duke University Press.

Palanques, Albert, Pere Puig, Pere Masque, Jacobo Martin, and Anabel Sanchez-Gomez. 2001. "Impact of Bottom Trawling on Water Turbidity and Muddy Sediment of an Unfished Continental Shelf." *Limnology and Oceanography* 46 (5): 1100–1110.

Pearson, Karl. 2011. *Walter Frank Raphael Weldon 1860–1906: A Memoir Reprinted from Biometrika*. New York: Cambridge University Press.

———. 1901. "Editorial (II). The Spirit of Biometrika". *Biometrica* 1, (October).

Povinelli, Elizabeth A. 2016. *Geontologies: A Requiem to Late Liberalism*. Durham: Duke University Press.

———. 2014. "The three figures of Extinction". Paper presented at the series of conferences on Extinction Marathon: Visions of the Future. London: The Serpentine Gallery. Accessed September 20, 2016. https://vimeo.com/111844660.

———. 2011. *Economies of Abandonment: Social Belonging and Endurance in Late Liberalism*. Durham: Duke University Press.

Povinelli, Elizabeth, A., Coleman, Matthew, and Yusoff, Kathryn. 2014. "On biopolitics and the Anthropocene". *Society and Space* (March).

Robinson, Robb. 1986. "The Evolution of Railway Fish Traffic Policies, 1840–66." *The Journal of Transport History* 7 (1): 32–48.

———. 1996. *Trawling: The Rise and Fall of the British Trawl Fishery*. Vol. 11. Liverpool: Liverpool University Press.

Rudloe, Jack, and Anne Rudloe. 2009. *Shrimp: The Endless Quest for Pink Gold*. Upper Saddle River, NJ: FT Press.

Sekula, Allan. 2014. "An Eternal Aesthetics of Laborious Gestures." *Grey Room* 55:16-27.

Simondon, Gilbert. *L'individuation et sa genèse physico-biologique, 213, and L'individuation à la lumière des notions de forme et d'information, 215.*

Solís Pérez, Marlene; 2010. "La construcción simbólica de un mercado de trabajo feminizado en la ciudad de Tánger: Una aproximación" [The Symbolic Construction of a Feminized Labor Market in Tangier: A First Consideration]. *Frontera Norte* 22: 55–80.

Ubermorgen. 2010. *Deeeeeeephorizon*. Accessed September 20, 2016. http://www.deeeeeeephorizon.com/statement.html.

Ugarte, Javier, *Sin derramamiento de Sangre: un Ensayo sobre la Homosexualidad.* [Without Bloodshed: an Essay on Homosexuality]. Barcelona and Madrid, Spain: Egales.

Weldon, Walter Frank Raphael. 1892. "Certain Correlated Variations in Crangon Vulgaris." *Proceedings of the Royal Society of London* 51 (308–314): 1–21.

White, Ernest W. 2013. *British Fishing-Boats and Coastal Craft.* London: Read Books Ltd.

Wolmar, Christian. 2009. *Fire and Steam: a New History of the Railways in Britain.* London: Atlantic Books Ltd.

Afterword: Reverse Executions in the Internet of Things

Jennifer Gabrys

Execution, as the chapters in this collection demonstrate, is a process and condition that might unfurl through code, but also overspills the edges of code. The range of contributions included here addresses the ways in which code could be comparable to the law — or a suspension thereof; to effects that are productive of violence or political encounters; and to extended sites and ecologies where the performance of code remakes relations and materialities. What might begin as a set of instructions to be compiled and executed, then inevitably moves beyond the mere carrying out of commands to open into a wider set of considerations about the effects that computing has in the world. To "execute" is not simply to run a script to effect a particular action. It is also to activate a set of material-political relations and transformations. Yet this is less a deterministic operation, and more of a shifting set of encounters and contingencies that play out through the performance of execution.

Among the many provocations and lines of analysis that emerge across the insightful chapters included here is a question that resonates across several contributions, namely: when does execution come up against the limit of the executable to become something else? Or, to put it another way, how does the process of execution create limit conditions or modes of "termination" that rework or even halt the ability to execute? This question could be asked in relation to the operations that code would set in action that fail to compute; or in relation to the environmental conditions that make the expansion of executions untenable; or in relation to the political effects of computation that enact violence or even murder; or in relation to the ability of processes of execution to destroy the very infrastructure of the executable. It is this last area that I would like to explore as a point of resonance through a discussion of the Internet of Things (IoT), and especially the Mirai botnet attack that has attempted to execute commands through IoT devices.

A dark disco with smart light bulbs

In his amusing primer, *Abusing the Internet of Things*, Nitesh Dhanjani provides an array of examples and simple steps for hacking and commanding IoT devices. An advanced home wireless lighting system, for instance, becomes an infrastructure through which to force blackouts or strobe lighting events by gaining control of the lighting system. IoT extends and expands computation into everyday objects and environments, as well as infrastructures and control systems. At the same time, as computation runs through the fabric of everyday things, it also creates conditions for rerouting devices from their original programs of use. Security and web cameras can be easily hijacked through brute force attacks that allow remote access to real-time video and audio feeds. Refrigerators can be commandeered to make perishables perish. Smart TVs and smart cars are similarly at risk, where display systems can be turned into monitoring devices, and vehicles can be made to veer off route. And farther afield, ice skating rinks with smart HVAC and refrigeration systems can be defrosted, energy systems can be shut down and life support equipment in hospitals can be powered off.

IoT devices often are not manufactured or developed with similar levels of security that are now routinely bundled into personal computers and mainstream operating systems. Smart things are typically cheaply made and sold with default passwords that are not changed by consumers, or that are hard coded into devices and so cannot be changed in the first place. Many IoT devices also use relatively open and accessible communication protocols, which can make it comparatively easy to gain access to a host. On one level, IoT seems to offer the promise of an enhanced ability to perform executions within everyday environments so as to realise efficiency, automation, sustainability and more. Yet on another level, this expanding array of devices opens up the ability to reverse engineer not just these things and their usual programs of use, but also to reverse execute the networked systems to which these things are connected and in so doing bring down larger infrastructures.

Malware, command injections and IP scanners are just part of the growing execution toolkit that has sprung up to enable the commandeering of IoT devices. Programming practices are then proliferating along with devices, with IoT offering up a tantalising array of executable options. Execution can as likely be about the proscribed commanding and controlling of devices as much as the prescribed operation of computational devices in environments, where there might seem to be a war of executions and executables unfolding. Within the Internet of Things, what programs are to be run? Who decides which programs are to be prioritised? And how are the conditions of the executable shifting to give rise to new problems of execution?

Mirai: Executing the executable

Within this context of proliferating IoT devices and reverse executions, one particular bit of malware has gained attention for its ability to take over a large number of vulnerable things. Mirai is the name of the malware that has taken command of security cameras and routers in order to create a distributed denial of service (DDoS) attack against websites and web hosts. From September to November 2016, the malware has been responsible for attacking a security journalist's website, a French web hosting provider, a major domain name service (DNS) provider in the US (Dyn), home broadband routers in Germany and a telecom provider in Liberia. The Dyn DNS attack in the US on 21 October 2016 made the biggest headlines, since its interruption affected sites including Twitter, Reddit and Netflix, among others.

Dyn's account of the event suggests that over "100,000 malicious endpoints" were used in a botnet attack to disrupt their DNS infrastructure. DNS translates domain names to Internet Protocol (IP) addresses so that the locating and organising of computer networks can operate more easily. The excess DDoS traffic, which some accounts estimated to be as much as 1.2 terabytes per second, not only interrupted the DNS system, but also created the problem of "recursive DNS retry traffic, further exacerbating its impact" (Hilton 2016). The "attack vector" shifted across several worldwide regions, beginning "in the Asia Pacific, South America, Eastern Europe, and US-West regions" and then shifting to the eastern US (ibid.). The attack was launched in two stages, the first lasting for two hours between 11:10 UTC to 13:20 UTC; and the second taking place from 15:50 UTC to 17:00 UTC.

Mirai is set within a wider landscape of increasing DDoS attacks, and is one of two now well-known botnets—the other being Bashlight—that together are estimated to have control of up to 1.2 million devices (Goodin 2016). Mirai works by first IP scanning for vulnerable devices, and then brute forcing devices with a list of over 60 default usernames and passwords, many of which are from devices made with components from XiongMai Technologies in China (Krebs 2016). Mirai targets Linux devices using BusyBox, which is free software that provides Unix tools in a single executable binary file. These devices that can read the language of an introduced binary file will treat it as a series of instructions, and the binary file does not require compiling or further action in order to run.

Once the Mirai botnet malware is on the device, it then performs a series of functions, including kicking off (or killing) other malware from the device and securing (or killing, again) port 22 (SSH traffic) to avoid restarting and port 23 (Telnet traffic) so as to avoid botnet competition (Bashlight being the most obvious next competitor that would be commanding vulnerable ports). Mirai also establishes a connection between the infected device and the home command and control (C&C) server to add it to the botnet, and to await instructions. A DDoS attack can then be undertaken through the controlled device. In principle, other types of distributed computing could also be undertaken with the botnet. In this sense, the botnet becomes more than a bit of malware, since through the execution of Mirai on multiple vulnerable devices a distributed computational infrastructure is formed that could be used for multiple purposes, although DDoS attacks have been the most common type of command. Activities are conducted from bots, and not directly from the main machine of attack, and an algorithm for assigning dynamic domain addresses can also ensure that the command and control server is difficult to trace.

After the Dyn attack, Anna-senpai, the hacker assumed to have executed several attacks, made the source code of Mirai openly available on GitHub (some suggest as a way to dump the code and cover the tracks of the attacker, thereby multiplying executors and executions through others taking up and using the code). On the GitHub repository for the Mirai source code, Anna-senpai notes in ForumPost.md that up to 300,000 hosts could be identified and infected per attack using Mirai (Anna-senpai 2016). Within the source code, there are instructions not only for gaining access to bots and ensuring communication, but also for setting the terms of a DDoS attack, such as the duration of the activity and maximum number of bots involved. Botnets of infected devices can also be rented out for attacks, and further analysis of the Dyn attack suggests that rented bots from multiple locations formed part of the attack on their DNS infrastructure (Gallagher 2016). In this sense, there is an economy of executions emerging, where executed and executable devices can be hired into "attack vectors" at key moments and for particular assaults.

The types of execution that the Mirai malware performs are notable in several ways. First, its infection of IoT devices demonstrates not only that these are vulnerable technologies, but also that they can be turned into vectors for attacking other computational devices and infrastructures. Second, it extends execution and executability into a network of distributed computing that reworks the "sites of execution" (Snodgrass on Howse) not only beyond a single machine, but also into anticipatory events and temporalities (Soon) that are here dependent upon attacks to be launched and money to be made. Third, it points to the moment at which execution comes up against the limits of the executable, since Mirai, Bashlight and its yet-to-be-developed competitors, could bring down Internet functions to make the communicative exchanges of "smart" devices untenable. This could generate a sluggish IoT device, or it could derail a key bit of smart infrastructure, or anything in between. Execution involves much more than running instructions, and Mirai further points to the ways in which these command and control dynamics are, as Gauthier suggests in this volume, severely "under-theorised". By way of concluding this Afterword and discussion of Mirai as a sprawling example of execution, I now turn to consider how these ways of reverse engineering devices and performing reverse executions might be theorised in relation to the chapters in this collection.

Reverse executions

If you make a motor turn in reverse, you do not break it: you build a refrigerator.
– Michel Serres, *The Parasite*

When Michel Serres suggested that the reversal of motors could produce entirely new mechanisms, he did so in the context of a discussion of how "systems function with several norms at a time" (1982, 68). A refrigerator as reversed mechanism does not break a system; instead it could introduce other motorised operations. Indeed, in relation to a system Serres further suggests: "The best way to succeed in it is to misconstrue it. The counternorm is never a noise of the norm but the same norm reversed, that is to say, its twin" (68). Such reversals to a system could be a way to "transform it in order to reinforce it" (69).

Taking up this philosophy of reversals in relation to executions, and especially in relation to Mirai, we then find a somewhat different approach that might first deploy malware as an example of "oppositional tactics" to rework and exploit power within networks (Cox). But this exploitation of power within networks works just to the point of ensuring that botnet executions can continue to disrupt and threaten the collapse of a system, without finally destroying the very system upon which they rely. Dyn noted that not only did the attack on their service draw attention to the security flaws of IoT devices, but also it raised questions "about the future of the internet" (Hilton 2016). In a related conversation, security researcher Bruce Schneier has suggested that "Someone Is Learning How to Take Down the Internet" through recurring and larger DDoS attacks that look "as if the attacker were looking for the exact point of failure" within any given system under attack (Schneier 2016).

But perhaps the execution that Mirai performs is not one of absolutely crashing the Internet, but of demonstrating that this is the possibility of an unchecked set of executions performed through distributed computing. The reverse engineering of IoT devices highlights how reverse executions could terminate the very ability to execute, but then the botnets would be terminated along with these final executions. The reversal does not absolutely break the motor, as Serres suggests. Instead, it builds another kind of machine within the same system. A botnet that could hold machines to ransom and decide when and how they operate, and under what conditions, would be such a shadowy refrigerator—performing reverse executions in order to ensure that some executions and executables have priority over others, and that some might even be silenced or extinguished.

Reverse executions are then potentially generative of other programmatic relations. While a DDoS attack might attempt to bring down web sites, hosts or infrastructures, security measures are also generated to counter and diffuse the attack.

AFTERWORD: REVERSE EXECUTIONS IN THE INTERNET OF THINGS

At the same time, a whole set of other actions are set in motion, from communities analysing and developing responses to the attack execution matrix, to policy measures for increasing security on IoT devices, to calls for manufacturer responsibility for the vulnerability of devices, to further attacks and hijacking of devices. The running of instructions, as many of the chapters in this collection indicate, is then only one part of an extended environment of execution.

Most "users" of infected devices do not know that their devices have been compromised. A sluggish performance due to reduced bandwidth could be one clue. Or an inability to access controlled ports could be another one. Numerous forecasts for the growth of the IoT suggest that billions of devices are still to be introduced. Krebs, the security journalist whose website was also targeted by a Mirai DDoS attack, notes:

> There are plenty of new, default-insecure IoT devices being plugged into the Internet each day. Gartner Inc. forecasts that 6.4 billion connected things will be in use worldwide in 2016, up 30 percent from 2015, and will reach 20.8 billion by 2020. In 2016, 5.5 million new things will get connected each day, Gartner estimates. (Krebs 2016)

While on the one hand the Internet of Things could be seen to be a questionable technological adventure in saturating environments with resource-intensive computational devices,[1] on the other hand the rise of these devices reworks the problems of executions and executables to enable surveillance, hijacking, ransoming, cybercrime and more. While technologies such as drones are rightly addressed in this collection as examples of "computational regimes" that raise questions of how to develop "a politics appropriate to these radical modes of calculation" (Schuppli), at the same time there are a whole host of more everyday devices that have become computational "attack vectors" that also fall within the scope of this question. If this is a form of "software insurgency" (Cox), then how might a malware-commanded botnet army of toasters and cameras begin to point toward other programmatic relations? From critter compilers (Pritchard) to "comfortable forms of catastrophe" (Gallardo and Samson), the openings made into and through executions can demonstrate the shadowy commitments that inform the living and dying of our computational systems.

Notes

1. For an extended discussion and critique of the environmental impact of the Internet of Things, see Gabrys 2016.

References

Anna-senpai. 2016. "ForumPost.md." Mirai Source Code, 30 September. https://github.com/jgamblin/Mirai-Source-Code/blob/master/ForumPost.md.

Dhanjani, Nitesh. 2015. *Abusing the Internet of Things*. Sebastopol, CA: O'Reilly Media, Inc.

Gabrys, Jennifer. 2016. "Re-thingifying the Internet of Things." In *Sustainable Media: Critical Approaches to Media and Environment*. Edited by Nicole Starosielski and Janet Walker, pages 180–195. New York and London: Routledge.

Gallagher, Sean. 2016. "How One Rent-a-Botnet Army of Cameras, DVRs Caused Internet Chaos." *Ars Technica*. http://arstechnica.com/information-technology/2016/10/inside-the-machine-uprising-how-cameras-dvrs-took-down-parts-of-the-internet.

Goodin, Dan. 2016. "Brace Yourselves: Source Code Powering Potent IoT DDoSes Just Went Public." *Ars Technica*. http://arstechnica.co.uk/security/2016/10/iot-ddos-mirai-botnet-details.

Hilton, Scott. 2016. "Dyn Analysis Summary Of Friday October 21 Attack." *Company News*, 26 October. http://dyn.com/blog/dyn-analysis-summary-of-friday-october-21-attack.

Krebs, Brian. 2016. "Hacked Cameras, DVRs Powered Today's Massive Internet Outage." *Krebs on Security*. https://krebsonsecurity.com/2016/10/hacked-cameras-dvrs-powered-todays-massive-internet-outage.

Krebs, Brian. 1 October 2016. "Source Code for IoT Botnet 'Mirai' Released." *Krebs on Security*. https://krebsonsecurity.com/2016/10/source-code-for-iot-botnet-mirai-released.

Schneier, Bruce. 13 September 2016. "Someone Is Learning How to Take Down the Internet." *Schneier on Security*. https://www.schneier.com/blog/archives/2016/09/someone_is_lear.html.

Serres, Michel. 1982. *The Parasite*. Trans. by Lawrence R. Schehr. Baltimore and London: The Johns Hopkins University Press.

Biographies

Geoff Cox is Reader in Fine Art at Plymouth University (UK) and Associate Professor in the School of Communication and Culture, Aarhus University (DK), currently engaged on a 3 year research project The Contemporary Condition funded by the Danish Council for Independent Research. As part of this, he wrote (with Jacob Lund) *The Contemporary Condition: Introductory Thoughts on Contemporaneity and Contemporary Art*, as the first in a new series of small books published with Sternberg Press (2016). With Alex McLean, he wrote *Speaking Code* (MIT Press 2013), and amongst other things is currently working on a multi-authored book project about live coding.

Olle Essvik is an artist working and living in Gothenburg. Essvik works with themes relating to the digital, and technology in a human context, touching on notions of everyday life, repetition and time. The outcome could be a book, a publication, or a sculpture in which traditional materials and techniques like wood and bookbinding converge with programming and code. He is a Senior Lecturer at Gothenburg University (Academy of Design and Crafts). jimpalt.org

Jennifer Gabrys is Reader in the Department of Sociology at Goldsmiths, University of London, and Principal Investigator on Citizen Sense, a project funded by the European Research Council (2013–2017) that engages with inventive approaches to participation and monitoring in order to test and query environmental sensing technology. Gabrys's books include a techno-geographical investigation of environmental sensing, *Program Earth: Environmental Sensing Technology and the Making of a Computational Planet* (University of Minnesota Press, 2016); and a material-political analysis of electronic waste, *Digital Rubbish: A Natural History of Electronics* (University of Michigan Press, 2011). She has also co-edited an interdisciplinary collection on plastics, *Accumulation: The Material Politics of Plastic* (Routledge, 2013). Her work can be found at citizensense.net and jennifergabrys.net

Francisco Gallardo is a spatial practitioner whose work explores forms of environmentally embedded violence as the interface between territory, technology and society.

Within the duo FRAUD, he is interested in exploring the material intractability of global trade, the diminishing virtual negantropism of maritime finalisation, networks of immiserate remote labour, and other forms of slow violence. He is a PhD candidate at the School of Geography of Queen Mary University (QMU) with affiliated appointments at the New Media Lab and Technology of QMU and the Center for Cultural Studies at Goldsmiths University.

David Gauthier likes to mangle many things, chiefly concepts, objects, languages, practices, and disciplines. He produces artworks that address the various regimes of illegibility of contemporary techno-scientific equipment and has exhibited in puzzling places in Europe and North America. David is currently a research fellow of the Netherlands Institute for Cultural Analysis (NICA) and a doctoral candidate at the Amsterdam School for Cultural Analysis (ASCA) of the University of Amsterdam. gautier.info

Linda Hilfling Ritasdatter is an artist exploring means of control (code, organisation and law) as well as geopolitical aspects of information architectures. Her practice takes the form of interventions reflecting upon or revealing hidden gaps within digital infrastructures — the place where a system fails and its inadequacies become visible. Linda has a passion for outmoded media apparatuses and obsolete programming languages. She was the co-director and -initiator of the media archaeological festival, The Art of the Overhead. Currently Linda is a doctoral candidate at the School of Arts and Communication, Malmö University, Sweden.

Brian House is an artist whose performances, installations, and interventions address the material articulation of time in digital culture. His work is informed by his background in computer science and reflects a preoccupation with the immediacy and relationality of sound. His work has been shown by MoMA in New York, MOCA in Los Angeles, Ars Electronica, Cincinnati Contemporary Arts Center, Tel Aviv Center for Contemporary Art, Eyebeam, and Rhizome, among others, and has been featured in publications including *WIRED*, *TIME*, *The New York Times*, *Neural*, *Metropolis*, and on *Univision Sports*. He is currently a doctoral candidate at Brown University. brianhouse.net

BIOGRAPHIES

Yuk Hui is currently researcher of the DFG project "Techno-ecologies of Participation" at Leuphana University Lüneburg. He has published articles in periodicals such as *Metaphilosophy, Parrhesia, Angelaki, Cahiers Simondon, Implications Philosophiques, Jahrbuch Technikphilosophie*, among others. He is co-editor of *30 Years after Les Immatériaux: Art, Science and Theory* (Meson Press, 2015), author of *On the Existence of Digital Objects* (University of Minnesota Press, 2016) and *The Question Concerning Technology in China: An Essay in Cosmotechnics* (Urbanomic, 2016).

Marie Louise Juul Søndergaard is a PhD candidate at School of Communication and Culture at Aarhus University, Denmark. Within the field of speculative and critical design and feminist technoscience her work explores intimacy and/in networked and datafied futures. She works with design as a critical practice to intervene and critique the neoliberal logics of digital technologies and focuses on how the entanglements of technologies, society and power have cultural and political impacts on our intimate everyday lives.

Peggy Pierrot works on projects linking information, media, activism, radio art and technology. She runs a publishing house, Venus Negra, publishing on popular cultures, Black Atlantic, music and science fiction. A sociologist by training, she holds a postgraduate degree in multimedia engineering. Peggy worked as a journalist (Transfert.net, *Le Monde diplomatique*, Minorités.org) and as editorial/technical webmaster in media and non-profit projects. She lectures on African-American and Caribbean literature and culture, science-fiction or related topics and is also a tutor for les Ateliers des horizons (ex-École du MAGASIN).

Andrew Prior is a media artist, musician and educator based at Plymouth University (UK). He completed his PhD at Aarhus University (DK) and holds postgraduate degree in Digital Futures from Plymouth University. He has released his music with Nonclassical Records and Yacht Club Records; and worked with John Matthias, Adrian Corker, John Richards, The Elysian Quartet, Consortium 5 on projects release on 4AD, and Counter Records, an imprint of Ninjatune. He has had work performed and exhibited in New York, Tokyo, Aarhus, Roskilde, London,

Brno & Zilina. His research interests are concerned with post-digitality, mediality and media archaeology explored from both a theoretical and practice-based perspective.

Helen Pritchard is an artist and researcher. Her work brings together the fields of Computational Aesthetics, Geography, and Feminist TechnoScience to consider the participation and entanglements of nonhuman animals and environments in computational practices. Helen is the Head of Digital Arts Computing and Lecturer in Computing at Goldsmiths, University of London. www.helenpritchard.info

Roel Roscam Abbing is an artist and researcher with strong interest in the issues and cultures surrounding networked computation. In an often collaborative practice he has worked on projects about the internet's infrastructure, DIY technologies and wireless community networks. Currently he teaches Digital Media at the department of Graphic Design at the Artez Academy in Arnhem. For more details, see roelof.info

Audrey Samson is an artist-researcher with a PhD from the School of Creative Media in Hong Kong. She explores erasure as a disruptive technology in knowledge production. She is currently resident at the Somerset House Studios as a member of the duo FRAUD, and a lecturer in the Art Department at Goldsmiths University of London. She has lived, exhibited and taught internationally. ideacritik.com | @ideacritik

Kasper Schiølin is a long-term research fellow in The Program on Science, Technology and Society at Harvard University. While his dissertation (2015) explored the intellectual history of techno-pessimism, his postdoctoral studies concern imaginaries of techno-optimism and their influence on policy and decision-making. Kasper has published several peer-reviewed articles, an edited volume on Heidegger's philosophy of technology, and a popular book on technology. He is currently working on the manuscript, *The Gospel of Technology: Hope, Tragedy and Continuity* (under consideration with Oxford University Press).

BIOGRAPHIES

Susan Schuppli is an artist and researcher based in the UK, whose work examines material evidence from war and conflict to environmental disasters. Creative projects have been exhibited throughout Europe, Asia, Canada, and the US. She has published widely within the context of media and politics and is author of the forthcoming book, *Material Witness* (MIT Press). Schuppli is Reader and Director of the Centre for Research Architecture, Goldsmiths University of London and was previously Senior Research Fellow on the Forensic Architecture project. In 2016 she received the ICP Infinity Award for Critical Writing and Research.

Femke Snelting works as artist and designer, developing projects at the intersection of design, feminism and free software. In various constellations she has been exploring how digital tools and practices might co-construct each other. She is member of Constant, a non-profit, artist-run association for art and media based in Brussels. With Jara Rocha she activates Possible Bodies, a collective research project that interrogates the concrete and at the same time fictional entities of "bodies" in the context of 3D tracking, modelling and scanning. Femke teaches at the Piet Zwart Institute (experimental publishing, Rotterdam) and a.pass (advanced performance and scenography studies, Brussels). For more details, see snelting.domainepublic.net

Eric Snodgrass is a senior lecturer at the Department of Design, Linnaeus University, Sweden. His research looks into the intersections of media, politics, and technology, with a focus on issues of materiality, infrastructures of power, and forms of intervention. His recent work includes the co-edited volume *Executing Practices* and a PhD dissertation: *Executions: Power and Expression in Networked and Computational Media*.

Winnie Soon is an artist-researcher-coder-educator who resides in Hong Kong and Denmark. Her works explore themes/concepts around digital culture, including internet censorship, data circulation, image politics, code and real-time processing, etc. Soon's projects have been exhibited and presented internationally at museums, festivals, universities and conferences across Europe, Asia and America. Her current research focuses on Computational Thinking, working on two books titled *Aesthetic Programming* (with Geoff Cox) and *Fix My Code* (with Cornelia Sollfrank). She is Assistant Professor at Aarhus University. For more details, see siusoon.net

Magdalena Tyżlik-Carver is a researcher and curator based in the UK and Denmark. Her research explores relational arrangements of humans and nonhumans and their biopolitical creations through posthuman curating and curating in/as common/s, future thinking, affective data, and data fictions. Tyżlik-Carver is Assistant Professor in Digital Design at Aarhus University. For more details see: magda.thecommonpractice.org

Index of all elements leading to the end of the world (in this book)*

Linda Hilfling Ritasdatter

accordingly 126, 150
aftermaths 32
altogether 63, 173, 281, 283, 286
analysts 91
atrocity 95
bourgeois 58
brutally 206
buttons 211
calculation 10, 11, 19, 31, 32, 64, 86, 92, 94 269, 272, 301
cassettes 12
causality 29, 92, 93
Christelle 277
compensate 93
compliancy 146, 150
composing 14, 72, 127
computer 8–13, 15, 18, 23–24, 30, 37, 56, 59, 61, 65–66, 70–71, 80–84, 100, 104–106, 112–114, 119, 125, 137–138, 141, 145, 150, 156, 184–185, 197, 243, 245–246, 250, 252, 254–259, 261, 265, 271, 274, 296–297, 304, 306
corporate 18, 52, 96, 146, 197, 202, 210, 214
corrupt 12, 61
Corvallis 292
criterion 57
disclosing 151
drummers 126
dystopic 9
electrons 13
eroticism 14, 197–205, 207–208, 210–212, 214–216
estimates 301
exception 20–21, 37, 55, 57–58, 63–64, 67, 72, 78, 83, 105, 142, 172–173, 187, 243, 286, 288, 293
excessive 14, 127, 197, 202, 214–215
executor 19, 251

explaining 30
falterings 264
fascination 26
foremost 71, 141, 214
formation 173, 176
fundamental 89, 105, 117, 184, 216, 252
governing 92
Hlavajova's 23
horrors 205
humanity 50, 199–200, 203
illusion 32, 105
indecipherable 76
indictment 93
initialised 238
initially 11, 66, 141, 204
Innsbruck 67
isometric 16
iteration 23, 77–78, 81
lucrative 282
lustful 200
maintaining 15, 38, 105, 120, 126, 279–280, 290
majority 20, 61, 257, 274
monetary 290
moreover 56, 207
museums 169
obfuscates 91
operative 100, 102–104, 111, 114, 179, 181, 248, 287–288, 292
opinions 62, 96
opposing 28, 283
outcomes 51, 72, 88, 92, 199
outlaws 76–78, 80
overtaken 185
partners 103
perceptible 99, 110, 127, 240
perfection 159, 182–183, 256
periodicals 305
pictures 198

309

platters 118
predictive 85, 273
proudly 39, 43
reinstate 267
repeatedly 56, 99, 101, 171
reports 39, 51, 53
reserves 87
response 8, 13–14, 18, 21–22, 38, 40,
    45–46, 50–51, 57, 60, 65, 85, 90,
    95, 157, 204, 252, 255, 261, 263,
    270–271, 275, 284
reverses 81
revision 180
revisited 169
rhythms 16, 21, 85, 108, 240
Schmitt's 58, 64, 66
severely 299
significant 31, 87, 95, 102, 108–109,
    118, 171, 265, 273
Slower's 127
somewhere 121, 244, 266
stratified 254–255
strength 200, 290
thinkings 29
truetime 15–16, 123–125
underway 100
unruly 17, 19, 255, 274, 276
usually 40, 59, 82, 88, 93, 107, 112, 174,
    205, 208, 282, 288–291
Wohlfarth 65–66

> *Generated through a numerological algorithm that results in certain words to correspond to the satanic number 666. The algorithm used here originally "proved" the computer to be the work of the devil. It is reenacted and set to monitor various sources in order to compile a complete index of all elements leading to the end of the world, for *DATA browser 06: Executing Practices*, resulting in 91 elements being added to the index. For more details see Hilfling Ritasdatter's contribution "Bugs in the War Room" (pp. 137–158).

www.ingramcontent.com/pod-product-compliance
Lightning Source LLC
Chambersburg PA
CBHW031609210526
45464CB00004B/1493